A Good Girl...Seldom

Jenni McMullan was born in Macclesfield, Cheshire, in England and was educated at Bailey in Fleetwood, Lancashire. She migrated to Australia with her mother in 1963 as a 'ten-pound Pom'. She completed her education in Canberra before joining the Public Service Board.

Highlights from a public sector career spanning more than forty years include Manager of the government's disposal arm known as Aussales; Team Leader of an IT group that won both silver and gold in the Government Information Technical Awards; Manager of the team providing IT services to the electorate offices of Senators and Members; Assistant Commissioner Information Technology at the Australian Electoral Commission; and State Manager for Victoria for the Electoral Commission, responsible for delivering the Federal election in that state.

On the death of her much-loved husband Brian in 2006, Jenni spearheaded the task of converting the only four-bed ward at the Canberra Hospice into four private rooms as she felt that when people were losing their life, they should not also lose their privacy. On retirement, Jenni was appointed to the board of Palliative Care ACT and is actively involved in fundraising for that group.

She has two daughters, Elizabeth and Kathryn, and four grandchildren. She remarried in 2015 and lives with her husband, John McNee, in Reid, ACT.

Jenni McMullan

A Good Girl...Seldom

This book is written in memory of my mother, Annie Gidman – a strong, intelligent woman who placed family above all else. She lived through extraordinary times and in the living of those times she became extraordinary herself.

'When everything goes to hell, the people who stand by you without flinching – they are your family.' – Jim Butcher

This book is dedicated with much love to Annie's grandchildren, Elizabeth and Kathryn McMullan, and to her great-grandchildren, Tom and Lucy Kearins, and Grace and Harriet McDownie.

I may not always be with you
But when we're far apart
Remember you will be with me
Right inside my heart.
Marc Wambolt, *Poems from the Heart*

A Good Girl…Seldom
ISBN 978 1 76041 959 2
Copyright © Jenni McMullan 2020

First published 2020 by
Ginninderra Press
PO Box 3461 Port Adelaide 5015
www.ginninderrapress.com.au

Contents

Introduction		7
Characters in the Story		11
1	My Arrival	15
2	My Mother's Family	22
3	My Father's Family	31
4	Nellie Ronan and Harry Gidman	36
5	The Gidman Girls	39
6	Dr Sommerville	46
7	The Terrible Trio	52
8	Wakes Week	55
9	Schooldays	59
10	Mum and Dad	63
11	Work and Home Life	66
12	Life As a Young Woman	72
13	My Business Start-up and Nellie's Antics	78
14	Harry Kirk	80
15	Louie	85
16	Alice	89
17	Harry and I	92
18	Frank and Ethel Kirk	100
19	Frank Kirk and Emmie Collins	102
20	Harry, the Baby and the Early Months of the War	104
21	Alice and Norman Rodman	108
22	The War Years	114
23	Harry and the Navy	123
24	Harry Gidman	127

25	Freddie Thornicroft	131
26	A Second Child	133
27	Rodney and the King's School	136
28	New Beginnings	139
29	Café Life and Staff	142
30	Alice and Loraine	149
31	Life at the Kings School	155
32	Café Life and Colourful Customers	159
33	Two Nasty Accidents	165
34	The Police	169
35	Rationing	172
36	Nellie and Louie	175
37	Harry and I – the Roller-coaster Ride	177
38	Café Life, Staff Dramas and Unwanted Pregnancies	183
39	Wilf Carson	187
40	Louie and Charlie Steele	189
41	Time To Call It Quits	191
42	George Collier	199
43	Hogmanay	203
44	The Children	205
45	Charlie Bullen, Australia and the Complexities of Life	210
46	A New Beginning in Canberra, Australia	216
47	The 1960s	220
48	The Church of England Boys' Home, Carlingford	226
49	Jennifer, Loraine and Louie	230
50	Phil Ward	238
Afterword		247
Postscript		252

Introduction

I have wanted to write my mother's life story for at least twenty years, but life simply got in the way. As I grew up, I would hear tales of Mum's childhood, of the hardships she endured, of the love she shared for her sisters, of her meeting my father and their life together, of the many loves she had in her life, of the people she interacted with, of the fun, the laughter, the sadness, and I always thought it would make a good story.

Then around 1998, when she was eighty-three, I thought it would be wise to capture her story on tape. Over about six months, my younger daughter Kathryn and I would slip down to Batemans Bay, where my mother lived, and start her talking about her life. Of course, I had heard many of the stories several times, so I was able to prompt her. She would begin with one part of her life and then go off on multiple tangents, so many of which were interesting. I finished up with about ten hours of her recollections on tape and I had good intentions of writing the book and having her proofread it.

However, a super-busy job and family life left me with little time, so the tapes were closeted away. Mum died in 2003 and I felt her loss profoundly. A short three years later, my much-loved husband Brian died; so the two people who had been my strongest allies, my supporters, my advocates, my metaphorical crutches if you like, were gone. I threw myself into work, my daughters were brilliant, my friends were loyal, but at the end of the day it was me that coped with the emptiness. I did think then about beginning to write the book to fill in the evening hours, but I did not feel emotionally strong enough to listen to Mum's voice. It would have been a tease to close my eyes and hear her there beside me, then open them to find only an empty space. I was not ready to live through loss again, so the tapes stayed in the cupboard.

At the end of 2007, I met John McNee, a wonderful man who had himself endured the loss of both parents, a brother and sister, and most of all his beloved wife, Bettie. We became instant soulmates. On our first outing, we spoke about love and loss, of the eulogies we had given at our respective spouses' funerals, of the difficulty in moving forward, and there was a mutual recognition that neither of us had a monopoly on grief. My friendship with John McNee blossomed, and as the relationship developed, I no longer felt alone. There was someone beside me who understood loss, and John's support gave me the confidence to open my treasure chest of memories. I felt strong enough to conquer that emotional mountain.

So, after I retired, I decided that the tapes had to come out of the cupboard. Listening to Mum's voice did not engender the angst I had anticipated. As I listened, and her voice swam around in my head, always challenging, always seeking the best, it filled me with a great many memories and so the writing began.

Many times in telling the tale I wanted to confer with Mum on small issues. As that was not possible, I have used the tapes, the knowledge I do have, together with considerable research, plus my imagination, to fill in the gaps. I have used the real names of all key people in the book, but there are some characters who have a minor, passing role whose names I did not know or could not recall, but to whom I have given a name for ease of writing.

One of the decisions I had to make in writing this story was finding a suitable title for the book. *A Good Girl…Seldom* was a phrase my mother used when I was little, and I would ask her whether I was good – usually as a prelude to seeking a chocolate or an ice cream – and she would nod and say, 'Oh darling, you're a good girl…seldom.' Of course, I had no idea what seldom meant but I would go off happy. It is a phrase I used with both my girls as they were growing up and as I wrote this story, it struck me that it seemed so apt for Annie.

During the writing, I was very fortunate to come across Beverley Rutter via ancestry.com, who turned out to be my first cousin once removed. My grandmother, Harriet Ellen, and her mother, Rose, were sisters, Harriet being child number one of ten and Rose being child number nine. I pay tribute to Beverley for the fantastic information she was able to provide about my great-grandfather, Edward Ronan, and my great-grandmother, Mary Elizabeth Ronan (née Hayes). I have included this information in the book. Beverley's research was meticulous, and I thank her for her contribution.

I also give credit to Wikipedia for information on the recruitment, training and deployment of the Accrington Pals, as well as providing information on where my great-grandfather died. Wikipedia also provided useful background on the HMS *Avenger*, where my father served in 1942, and on HMS *Warsprite* and the Normandy landings.

I visited Macclesfield, Cheshire, where my mother was born, and spent time researching in the library. Sincere thanks go to the library staff for their generosity of time and passion in assisting me to identify information that gives the story colour. I pay tribute to the librarian, Katherine Yates, as well as Ken Bolton, and make special mention of James Hough, who has given up personal time to assist with research. Their contributions have been outstanding, and I acknowledge their excellent input.

I also pay tribute to Dr Robin Doherty and Dr Jean Doherty, both retired Canberra GPs, who provided valuable information on the various medical incidents in the book.

Sincere thanks go also to Lolita Butler, who spent many hours reading my work and providing suggestions for improvement. I also extend my warmest thanks to Ara Nalbandian, who edited my writing and encouraged me to flesh out certain parts, identifying them as poetic opportunities.

The book is written in the first person as that is how Mum told me her story and so many of the quotes are directly from her lips. I have chosen to tell the tale chronologically as I feel it gives a better picture of the little girl growing to womanhood, and the woman into the wise, feisty person she became.

I do not claim that this is a literary masterpiece, but I hope you will find it is a good story. So, I give you the life of Annie Gidman.

Jenni McMullan

Characters in the Story

There are over a hundred people featured in this story, but many are simply incidental to the tale. However, in the interests of clarity, I have listed the main characters. Where someone has been mentioned more than once, I have tried to include a reminder of who they are. Sometimes, though, readers will put a book down and not get back to it for a while, forgetting who the person is. It happens to me quite often, so if it happens to you, this list might help.

The Gidman family

Annie Gidman	central character
Louisa Gidman	known as Louie-Annie's oldest sister
Alice Gidman	Annie's other sister
Harry Gidman	Annie's father
Harriet Ellen Gidman	née Ronan: Annie's mother, also known as Nellie
John Gidman	Annie's grandfather
Emily Gidman	née Simms: Annie's grandmother
Selina Gidman	sister to Harry Gidman and one of John and Emily's twelve offspring
Jimmy Gidman	brother to Harry Gidman and one of John and Emily's twelve offspring
Annie Gidman	sister to Harry Gidman and one of John and Emily's twelve offspring; became Annie Beard on her marriage to James Beard, aunt of Annie Gidman

The Hayes/Ronan family

John Hayes	grandfather to Harriet Ellen Gidman, great-grandfather of Annie
Elizabeth Hayes	previously Elizabeth Lovatt, wife of John, grandmother of Harriet Ellen and great-grandmother of Annie
Mary Elizabeth Hayes	daughter of John and Elizabeth, mother of Harriet Ellen, grandmother of Annie
Edward Ronan	husband of Mary Elizabeth Hayes, father of Harriet Ellen, grandfather of Annie
Matthew Ronan	Edward's father, grandfather of Harriet Ellen and great-grandfather of Annie
Harriet Ronan	previously Webster, née Johnson, wife of Matthew Ronan, grandmother of Harriet Ellen and great-grandmother of Annie
John Keefe	second partner of Mary Elizabeth Ronan (née Hayes)

The Kirk family

Harry Kirk	Annie's husband
Frank Kirk	Harry's father, Annie's father-in-law
Ruth Ethel Kirk	née Baguley, Harry's mother, Annie's mother-in-law
Arthur Kirk	Harry's brother
Emmie Kirk	née Collins, Frank Kirk's second wife
Auntie Lil	Harry's aunt
Dorothy Darby	Harry's cousin
Stephen Kirk	Annie and Harry's first child
Rodney Kirk	Annie and Harry's second child
Jennifer Kirk	Annie and Harry's third child

The Steele family

Charlie Steele	Louie's husband and brother-in-law to Annie
Michael Steele	Charlie and Louie's son, nephew to Annie
Fred and Fanny Steele	brother and sister-in-law of Charlie Steele
Jimmy McMahon	taxi driver and close friend of Louie's

Unwin/Rodman/Dutton/Muir

Jack Unwin	Alice Gidman's first husband
Norman Rodman	Alice Gidman's lover and father of Loraine
Charlie Dutton	Alice Gidman's second husband
Loraine Dutton	Alice Gidman's daughter, adopted by Annie
Malcolm Muir	Loraine's husband
Dawn Muir	Malcolm and Loraine's daughter
Simon and Aaron Muir	Malcolm and Loraine's twin sons

Other characters

Dr Sommerville	family doctor to the Gidmans in early years
Dr Gillies	family doctor to the Gidmans in later years
Dr Yule	family doctor to the Kirks in Fleetwood
Mrs Isherwood	owned a gown shop in Macclesfield and friend to the Gidman girls
Mrs Dale	one of the ladies Annie helped out
Mrs Goodyear	one of the ladies Annie helped out
Miss Hardcastle	Annie's teacher
Amy Brierly	Annie's best friend
Marjory Finlow	Annie's friend
Elsie & Emma Bradshaw	Annie's friends
Freddie Thornicroft	Annie's mentor and friend
Alice and Frank Wall	employees of Freddie Thornicroft
Maureen Bamford	Annie's employee and second-in-command at the Wyre Dock Café
Mary Ebdell	Annie's employee at Wyre Dock Café

Flora Fitzgerald	Annie's employee at Wyre Dock Café
Mavis Harris	Annie's employee at Wyre Dock Café
Brenda Wright	Annie's employee at Wyre Dock Café
Sheila Wright	Annie's employee at Wyre Dock Café
Mary Robinson	next-door neighbour in Manor Road
Clifford Hodgson	Annie's accountant
Jean Fish	abortionist and Annie's friend
Charlie Bullen	Annie's lover
George Collier	Annie's lover
Dougie Walters	Annie's lover
Phil Ward	Annie's partner of twenty-six years

1

My Arrival

'Our Louie, run to Grandma Gidman's and tell her the baby's on its way. Hurry, child, then come straight back 'cos I want you to run a message for me,' said my father, Harry Gidman. He quickly scribbled a note to the midwife, saying his wife was in labour and asked that she attend as soon as possible.

Louie, my six-year-old sister, returned quickly from Grandma's then raced up the Buxton Road and knocked frantically at Mrs Drinkwater's door, thrusting the note into the midwife's hand. 'You must come now, Mrs Drinkwater, the baby's coming,' she yelled.

Meanwhile, Grandma Gidman bustled into the bedroom and shooed out my other sister Alice, who had just turned four. 'Go outside and play, Alice. Our Louie will be back shortly,' she said as she turned round and gently wiped my mother's forehead. My grandma was no stranger to childbirth, having birthed twelve children herself. 'Now then, Nellie,' she soothed as she spoke to my mother, 'it will all be over soon.'

*

We live at 42 Fence Street, in the silk-weaving town of Macclesfield, Cheshire. It is a very old market town whose history dates back to the Domesday Book. St Barnabas is the patron saint of silk workers, and in 1595 Queen Elizabeth I officially granted the Barnaby holiday fortnight, taken from the nearest Sunday to the feast of St Barnabas on 22 June.

Although commonly referred to as 'Silk Town', Macclesfield was nicknamed 'Treacle Town', after a horse-drawn wagon overturned, spilling its load of treacle onto the street, and the poor scooped the treacle off the road. Since the early 1800s, the town has produced some of the finest silk in the world.

Macclesfield is also the original home of Hovis bread, a cheap but nutritious loaf which provides excellent nourishment to the mill-workers. The Hovis factory is significant in my life as my dad, and later my husband, both worked there. It is built on a canal which facilitates the transport of flour to the factory and the distribution of bread to towns along the canal banks.

There are rows and rows of houses like ours, built as part of the Industrial Revolution. The silk mills are the lifeblood of the town and my mother is a weaver at Lomus's mill. Our house is in a row of terraces, with two bedrooms upstairs and a front room and kitchen downstairs. You walk straight off the street into our front room with its large flag-stone floor covered in yellow oilcloth. Dad has managed to get the floor surface reasonably even by stuffing newspapers under the oilcloth. There is a large rug embossed with hydrangeas over the oilcloth and my mother thinks it makes us look rather posh.

In the front room, we have a fire grate with an oven on one side and burning coals from the fire are placed into a drawer under the oven to create heat for cooking. There is a large, overstuffed, Victorian settee with a grey flower pattern on it as well as a dresser with all our good plates set out on display. We have a mantel over the fireplace with two pottery dogs which face each other, and there is a clock right in the middle which my father winds up every night at six p.m.

We do not have a bathroom or laundry but there is a toilet up the backyard that is shared between three houses. Since next door has thirteen in the family, you can imagine how hard it is to find a toilet when we need it. We do not have electricity but there is a gas lamp, nor do we have hot water, but we do have a tap with running water in the kitchen and a large wood stove with a hob for the kettle, so we always have hot water for a cuppa or a wash. By today's standards, this was a very primitive home, but it was the home I was to be born into.

*

Within fifteen minutes of Louie leaving home, Mrs Drinkwater, with her straight back and firm voice, walked into the house and issued her orders. 'Get that water boiling, Mrs Gidman, and let me have three towels, plus a cloth to swaddle the baby in.'

Louisa, or Louie as she prefers to be called, kept Dad company for a while and then went out to play with Alice.

Grandma Gidman told the girls, 'You must stay outside, not bother your dad or me and play until I call you.'

It was two p.m. and the contractions were getting closer.

Mrs Drinkwater examined mother internally. 'I don't like the way the baby is lying, Nellie. I'm going to try and turn it.'

Mother yelled out in agonising pain as first one attempt and then another was made to turn the baby round. Perspiration streamed down her face, and Grandma Gidman mopped Nellie's brow and told her how well she was doing.

'It's going to be a difficult birth, Nellie. This little one is too far down the birth canal for me to turn it, so just bite on to this rag. The baby's heartbeat is strong. You'll be all right. I won't leave you.'

Grandma Gidman with her soft, lilting voice broke into song:

> It's a long way to Tipperary, it's a long way to go,
> It's a long way to Tipperary to the sweetest girl I know.
> Goodbye Piccadilly, farewell Leicester Square
> It's a long, long way to Tipperary, but my heart lies there.

'I wish I was a bloody long way from here,' yelled Nellie. 'I can't do this any more.'

'Yes, you can, Nellie,' whispered Grandma Gidman. 'You can do it.'

Mrs Drinkwater and Grandma Gidman looked at each other, and Mrs Drinkwater gave an imperceptible nod and they left the room together.

'We need Dr Sommerville, Mrs Gidman,' whispered Mrs Drinkwater. 'Get your Harry to cycle over to Dr Sommerville's surgery and tell the doctor that I'm needing his expertise now…and hurry.'

Grandma hitched her long skirts, patted down her bonnet, braced her shoulders and raced downstairs. 'Harry, this baby needs some help to come into the world. Get on your bike and fetch Dr Sommerville. Be as quick as you can.'

Returning upstairs, Grandma Gidman found Nellie drifting into a dreamlike state. The pain was making her cry out in a pitiful deep moan, but between contractions she disappeared into herself and her breathing became shallow.

'Get the smelling salts, Mrs Gidman, and put them under your Nellie's nose. Then turn her on her side and rub her back. We'll get this baby out, if it's the last thing I do.'

Time dragged on, and the contractions became closer: three minutes apart, then two minutes.

Dr Sommerville arrived on his bicycle, an elegant gentleman with dark hair poking from under his trilby, a short beard and a handlebar moustache; he wore a starched collar, tie and tweed jacket. But under his stiff exterior lay a soft heart and in his broad north English accent he spoke gently as he examined Nellie.

'Nellie, this baby's in the breech position, which means that its buttocks and feet will come first. I'm going to have to guide the child out, and it will hurt. I have some medicine called laudanum which I'm going to give you to take the edge off the pain. It works quickly, and it will help.'

'I can't take this any more, doctor. The other two babies were no trouble. I can't understand why this is so different.'

'All babies are different in my experience, Nellie, and we will get through this together. Keep breathing steadily. Where's Harry? We should tell him what's happening.'

Grandma Gidman chimed in, 'Harry will be downstairs awaiting the arrival of his son.'

Nellie added, 'He's not one for the birthing, Dr Sommerville… Oh, here's the pain again.'

'You're doing well, Nellie. Push when the pain arrives. It won't be long now.'

'Good work, good work,' encouraged Dr Sommerville. 'Mrs Drinkwater, I can see baby and I'm going to help the child out. Please hold on to Nellie's hand. Push again Nellie, we're nearly there.'

With great skill, Dr Sommerville eased his hand around the baby's buttocks and gently pulled. 'Push again, Nellie, push, push'...and with that final push the baby slid out and Nellie leaned back against the bed head and let out the longest sigh.

'Thank God that's over,' she whispered.

'Congratulations, you have another daughter,' said Doctor Sommerville with a huge grin on his face.

'Oh God, what will Harry say? He so wanted a boy this time,' said Nellie weakly.

Dr Sommerville tied off the umbilical cord and passed the baby to the midwife to check and swaddle and then smiled down at Nellie, pushing the wet lock on her forehead back from her brow. 'You were a brave girl, Nellie. I know Harry, he'll be just as pleased with this little one as he was with Louisa and Alice. We just need to finish the job now. One more push and it will all be over.'

Nellie pushed and what appeared to be the full placenta was delivered. She smiled.

Dr Sommerville then turned his attention to the baby, checking the child over before turning back to Nellie. He noticed how pale she had become, and he shook her by the arm.

'Nellie, are you OK?' asked Dr Sommerville with great concern.

But Nellie was far from OK. She had turned a ghostly white and her silky cheeks were as translucent as gossamer.

Dr Sommerville took her pulse, which was now running extremely fast. Nellie was losing consciousness.

He then looked down and saw a mass of blood. 'Oh, no,' he muttered. 'Mrs Drinkwater, we have a post-partum haemorrhage.' Quickly, Dr Sommerville began to palpitate the uterus. 'Come on, contract, contract,' he mumbled urgently to himself, but still the blood flowed.

He then placed one hand below the uterus in the vagina and with the other compressed from above through the lower abdominal wall. He pressed again and again, but nothing happened.

Nellie's pulse began to weaken.

'Come on girl,' urged Dr Sommerville in an earnest whisper. 'You can do this.'

He tried yet again but there was nothing; the blood flooded his hand. He did another compression and suddenly he sensed just the slightest contraction of muscle. He compressed again and once more felt a response. One more time and suddenly nature clicked in and the uterus contracted. Perspiration soaked his shirt; sweat trickled down his cheeks, he breathed in deeply and whispered a quiet prayer of thanks.

'That was a close one, Nellie. I don't want to experience that again any time soon. You were very fortunate this time. You have a beautiful baby and given a few days' rest you'll be fine, but this must be your last child. There can be no more. The risks are too high.'

Dr Sommerville went downstairs and congratulated Harry. He then asked Harry to sit down. 'Harry, Nellie came very close to losing her life with this baby. It's the closest I've come in a long time to losing a mother in childbirth. You cannot risk her life with another child, Harry, so be very careful in future.'

'Aye,' said Harry, 'and thank you, doc.'

With that, Dr Sommerville rolled down his sleeves, put on his jacket, doffed his trilby, mounted his bicycle and, no doubt with relief in his heart, he pedalled off.

Nellie cradled the baby in her arms then turned to her mother-in-law and said, 'Can you slip up to the off-licence and get me a gill of milk stout. It'll help me build up my strength and I can give a sip to the baby.'

And so I arrived in the world around five p.m. on 24 June 1915 and had my first taste of alcohol. What a world I was entering! The war was in full swing: Mesopotamia had been captured by the British; U-boats had sunk the British liner *Lusitania*; my grandfather was fighting with the East Lancashire Regiment; and the British advance up Gully Ravine at the Dardanelles was about to take place. And then my dad was called up.

2

My Mother's Family

Let me tell you what I know about my mother's family. She came from a working-class background – as working-class as you can get. My mother was the granddaughter of John Hayes, cotton factory worker, and Elizabeth (Lizzie) Lovatt. John was fifteen years older than Lizzie, who already had four children when they met: Ann Elizabeth (b. 1852), Emma (b. 1854), Job (b. 1857) and Ellen (b. 1861). It appears that she never married the father of these children, as Lovatt was her maiden name.

According to the 1861 Census, Lizzie was living at the poorhouse in Walker Lane, Sutton, an outer suburb of Macclesfield. Poorhouses were very sad places in the 1860s, as they were governed under the harsh provisions of the New Poor Law Act of 1834. Each parish had responsibility for their local poor folk, but as most parishes could not afford to build a workhouse or poorhouse, they joined forces with the unions and built the premises jointly. Men were usually separated from their wives, and children were often separated from their parents. It would appear, though, that Lizzie kept her children with her, perhaps because Ellen was only four months old at the time and was possibly still being breastfed.

Poorhouses provided basic food, medical care and shelter, known as Indoor Relief, but the rules were strict and conditions deliberately unpleasant in order to deter as many people as possible from seeking shelter. All able-bodied people were required to work: men would do the hard, manual labour and work in the garden while women worked in the laundry, washing for the household as well as for the wealthier folk who sent their laundry out. There is a wonderful Victorian nursery rhyme that Louie, Alice and I used to recite as kids; it goes like this:

> They that wash on Monday
> Have all the week to dry;
> They that wash on Tuesday
> Are not so much awry;
> They that wash on Wednesday
> Are not so much to blame;
> They that wash on Thursday
> Wash for shame;
> They that wash on Friday
> Wash in need;
> And they that wash on Saturday
> Oh! They are sluts indeed.

Goodness knows what the people were who washed on Sunday, because when we were all working five-and-a-half days a week, Sunday was normally our washing day! But I am digressing.

It was not unusual for people to move in and out of the workhouse, usually in accordance with the availability of seasonal work, and I know that at some point Lizzie obtained a position in service at Adlington Hall. John and Lizzie met at a local fair and he thought she was a real beauty. He would go up to the hall every Sunday to meet Lizzie, then they would collect the children from the poorhouse and go roaming the hills around Macclesfield on her afternoon off. The Cheshire countryside was truly beautiful, and John, Lizzie and children loved the serenity of the woodland, where the silence was broken only by the call of chaffinches and the trill of wrens.

Adlington Hall is a grand edifice set in 2,000 acres of superb garden. In the spring, the laburnum arch makes a stunning feature, while the pathways wend through carpets of bluebells and wild flowers. The hall itself can be traced back to Saxon times and embraces the changing architectural styles in Britain, with the northern front reflecting the Restoration period, the eastern being built in Tudor times, and the southern and western fronts showcasing Georgian grandeur. Inside the great hall is an organ, reputed to be one of the finest in England, and rumour has it that it was once played by Handel.

Lizzie married John Hayes in 1868 and the whole family moved into Blagg Street in Hurdsfield, where on 4 July 1869 my grandmother, Mary Elizabeth Hayes, was born. Great-granddad Hayes was fifty-one years old at the time and great-grandmother Elizabeth was thirty-six. He could neither read nor write, so he signed Mary Elizabeth's birth registration form with an X.

Mary Elizabeth had little schooling, entering service at Adlington Hall, just as her mother had done twenty years earlier. She was thirteen years old. At the time, Charles Richard Banastre Legh of Adlington was squire at the hall. It was a hard life, rising at five a.m. to clean and set the fireplaces in the great hall and the drawing room before the family came down for breakfast. The elegant rooms, the silverware, the china, the lush velvet chairs and the deep red carpets, so thick that they felt like a cushion, must have been a stark contrast to the humble surrounds of her family home.

Mary Elizabeth was an enterprising girl and she used her good looks and sparkling demeanour to find a way out of domestic drudgery. When she was nineteen, she met Edward Ronan, who was described on their marriage certificate as a 'mineral water manufacturer'. He was a tall and distinguished-looking young man with bright red hair and a big red beard. Edward's father, Matthew Ronan, who was born in 1821 but did not marry until he was forty, was a furniture broker by profession and the family was moderately comfortable by the standards of the time. Matthew married a widow, Harriet Webster (née Johnson), aged thirty, on 20 August 1861, and had three sons: Matthew junior in 1867, Edward in 1869 and Frederick in 1873.

Edward's father was none too pleased that Edward would consider a partner in life who was below his station, and Matthew worked hard to break up the relationship. However, Mary Elizabeth fell pregnant, so Edward felt he should do the right thing and marry her. The wedding took place on 13 October 1889; both were aged twenty. Mary Eizabeth signed her marriage certificate with an X. Five months later, on 5 March 1890, she gave birth to my mother, Harriet Ellen Ronan, although right from the start she was known as Nellie, probably to differentiate her from her grandmother Harriet.

When Matthew senior passed away in 1882, his wife, Harriet, moved to 106 Chestergate and lived in more humble circumstances. For a while, Edward, Mary Elizabeth and young Nellie lived with Edward's mother and her other two sons, Matthew junior and young Fred, but they later set up house by themselves. Edward joined the Irish Guards, leaving Mary Elizabeth alone for extended periods with young Nellie as a baby. Mary Elizabeth would frequently leave the house and go to town, or to the local pub for a drink in the snug, leaving Nellie by herself at home.

One day, Edward's older brother Matthew visited and found Nellie alone in a cot by the side of the fire. She was crying, she was hungry, and her nappy was soiled. It was clear that Nellie had been left on her own for quite a while. Matthew searched the house and around the area for Mary Elizabeth but there was no sign of her, so he scooped the baby up and took her to his own mother. All contact with Mary Elizabeth was severed.

The fact that neither Edward nor Mary Elizabeth appeared to fight for the return of their firstborn is interesting. Whether that was by arrangement or circumstance I am unaware. Mary Elizabeth went on to have a second child, Frederick, in 1891 but he died the following year. Then William was born in 1893, followed in 1895 by another child who Mary Elizabeth chose to call Harriot. Harriot died the day she was born but I think it is significant that she called another girl by the same name, although different spelling, as the child she had abandoned. Edward Ronan junior was born and died in 1899, and in 1900 Harold was born.

The 1901 Census indicates that Mary Elizabeth had moved in with her sister Alice and her husband Henry Potter, who were living at 15

Green Street, Macclesfield. She took her sons, William Alfred, aged seven, and Harold, aged ten months, with her. I am speculating that during 1900–1902 my grandfather was away fighting in the second Boer War, as no children are recorded as being born. After the Boer War (1899–1902), two more children arrived, Arthur in 1903 and Gladys in 1904, but neither lived for very long.

The 1911 Census shows that Mary Elizabeth had left Edward and was living with a man called John Keefe in Bank Street. She must have left soon after Gladys's birth, as Rose, the first of the two children she bore to Keefe, was born in 1905, and lived to 1995. The other child was Alexander, who arrived in 1909, but he only lived to his sixth birthday. So, in the space of nineteen years, Mary Elizabeth gave birth to ten children, eight to her husband and two to John Keefe. Interestingly, they all bore the surname of Ronan.

Of the ten, only four survived to adulthood, the rest dying at birth, soon afterwards, or as young children. In today's world, it is impossible to imagine that sixty per cent of your children would never see adulthood, but perhaps, given the poverty they endured, it was, in some ways, a blessing to have fewer mouths to feed.

*

Meanwhile, my grandfather Edward had moved to Oldham, twenty-six miles north of Macclesfield. When World War I was declared in 1914, he rallied to the call of Captain John Harwood, mayor of Accrington, a town twenty-four miles further north from Oldham. Mayor Harwood had vowed to raise a complete battalion of men from Accrington and surrounds. Edward was forty-five at the time. When recruitment began on 14 September, 104 men were accepted in the first three hours. My grandfather signed up on 17 September 1914 under the false name of Edward Nickson. There are two possible reasons for the name change: the first is that there was an age limit of forty years for recruiting men for the army in World War I, and the second is perhaps that he had wished to escape any garnisheeing of his pay by Mary Elizabeth, who by then was living with Keefe.

Brothers, cousins, friends and workmates enlisted together, and by 24 September 1914 the Accrington Battalion had all but reached a full-strength of 1,100 men. They were known as the Accrington Pals.

My research in later life revealed that the Accrington Pals trained at Caernarvon before moving in May 1915 to Penkridge Bank Camp near Rugeley, where the battalion joined the 12th, 13th and 14th Battalions of the York and Lancaster Regiment to form the 94th Brigade, 31st Division. In December, they embarked for Egypt to counter a Turkish threat against the Suez Canal. In the last week of February 1916, the 31st Division was ordered to France to take part in a joint British–French attack on the Somme.

In January 1916, the commanders-in-chief of the French and British armies, Joffre and Haig, had reached agreement to mount a joint offensive on the Western Front in the coming summer. Although Haig had argued for an offensive in Flanders, the decision was taken to attack along a wide front at the point where the two armies met close to the Somme River. It was a poor choice: the chalk-based nature of the ground there had allowed the Germans to construct deep underground shelters, largely untouchable by artillery. North of the Somme River, the German lines ran along the higher ground, protected by dense concentrations of barbed wire.

Over the coming months, German pressure to the south against the French town of Verdun forced a change in plans for the offensive. The bulk of the attack was now to be made by the British army on a fifteen-mile front, extending south from Serre to Fricourt, then east to Maricourt on the north bank of the Somme River.

The objective of the Accrington Pals battalion of the 94th Brigade was to capture the hilltop fortress of Serre and form a defensive flank facing north-east and north. The attack was to be led by the 11th East Lancashires (the Pals) on the right and the 12th York and Lancasters on the left. The 13th and 14th York and Lancasters were to support the two leading battalions.

On 24 June, the day of my first birthday, the British artillery opened a bombardment that was intended to destroy the German defences completely, but it failed to penetrate through to many of the underground shelters and left much of the barbed wire intact.

In the early evening of 30 June, the 11th East Lancashires left their camp at Warnimont Woods for an arduous seven-mile trek to the trenches in front of Serre. At two-forty a.m. on Saturday 1 July, the leading companies of the battalion reached the front-line trenches to find them already heavily shell-damaged. The build-up had not gone unnoticed and, as daylight broke, the forward lines were pounded by enemy shellfire.

At seven-twenty a.m., the men went over the top and were immediately cut down by machine-gun and rifle fire. One British observer likened the lines of dead to 'swathes of cut corn at harvest time'. Incredible as it now seems, groups of the Accrington Pals defied the machine-gun fire, threaded their way through the barbed wire and dropped into the German front line. Some of the Pals, their officers killed or wounded, pressed on towards Serre, never to be seen again. The remaining survivors in the German front line, bereft of reinforcements, were forced to withdraw. By eight a.m., the battle for Serre was effectively over. Of the 720 Accrington Pals who took part in the attack on 1 July 1916, 584 were killed, wounded or missing. My grandfather, Edward Ronan, lost his life that day at the Somme. Although he enlisted under a false name, his commemoration appears on Panel Pier and Face 6 C of the Thiepval Memorial in France, where he is shown as Lance Serjeant Edward Ronan.

It is likely that Nellie knew of her father's death because a pay credit of nine pounds four shillings was divided between Mary Elizabeth (three pounds two shillings), Nellie and her brother William, each of the children receiving three pounds and one shilling.

*

Coming back to Nellie, as I have mentioned, she spent all her early life being raised by her grandmother Harriet, who by then had moved to the almshouses on Buxton Road. When she was thirteen, Nellie began work at Rudyard Lakes, near Leek in Staffordshire. Rudyard Lakes is a picturesque tourist destination about forty minutes by bus from Macclesfield. It was popular in the late 1800s for workers from the Potteries who came to enjoy the beauty of the lake and the outdoor facilities. Rudyard Kipling was named after the place, as his parents had spent their honeymoon there.

Nellie worked at the Hotel Rudyard, a grand edifice with a splendid ballroom and extensive grounds for archery, bowls and quoits. She started in the laundry, progressed to the kitchens and later served in the dining room. Nellie was a strong and pretty young girl; she had her mother's big blue eyes and there was a tinge of red in her long curly hair. She was feisty and, in many ways, quite cunning, much like her own mother; she also knew the value of hard work and was shrewd enough to recognise she was lucky to have a position at the hotel.

Although Mary Elizabeth had abandoned Nellie, she did keep a remote eye on her, with the intention of claiming her back when Nellie became of working age.

One day just after Nellie had turned fifteen, she was walking down Chestergate when her birth mother spied her.

Mary Elizabeth approached Nellie and slapped her right across the face saying, 'You're a rude girl not acknowledging your own mother,' to which Nellie responded, 'But I thought my mother was dead as I was raised by my grandmother.'

Unsurprisingly, Nellie had not been told the truth about her parents.

As Nellie had a room at the Hotel Rudyard, she resisted returning to her mother and willingly spent her brief time off with her ageing grandmother. Life was tough, and although she had a pleasant disposition, there was a hard streak in my mother. My relationship with her was not close. As a child, there were times when I really hated her, but as I grew older, I better understood the hardships she had lived through: being abandoned by her mother as a baby, having a father who took no interest, and being raised in quite poor circumstances. To this day, though, I cannot put together the words Mother and Love, so I will frequently call her Nellie in my story.

Nellie made the best of what she had, attending church every Sunday, and walking out with her friends. Then, one afternoon, she met the man she would marry, my father, Harry Gidman.

3

My Father's Family

My grandparents on my father's side were John Gidman and Emily Simms. They produced twelve children, seven boys and five girls, the youngest being my father Harry, who was born on 2 August 1888 at 5 Wellington Street, Hurdsfield. One of the twelve died at birth; as far as I am aware, they named him Paul. As if bringing twelve children into the world was not enough, Emily then took in two more, both called Harriet, and they become known as Big Harriet and Little Harriet. The older children brought the younger ones up and my father was uncle to children who were actually older than he was.

My grandfather, John Gidman, died when he was forty-six, leaving Emily a widow at forty-four. Grandma Gidman was as slight as a sapling, but as strong as an oak. With so many children to support, and no social security, she developed steel in her spine. She was always ramrod straight, wore long skirts with a pinafore over the top, and her hair was twisted up and held in place with a bonnet. In so many ways she was quite prim and proper; she was like a lioness with cubs, fiercely protective of her brood, but beneath the shell there was a core of love that bubbled from her like lava from a volcano.

Interestingly, she was a woman of her time and most certainly did not trust new inventions. She liked the street gaslights and did not trust electricity and as she grew older, she would say, 'When the dear Lord calls me home, I'm not going in one of those newfangled motors; I want a horse-drawn carriage.'

When I close my eyes and think of her, I can recreate the smell of lavender. She used to buy sprigs of fresh lavender from the florist and dry them out, then make small sachets out of gauze, stuff them with the dried lavender and pop the sachets in her clothes. For me, the smell of lavender always engenders a feeling of security.

As Grandma Gidman grew older, her children were intensely loyal to her, such was the love and support she generated. When things were sad in my life, it was always her, or later, my own dad, who I turned to.

*

I know a little about my father's brothers and sisters, but surprisingly, despite my father having so many siblings, I have very few first cousins. Let me tell you what I do know.

There was Mary (b. 1869), known as Maggie, who died in childbirth with her first baby; both mother and baby were buried together in the same coffin. Next was Louisa (b. 1870). She moved to Staley Bridge when she married, and she had two girls, Emily and Alice. James (b. 1871), or Jimmy as we knew him, was a butcher; he married but had no children. The fourth child was Edward (b. 1876), but I know little about him. Annie Gidman (b. 1878) came next and became Annie Beard when she married Jim Beard. She was a crusty old soul who did not produce any offspring either. Then there was Ernie (b. 1879) who was an engine driver and lived in Crewe. He had one daughter, Phyllis. John Gidman (b. 1880) followed. He was always known as Jack and worked on the railways. He was married and had two boys and a girl.

Next came Emily (b. 1882), a pretty little thing with a button nose, deep blue eyes and long, fair curly hair. Her life was the saddest of all. She was eighteen when she met a very handsome labourer called Paul Stubbs. He was tall, with dark eyes and dark hair. He had an engaging smile, a persuasive way of talking and seemed to charm his way through life. They were married when she was nineteen and he was twenty-three. He was, however, quite a heavy drinker and a bully. He lived by the mantra that his wife was his property, to do with as he pleased. If he decided that Emily should drink with him, then he would brook no discussion on the matter. She would frequently plead to go home, but Paul had a violent temper and when Emily failed to do as he bade, he was quick to slap her around.

Things went from bad to worse. When he was out of work, he would get Emily tipsy, then have men pay him to sleep with his wife. It was not unusual for three or four different fellows to sleep with her on one night. He was a disgusting and depraved animal. She hated being pimped out, but whenever she raised the matter with Paul, he put his fist in her stomach or he would blacken her eye. I never understood why none of Dad's older brothers did not deal with Paul Stubbs, but Dad said that people tended not to interfere in other people's lives then. Emily died at the age of thirty. It was rumoured in the family that she had succumbed to syphilis. Paul died about three years later.

Selena was the next child, born in 1884. She married Harry Fisher. They had one son, Ernest, who worked at the mental asylum in Broken Cross. Ernest had two daughters, one of whom joined the navy. Fred Gidman followed (b. 1885). He married Lizzie and had two boys and one girl, but Fred was killed in World War I, so Lizzie married again and had another daughter, who died of pneumonia.

Finally, there is my dad (b. 1888), whom I love with all my heart. When my father was five, he contracted rheumatic fever and was so ill that it was painful to even be touched. To change his bed linen, his brothers used to lift him from the bed by the corner of the sheet, place him on another bed, then gently return him to his bed once the new sheets were in place. As a result of his continuing sickness, Dad missed a great deal of school. When he did go, he was well behind his peer group, so he hated attending classes. Grandma Gidman was determined that he should learn his letters, so she forced him to school, where he was strapped into his seat for two hours each day and made to read and write. At home, his brothers helped him, and over time he developed a basic understanding of reading and writing. Interestingly, as he grew older, he came to love books but as a child he was embarrassed that he did not have the same skill level as his peers.

I think that Dad's childhood illness moulded him into a gentle soul. He always had the ability to see the good in people. If he chastised us as children, we would take it to heart, for cross words seldom passed his lips. Despite his lack of formal schooling, he was a wise and caring man, and Grandma Gidman held a really soft spot for him, as he was the youngest.

'Now then, young Harry,' said Grandma Gidman one morning just before Dad's tenth birthday, 'I know you have no love of learning. You also know that since your Grandpa was taken by the Almighty, things have been tight for us financially. While your brothers bring home their wages, both Jimmy and Ernie are to be married soon. Their wages will then go to their wives, so I've been thinking. I've spoken to Mr Stacy, the foreman at Lomus's mill, and he'll take you on picking up the ends for the weavers. I know you're only a young 'un but you'll do a good job there. So, what do you say, boy?'

Dad jumped at the chance. 'Righto, Ma, if you think that's the right thing for me,' said Harry.

And so Dad started work at the mill, preparing the spools, running errands and generally being everyone's dogsbody.

'He's a good lad,' said Albert Stacy to Grandma Gidman, 'and works hard. If he goes on to the weaving, he can make a good life for himself.'

So Dad stayed on at the mill for almost four years.

Then, one afternoon, while walking home, he helped an elderly lady who had been knocked to the ground by a passing horse and carriage. 'Are you all right?' Harry asked as he helped her stand. 'Let me help you home.'

'What a thoughtful lad you are! What's your name, young man?'

'Harry, Harry Gidman,' Dad replied.

'Are you one of John Gidman's lads?' she asked.

'Yes, I'm the youngest. I work at Lomus's. Been there for nigh on four years.'

'And are you happy there, young Harry?' she questioned.

'Oh, it's a fine job. Why do you ask?' he said.

'Well, if you were looking for a change, I could speak to my husband, Mr Arkwright, and see if there's an opening at the Hovis. Hovis is the best bread in England and you could help feed the country. I reckon they could use an enterprising lad like you.'

This chance encounter led to Dad moving from Lomus's to the Hovis. He started out in the bakehouse, greasing the bread tins, and when he turned fourteen, he became an apprentice baker. It took five years to become a journeyman baker, then for two years he did extra training and at twenty-one he qualified as a master baker. He spent forty-one years of his life working through the night to put fresh bread on the table each day. But he paid a price for this unrelenting toil, as years of breathing in wheat-flour dust left him with significant respiratory problems.

4

Nellie Ronan and Harry Gidman

Harry was four years into his apprenticeship when he met Nellie at the Congleton Fair Shooting Gallery in May of 1907. He was there with his big brother Ernie, who was now working on the railways. Harry was quite shy, but Nellie took his eye with her outgoing personality and lovely smile. She was wearing an ankle-length brown skirt, cream blouse and neat brown jacket with a jaunty little hat perched on her head. She wore cream-coloured hose and boots that buttoned up one side. She was seventeen but had a worldliness that defied her tender years.

Ernie sidled up to Nellie, doffed his hat and introduced himself. Nellie was with her friend Ida Darby, and the two girls giggled at Ernie's forthright approach.

Harry lingered hesitantly behind Ernie, then shyly stepped forward to introduce himself. 'My name is Harry Gidman and I'd be pleased to show you round the fairground, miss,' said Harry to Nellie.

As Grandma Gidman had brought him up to be respectful to women, Harry was formal and gracious, and Nellie thought him rather a gentleman. The foursome spent a relaxed afternoon, each boy displaying his prowess at the shooting gallery.

As the afternoon drew to a close, Harry asked Nellie if he could call on her on her day off from the Hotel Rudyard.

'Well, I might let you do that,' said Nellie. 'You seem a nice enough lad. But you realise it's at least a half-hour ride on the bus each way.'

'Ah, lass,' said Harry shyly, 'I don't mind, I really don't.' And so began a two-year courtship. Grandma Ronan, who had raised Nellie, quite approved of young Harry Gidman but was always telling him to mind his manners and treat a girl with respect.

The months drifted on, and Nellie and Harry found themselves more and more attracted to each other. One Sunday afternoon, they sauntered leisurely from the hotel to Rudyard Lake. The sun was shining on the rippling water, the spring blossoms were in full bloom, the finches were chirping happily in the background and Harry, the gentleman that he was, went down on one knée and proposed. Nellie did not hesitate in accepting. She knew a good man when she saw one. I am sure there was genuine affection but, knowing Nellie's calculating ways, I would not be surprised if she also saw this as an opportunity to leave the drudgery of hotel work.

Being engaged led to a greater degree of intimacy and Nellie soon fell pregnant. They confronted Grandma Ronan with the news and then Harry had to tell his mother. Neither Grandma Ronan nor Grandma Gidman was pleased but both conceded that a baby should be brought into the world inside the holy state of matrimony, so on a Saturday afternoon in September 1909, Harriet Ellen Ronan became Mrs Harry Gidman.

As soon as she fell pregnant, Nellie left the hotel, moved back to Macclesfield and found herself a job at Beresford's mill. Initially she started off on five shillings and sixpence per week. Harry by then was a journeyman baker earning twelve shillings a week, so on marriage their combined weekly income was seventeen shillings and sixpence. They should have lived modestly well on this amount. However, Nellie had three great failings: she loved a punt on the horses, she was partial to a snort of snuff, and she could not do without her tipple of brandy and her glass of beer. Dad, being such a softy, would hand his weekly pay packet over to Nellie but, with her love of gambling, it was not unusual for the weekly income to be frittered away.

When they first married, they moved in with Grandma Gidman, as most of the others had left home. Grandma Gidman lived in Davies Street – just two streets away from Fence Street, where Harry and Nellie eventually set up home. The Davies Street house was a terrace beside an entry, so there was an extra bedroom over the entry, making it a three-bedroom house. Grandma Gidman was very kind to Nellie, who really had no mother of her own, and she tried in her firm but fair way to steer Nellie in the right direction. When Grandma Gidman would suggest to Nellie that she stay home in the evening when Harry had gone to the bakery, Nellie would push back. 'Life's for living,'

Nellie would say, 'None of us know what's around the corner.' Even pregnancy failed to stifle Nellie's social life.

Louie, my eldest sister, arrived on 28 December 1909, three months after their marriage. It could hardly have been described as a premature birth, although Louie was a tiny child with fair skin, dark hair and cobalt-blue eyes. All her life, Louie suffered from respiratory problems, had a permanent cough and experienced difficulty in breathing. As an adult, she only reached five feet three inches and was petite, but while she might have been small in stature, she was large in spirit and had a daredevil streak. I loved Louie because she was a fighter and she had a cheekiness about her that was endearing.

My sister Alice arrived fourteen months after Louie on 1 March 1911. She was a beautiful child and quite the opposite in looks to Louie. Where Louie was dark, Alice was fair; where Louie was short, Alice was tall. Louie had spunk, but Alice was timid by nature, and it was not unusual for tiny Louie to fight Alice's battles for her. Alice grew up into a true beauty with her long wavy hair, slim figure and her big blue eyes.

With my arrival in June 1915, the trio was complete, and we were always known as the Gidman Girls.

5

The Gidman Girls

Dad was conscripted soon after my birth and was assessed by the army doctors as being A1 despite having a record of ill-health and a weak heart from the rheumatic fever. He was posted to Baghdad. I was three by the time the war ended and he came home. I can still remember him lifting me from my bed, taking me downstairs and standing me on the kitchen table.

'Did you know about me before you went away?' I asked him.

The question amused him greatly. 'Yes, I knew about you, Annie, before I went away, and what a wonderful little girl I had to look forward to when I came home!' Whenever Dad had had a few drinks he would relate that story.

Our life at 42 Fence Street was not easy. With a constant shortage of money, there were no blankets for our bed. Instead, coats were laid over the sheet, which rested on a lumpy flock mattress. On winter nights, the shelves from the oven would be wrapped in brown paper, covered with an old piece of sheeting and placed under the coats. Sometimes, we would take a piece of broken brick and heat it up so there would be warmth at our feet.

With Dad being away at war and Nellie working at the mill, Louie and Alice were often left to look after me with an overview from Grandma Gidman, who had moved to live next door to us at number 44. Apparently, she was required to surrender the Davies Street house as most of her children had left home and the three-bedroom place was deemed more appropriate for a larger family.

I remember Grandma Gidman relating the story of Louie and Alice being told to take me to Victoria Park for a play when I was about two years old. Louie would have been about eight, and Alice seven. I was still in my pram and they parked me on a grassy slope under a large elm tree. It was around four in the afternoon and I fell fast asleep in the warm afternoon sunshine. At five-thirty, the park keeper was locking up, so the girls headed home. They were preparing tea when Nellie came in, having had a wee dram at the pub on the way.

'Girls, where's our Annie?' asked Nellie.

'Oh, my goodness!' said Louie. 'We left her at the park.'

It must have been around six-thirty when Nellie went around to the park keeper's house.

'Mr Withers, you'll be needing to go down to the park gate and open up. I think my youngest is still in there.'

'Oh, Mrs Gidman, how careless of you to leave a young 'un in the park by their self.'

'It wasn't me, you dozy bugger. It was my two older ones. Took off playing, they did, and left the little 'un behind.'

So reluctantly Mr Withers gathered his keys and walked down Park Lane to open up, and there I was, still fast asleep in my pram under the tree, just where my sisters had left me. Grandma Gidman was not so fussed about my being left behind; she was more concerned that I might have an earwig in my ear. What a strange thought to have!

*

Grandma Gidman worried about all things that wriggled. One day, Louie was having a major coughing fit and Grandma Gidman could hear the rasping wheezing noise from next door. She stepped in and saw how Louie was struggling to breathe, then noticed something extraordinary.

'Nellie, there is something wriggling up this child's nose,' she cried. 'Now then, our Louie, you must lie very still,' said Grandma Gidman while she carefully placed her forefinger and thumb at the end of Louie's nose. Very slowly and very carefully she pulled.

'Oh, my Lord Jesus!' exclaimed Grandma Gidman. 'Would you look at this,' she said as she extracted an enormous tapeworm from Louie's nostril. She laid it out on the table and took out her tape measure. It registered a full twenty-four inches long.

Our family doctor said that Louie was lucky the tapeworm had not wrapped its way around her brain, as it would have killed her.

*

The underlying cause of Louie's perpetual cough was never properly investigated. Whether it was asthma, chronic bronchitis or a persistent allergy was never really known but her respiratory function was poor all her life. Mind you, the environment we lived in was hardly the healthiest. Our house was close to the railway station with its steam trains, plus the gasworks and coal yards produced atrocious smells. The River Bollin, which ran through Macclesfield, was a major tributary to the River Mersey. It was full of chemicals and waste from the local factories, not to mention decomposing animals and bags of kittens and puppies. None of these conditions could have been good for someone with poor respiratory function.

Perhaps the medical profession had no ability in those days to diagnose her problem, or perhaps it was lack of money that led to what almost appeared indifference to Louie's ailment, but I remember as a child Louie would often cough her way all through the night. It was a dry hacking sound, almost like a dog barking.

When I grew out of my cot, we all shared the same double bed and Louie's coughing often made it hard for Alice and me to sleep. I recall one time when Louie was coughing so much that mother came in and smacked her right across the face for making too much noise. Poor Louie crept downstairs and stuffed rags in her mouth to try and stifle the sound.

As children, we did not dare to challenge our mother's ruling. While we talked among ourselves about how mean she was, we had no capacity to fight back. Certainly, as I grew older and looked back on my childhood, I used to wonder how she could be so heartless, so lacking in compassion.

We would cower in her presence, particularly when she had been drinking, as we were afraid that any slight wrong she perceived us to have done would be punished. Louie, in particular, must have felt uncherished and unloved, and when I think back on it, it is no wonder that there was a lifelong friction between Louie and our mother.

*

My other sister, Alice, was a different child; very quiet and very obliging. Not only was she the prettiest of us three girls but she was also the one who never answered back and who never defied our mother or father. In some ways, Louie and I were a little jealous of Alice because she was the favourite of all our aunts and uncles. This favouritism was particularly evident at Christmas.

Christmases for us were usually simple affairs. We loved attending the Sunday school Christmas party as there were mince pies, sausage rolls and Swiss buns – food we rarely ever tasted. At home, though, a typical Christmas dinner would be a broiling fowl (one which had finished laying) together with some roasted potatoes and peas. For presents, we were each given two comics, an orange, an apple and a banana. Louie and Alice received four ounces of liquorice allsorts while I, being so much younger, used to get four ounces of dolly mixture lollies. The liquorice allsorts were larger than the dolly mixtures, so my sisters would only give me part of their lolly in exchange for one dolly mixture or a whole licquorice allsort in exchange for two dolly mixtures. It was so rare for us to receive such treats that we would make an orange, once peeled, last three days, savouring each segment at a time. Our sweets would last up to two weeks because we knew there would not be any more for a long time.

I will never forget the Christmas of 1920. I was five and a half; Alice almost ten and Louie nearly eleven. Both Mum and Dad were ill and in hospital. Dad had chest problems and Nellie had Ménière's disease, which badly affected her balance. So it was decided that I would spend Christmas with Grandma Gidman as I was the youngest. After much whispering behind doors, I was later told I would be staying at home with Louie to look after me while Alice was chosen to stay with Grandma Gidman. I think it was because Uncle Jim, who lived with Grandma Gidman, had taken a real shine to our Alice.

That Christmas, Uncle Jim had had a few drinks when he decided, as a joke, that he would climb into a cot that was placed in the room where Alice had been sleeping. However, it was rather small and when he fell in, head first, he became stuck. He turned over, attempting to get out, but the alcohol added to his clumsiness and the harder he tried, the clearer it became that he needed help. He flopped back in the cot and yelled. 'Oy, you lot, come up and give me a hand, I'm stuck up here.'

Louie and I, who were having Christmas lunch at Grandma's, rushed upstairs and there was Uncle Jim, his feet in the air, legs pedalling away at ten to the dozen but getting nowhere. Then he stopped and sighed. Squashed up in the tiny space, he was like a fat puppy dog lying on its back groaning after a tummy rub. We all rolled around laughing because he had made such a goose of himself.

It was while we were helping Uncle Jim out of the cot that Louie and I noticed a doll on Alice's bed. Uncle Jim had given it to her for Christmas. It was the most beautiful doll I had ever seen. It had a wax head and an exquisitely painted face, while the body was made of cloth and was soft to touch.

'Look what our Alice got for Christmas, Annie,' said Louie. 'Isn't it beautiful?'

We stared at the doll with real envy. '

When Uncle Jim had gone downstairs, Louie turned to me and said, 'Why did she get a doll and we didn't? It isn't fair. We do just as many jobs around the house as Alice, and we help Grandma and Uncle Jim, but we didn't get a doll.'

'Let's hide it from her,' I remember saying. 'I know she'll cry but if there's only one doll, we should all have a turn at playing with it as well.'

'I have a better idea,' said Louie. 'You wait here.' And with that Louie crept downstairs, returning with Uncle Jim's open razor that had been lying on the kitchen windowsill.

'What are you going to do with that, Louie?' I asked.

'Well, if we can't have a doll, Alice can't either,' said Louie.

In my naivety, I asked, 'Are you going to kill the doll?'

'Don't be stupid, Annie. You can't kill a doll,' she replied.

Louie then turned the doll on its face and slit the body open from the neck to the foot.

'Oh, my goodness!' I cried as the sawdust from the doll spread over the bed.

Even Louie got a fright as the fine dust puffed out everywhere. It was over all the bedding and the lino floor; it was worse than confetti at a wedding. Frantically we tried to gather it up and stuff it back in the doll, but the sawdust was just too fine. So we pulled the back of the doll together and placed it carefully on Alice's bed.

'If they say anything to us, we'll just say the doll must have been faulty,' said Louie. With that, she secretly returned the open razor to the kitchen windowsill.

When Alice went upstairs, she burst into tears. She so loved her doll and had guessed that Louie and I had destroyed it. Uncle Jim was really cross with us, as was Grandma, and a couple of weeks later, once Nellie was up and about, we received quite a hiding from her for being jealous children. Looking back on that incident as an adult, I still think it was not fair; Louie and I had so little and we felt very left out and unloved.

This favouritism carried right through to adulthood because on my sixteenth birthday, it was Alice who was given a new dress while Louie and I were each given an apron. We knew Alice was not to blame, but it did make us both feel so much less important.

*

Louie and Nellie's relationship was a tempestuous one. Whenever Nellie hit our Louie, it made Louie more defiant, and never more so if Nellie had been drinking. Once, in an argument after Nellie had been to the pub, she grabbed our Louie, shook her, pushed her on the settee, snatched a nearby pillow, covered Louie's face, then sat on the pillow. Louie could not breathe! Alice and I had heard the argument from upstairs but when everything fell quiet, we hurried downstairs.

'Stop it, Mother,' Alice and I yelled in unison. 'Get off. You'll suffocate her.'

'Well, she shouldn't answer me back, the little cow,' said Nellie.

Although Alice and I were still relatively young, we pushed Mother with all our might until she fell off the pillow and on to the floor.

Louie's face was blue, she gasped for breath and, struggling to speak, she turned round to Nellie and with all the venom she could muster, shouted at Nellie, 'I hate you. I hate you.'

Truly, if it had not been for Alice and me, I think that day Nellie would have killed our Louie.

In my later years, as a mother, I simply could never imagine circumstances where I would treat my child as Nellie treated Louie. Yes, Louie was outspoken, perhaps even disrespectful, but Nellie's cruelty was unforgiveable.

6

Dr Sommerville

I was very fond of Dr Sommerville. He brought me into the world and was our doctor for years. He was probably in his early fifties when I was a young girl. He was such a gentle man that I was definitely infatuated, if not a little bit in love, with him. But I am getting ahead of myself.

Let me tell you a couple of wonderful stories about Dr Sommerville. He often popped into our house. Now that I am older, I realise that in many ways we were 'at risk' children. Dad worked every night at the bakery and Mum worked days at the mill and spent most of her evenings at the pub. We were like three little orphans left to fend for ourselves. In some childish way, we thought of ourselves as the Three Musketeers because we only had each other to rely on.

I recall that it was the school holidays, because we were home, Dad was asleep, and Mum was at work. Dr Sommerville called and asked what we had eaten that day.

I was about six, but I remember telling him that we had eaten well. Very proudly, I said, 'We had sugar butties for breakfast, Dr Sommerville, and treacle on bread for lunch.' A confident smile crossed my lips as I thought he would be impressed.

'Well, that sounds quite a treat,' he said in his kindly way.

Then the very next day he called again, this time bringing with him a bottle of cod-liver oil and malt, and he told us to have a dessertspoonful every day. I did not like the taste at first, but we soon got used to it.

Dr Sommerville said it would help us fight off a cold. When we had taken our medicine, we always gave the spoon to Snowy, our dog, to lick.

*

I must digress to tell you about Snowy. He was a Heinz 57 variety, white all over, with a black stripe down his nose. Our Louie found him in the park one day and brought him home. We had been told that we could not have any animals because they were too much trouble, but Louie smuggled him upstairs and we all tried to keep him quiet. We thought he was wonderful. He was our secret for almost twenty-four hours but eventually he barked, and Mum was up the stairs in a flash to see where the noise had come from. We could barely afford to feed ourselves let alone a dog, and Mum insisted that the dog be returned to the park. She was not keen on children, never mind animals, but we pleaded with Dad, promising to look after the dog and take him for walks. After much begging on our part, Dad said he could stay. He became very fond of Snowy, who was a super-clever dog.

It was tradition in our house that we had tea together before Dad headed off to the Hovis. So when Dad woke up he used to say to Snowy, 'Go and find your mother,' with which Snowy would take off and do the rounds of the pubs.

If she was not in the Nag's Head, he would go to the Water's Green. If she was not in the Water's Green, he would go to the Fence Tavern, and if she was not there, finally he would go to the Waterloo. Even if Nellie moved pubs three or four times, Snowy would always find her. He would then paw at her and not leave her alone until she came home. Clever Snowy!

*

Coming back to Dr Sommerville, it was December 1923. I was eight, Alice twelve, and Louie thirteen. Dad came down with rheumatic fever and was sent to Buxton Sanatorium. At the same time, Nellie was admitted to hospital with a diseased sciatic nerve and we girls were again left by ourselves, although Grandma Gidman kept an eye on us. I remember it being very cold in the house. The coal hole was empty and there was nothing to eat in the cupboard. So, brazen as you like, Louie went up to Mr and Mrs Farrar at the Selling Out shop on the corner of Wellington and Waterloo Streets and bought some food on tick; however, that did not last long, because we were already in debt and, with Dad and Mum sick, there was no money to pay it off. We survived through sheer ingenuity.

I regularly ran errands for Mrs Dale or I paid the Provident for Mrs Goodyear, and they both gave me a few pennies. The Provident was like an account system whereby clothes, shoes and other goods were purchased on credit and paid off at a few shillings each week. So this December morning I popped around to Mrs Goodyear, and asked whether she wanted me to do anything.

'Oh, Annie,' she said, 'you're just the person I need. Can you get my bits and pieces and pay sixpence into the Provident for me?'

Talk about a blessing! I did the jobs as quickly as possible and as usual she gave me threepence. So I went down to Market Street and bought a rabbit.

'That will be threepence,' said the butcher.

'But I only have tuppence,' I said.

'Oh well, since it's you, Annie, you can have this small rabbit for tuppence.'

I took that rabbit home and with Louie's help I skinned it, then took the skin to Mr Sheraton, who gave me a ha'penny (half a penny) for it. I then bought some lard from the butcher. With the remaining penny, I bought some damaged apples from Mrs Wilson. I took my shopping home, washed the rabbit and prepared it for roasting; I cut all the bad out of the apples, stewed them, then made some pastry for an apple pie. At eight years of age, I could mix flour and butter, add milk and pound the dough, making a really good short pastry.

Another problem was how to cook without fuel. Coke for a fire was sixpence a bag, or with an unemployment card it could be bought for fourpence, but this was a fortune for me. However, we were allowed to pick up for free the coke cinders that the lorries from the gasworks dumped, creating great big slag heaps. Coke is made by burning the outer layer of coal, which increases the carbon inside and it makes for a good fire. The trouble was I was too little to hump a full bucket of coke all the way home, but I sweet-talked my friend Freddie Olsen and he carried the bucket for me all the way home.

With the fire going and the rabbit roasting, I rolled out the pastry in preparation for the apple pie; then late in the afternoon Dr Sommerville knocked on the door. This was a surprise. He said that dinner smelled good and he asked me what I was cooking. He also looked into our cupboards and our coal hole, and I recall thinking that he was being a bit of a nosy parker.

'Have you done all this by yourself, Annie?' he asked.

'I have, Dr Sommerville.' Very proudly, I told him how I had done errands for Mrs Goodyear, bought the rabbit and made the pie. 'My only trouble is that the oven door is stiff, but Louie can undo that for me.'

'I'll pop back a bit later,' said Dr Sommerville, and with that he went off on his evening rounds.

About an hour later, he came back. There was the apple pie nicely cooling on the table.

He could not take his eyes off it. 'May I have a slice of your apple pie, Annie? It looks so good!'

Well! I have to say, if looks could kill, then Dr Sommerville would have been a goner right there and then. I thought to myself, How dare he ask for a slice of my pie when he's so rich, and we have so little! I was not very gracious with him as I cut the thinnest slice I could manage and put it on a plate. I then stared at him intently, watching him eat my pie and begrudging him every mouthful. Then off he went, but I was not happy that he had 'stolen' some of our pie.

The following day, two bags of coal arrived, together with a large bag of groceries. We had never seen such a big bag of goodies in our life.

When the delivery man knocked at the door and I saw what he had brought, I said, 'This can't be for us.'

He then asked, 'Well, is your name Gidman and is this 42 Fence Street?' When I replied that it was, he said, 'Well, these are for you.'

There was a pot of jam, a tin of salmon, some butter, six rashers of bacon, a halfdozen eggs, some cheese and a tin of peaches. It was years before I knew who had sent them. It was not until I was a young adult and in the Co-op one day when Walter, who worked there, told me that it was Dr Sommerville. Dear Dr Sommerville.

*

He looked after me the day I burned my leg. Dad had gone to work. Nellie had, as usual, gone to the pub. It was summer, and we were allowed to play outside until it was dark. Anyway, I had gone inside and put the kettle on the hob so I could have a cup of tea before going to bed. As I picked up the kettle, the intense heat seared my hand, so I dropped it and the boiling water spilled down my leg, scalding it really badly. My leg was on fire and and I screamed out at the top of my voice, 'Louie, Alice, come quick'

Alice ran next door to Grandma Gidman, who came in and poured oil on the burn. I was sobbing in excruciating pain, so Grandma Gidman told our Louie to run for the doctor. She raced to Dr Sommerville's house, banged hard on his door and told him what had happened. He came quickly and was appalled by what he saw. He covered my leg with calamine lotion to ease the pain and wrapped it in bandages. He gave me something to help me sleep.

Twenty-four hours later, I was still in agony and over the next few days, Dr Sommerville popped by to check on me. I soon developed the most enormous blisters on my leg. They were so huge that I had to walk like a duck with my legs set well apart. I was off school for three weeks, with Dad keeping an eye on me in the day.

When I think about it now, I marvel at how we survived. These days, someone would question the lack of care that we girls faced, but back then no one seemed to worry.

It was a different age. Children were born, children died. I suppose in some ways it was the survival of the fittest.

7

The Terrible Trio

Nellie was very strict and harsh with us and she hardly took any interest in what we were doing. She never attended school to see how we were progressing, nor would she go to school concerts to see us perform. Alice was in a club and became quite an expert at juggling, winning a local competition, but Nellie was as uninterested as ever. So you can see how we girls stuck together because we only had each other for support.

On the weekend, Nellie would often have an afternoon lie-down and if it was raining, she would put all three of us in the back bedroom and lock the door. We were prisoners in our own home. One Sunday afternoon, Alice and Louie decided they were not going to stay cooped up in the bedroom like caged animals, so they opened the upstairs window and climbed on to the roof of the garden shed below. They shouted for me to follow but that woke Nellie up and she stormed into the room just as I was trying to get through the window. Nellie grabbed my legs and pulled me back while the other two took off, and it was me who took a belting for all three of us. I was not happy about that.

We would often while away time making peg rugs. These were mats made from any old rags we could scrounge from family or friends – the more colourful, the better. We would cut the rags into strips and then weave or stitch the strips together, making a mat. One afternoon, we had promised to sit quietly in the kitchen making rugs while Nellie slept, but Louie got bored and said it would be more fun if we went to play Riley O with the Brierly kids up the Buxton Road. We tiptoed out of the back door, hoping that the squeaky hinge would not wake Nellie.

Louie went first. She scaled the wall behind the toilet at the end of the yard. It was about six feet high and in climbing over she put her foot right through Mr Abercrombie's greenhouse window. Alice and I were still in the yard, so we helped Louie back over the wall and raced quickly into the house. We seized our rug-making and began stitching in earnest while trying to slow down our breathing.

Another neighbour had seen the incident and told Mr Abercrombie that one of the Gidman girls had caused the damage, so about a quarter of an hour later he was hammering on our door.

'Mrs Gidman, one of your girls was seen scrambling over the back wall and she put her foot through my greenhouse window,' he said angrily, 'and I want payment for the broken glass.'

'I don't think it was one of my girls, Mr Abercrombie. Come in. I'm sure they're in the kitchen.'

And as she opened the door, there we were as innocent as babies, busy making the peg rug.

'Girls, have you been out this afternoon?' Nellie asked.

'No, Mum,' we said in unison, 'we've been here all afternoon working on the rug. We swear we haven't been anywhere.'

'There you have it, Mr Abercrombie. I don't know who told you it was one of my girls, but they wouldn't tell me a lie,' said mother.

With which, Mr Abercrombie shook his fist. He had not actually seen the incident himself, so it was the neighbour's word against ours, but I tell you it was a very close shave.

*

We had no radio or TV to keep us amused as today's children do, so we made our own fun. We would play Top of the Whip, Ball and Hoop and Riley O, singing at the top of our voices, 'Riley O, Riley O, we shall not follow.' We regularly played outside to avoid disturbing Dad, who needed his daytime sleep. We became streetwise at a young age and we learnt to stand up for ourselves.

There was a family called Black who lived up the road. Fred Black was sixteen when I was only about eight. He was in the street one day eating an apple.

I was really hungry, and my mouth was drooling at the thought of having a bite of a crisp, hard bright-red apple. So I said to Fred, 'Give us a bite of your apple.'

But Fred would not share. I pleaded with him; I even offered to give him a kiss, but he still would not share his apple, so I hit him. I knocked the apple out of his hand and landed him a punch on the arm. I grabbed the apple, deciding I was not going to share with him. Fred went off in a huff.

That night there was a knock on our front door. Mum answered and there stood Mrs Black in high dudgeon.

'Mrs Gidman,' she said, 'your Annie hit my Fred this afternoon and stole his apple. This is disgraceful behaviour. What sort of heathens are you rearing?'

'Mrs Black, are you telling me that your Fred, who is six feet tall and sixteen years old, was injured by my Annie, who is four feet six inches high and eight years old?' said Nellie. 'Well, that's a rum situation, I must say. And anyway, my children are not heathens.'

'Well, Fred came home with a sore arm and told me it was your Annie,' said Mrs Black.

Nellie laughed and told Mrs Black that her Fred needed to grow up and fend for himself, at which point she slammed the door in Mrs Black's face.

Needless to say, though, I got a rollicking for my behaviour. When I told Mum that sometimes my tummy felt like it had a huge hole in it because it was so empty, she told me not to complain so much, shrugged and walked off.

8

Wakes Week

Despite not having much money, we did have a family holiday during Wakes week every year. Mum and Dad loved Blackpool, a seaside resort on the Lancashire coast in north-west England, and, of course, we girls thought a holiday anywhere was wonderful. Blackpool is famous for its tower, which opened in 1894, and is modelled on the Eiffel Tower in Paris. It is also home to the Winter Gardens, a huge entertainment complex comprising a theatre and very large ballroom, as well as the Blackpool Pleasure Beach, a vast amusement park which has been operated by the Thompson family since its inception in 1896.

Wakes was one of the two traditional holiday periods for the mill towns, the other being Barnaby week. Wakes originally began as a religious festival in the Middle Ages and over the years it morphed from a one- or two-day event into a whole week, so the mill owners could close their factories and overhaul machinery. Wakes in Macclesfield usually happened around the first week of August, although other industrial towns in the north like Burnley and Bradford celebrated just before or just after as Blackpool, the most popular of the seaside towns, could not cope with the huge influx of visitors.

Nellie joined the Wakes Club, sometimes called the Going Off Club, at Beresford's mill and she put one shilling by every week for the Wakes holiday. We girls loved Wakes as it was the one and only time our parents bought us a new outfit.

Most of the mill workers went to Blackpool, although the posh folk would take their holiday in Morecambe just across the bay. Some years,

Beresford's would hire a charabanc and we would pack our carpet bags and tin boxes with our clothes, plus I always made a handkerchief bundle for my bits and pieces. When the service improved, Dad let us take the train, and that was super exciting, even though we travelled third class. The railways were not permitted to charge more than one penny a mile for third class travel and the fares were tax-exempt. While it was slightly dearer than the charabanc, the train was much more fun. Our family always stayed in the same boarding house, and we girls thought it was really posh because there were blankets on the bed rather than us having to keep warm with coats.

Mum and Dad were of the view that bathing in the sea during August or September was the most beneficial as there was said to be 'physic' in the sea. I cannot ever recall them putting on bathing suits and going for a swim, though Dad would roll up his trousers, and with a hankie knotted at all four corners to protect his head, he would paddle in the water. More often, they preferred to sit on the beach in their deckchairs, hired for a penny each, while we built castles in the sand. One year we even got a ride on a donkey.

I remember one Wakes Week when I must have been around nine years old. Mrs Isherwood, who owned a gown shop in Macclesfield, was very generous to us girls. As her own daughters grew out of dresses, coats and shoes, she would pass them on to us. When the coats became too shabby, we used them as blankets. Similarly, when old dresses became too shabby, we cut them up to make peg rugs.

This particular year, Mrs Isherwood gave us a pair of pretty black patent shoes with a bow on the front. Both Louie and Alice's feet were too big, but the trouble was, so were mine. Anyway, someone had told me that if I wet the shoes and put them in the oven they would stretch. So I found some old newspaper, soaked it through, stuffed the toes and put the shoes in the oven. But, lo and behold, quite the opposite happened: instead of stretching, they shrank, and all the patent peeled off. My beautiful shoes looked a sight and there was no way I could get my feet into them. I really believed this would do the trick but when I think back now, I can only smile at my innocence and gullibility. I showed the shoes to Dad and he shook his head.

'Well, our Annie, that will teach you not to listen to silly advice.'

'But, Dad, I loved those shoes,' I replied.

'Well, there's no way you'll get your feet into them, but here's sixpence. You go down to Woolworths and buy yourself a pair of pumps.'

I picked up the money and walking down to Woolworths I remember shedding a tear because those shoes were so lovely, and I had spoiled them.

*

From a very early age, I learnt the value of money. I was a good saver as a kid. Apart from running messages for Mrs Dale and paying the Provident for Mrs Goodyear, Louie, Alice and I would collect empty bottles and take them to the Selling Out shop, where we would be paid anything from a ha'penny to a penny for returning them. Sometimes we would be really cheeky and, in the evening, go to the back of the Selling Out shop where the empties were stored, help ourselves to them, then the next day go in the front door and get paid again.

At Christmas, we would go carol singing and might get as much as a ha'penny from each of the houses we visited. The parson from St Paul's church used to give us a penny when we sang at his door.

In addition, Dad always gave each of us one penny every Friday for the penny bank. If I had run messages and perhaps also scrubbed Mrs Swain's kitchen for a couple of pennies, I would bank as much as seven pence on a Friday. It took me almost two years to save thirty shillings, which, for me, was an absolute fortune. I was so proud of my saving, and when mother asked me how much I had, I blurted out that I had saved thirty shillings.

'That's wonderful, our Annie, now you'll be able to help pay for the holiday this year,' she said.

I was shocked, dumbfounded, hurt and could not believe what I was hearing. Nellie told me to take all the money from my savings account and give it to her. I remember she gave me sixpence back and she kept the rest. I felt as though I had been physically assaulted. I had gone without little treats; I had scrubbed floors; I had saved where my sisters had spent; and in that one act, she destroyed two years of solid effort. She did not seem to recognise, nor care, about the sacrifices I had made to accumulate my savings; she did not acknowledge that it was my money; she simply saw a sum of money that she could take. At the time, it felt as though she had trampled on my dreams and broken my heart.

I ran to the bakehouse to tell Dad what had happened. He put his arms around me, and I sobbed into his shoulder. I was distraught. He soothed my hair and rocked me back and forth and once I had quietened down he gave me the best piece of advice ever.

'Annie, never ever tell your mother how much money you have. You've learnt this lesson the hard way but mark my words, it's a lesson you'll never forget.'

How right he was! For ever afterwards, whenever Nellie asked me how much money I had, I would say, 'Mother, what do you think I am? A money tree?' and deflect the question.

Growing up and never having enough to eat or decent clothes to wear made me dream of a better life. Dreams were my escape from the reality I knew. I used to say to my darling Dad, whom I loved dearly, 'One day, Dad, I'll have a motor car and I'll take you for a ride in it.' Sadly, he passed away before this happened, but I can recall driving out of the garage in my first car thinking of my promise to him.

As I have told you, Dad was a very gentle soul, so different from our mother. But he would never hear a bad word said against her. I guess they loved each other once upon a time but I am not sure as they grew older whether they stayed together more from habit than affection, or whether they stayed together simply because of us three girls.

9

Schooldays

I adored going to school: I learnt to read and write quite easily and was always good with my sums. I also had a reasonable singing voice. In fact, I recall one Saturday afternoon when I was around nine years old, I had gone to the pictures with Louie and Alice when the projector broke down, upsetting everyone. There was a piano at the side of the screen, used to accompany the silent movies, and while the projector was being fixed, one of the ushers asked the three of us to go on stage to sing – he wanted us to be a sort of 'fill-in' act. Louie would not be in it and Alice said she would cry if she had to get up in public, but I climbed up there and gave it a go. One of my Dad's favourites was an old song, 'The Rose of Tralee', and I belted out that song for all I was worth:

> She was lovely and fair as the rose of the summer,
> Yet 'twas not her beauty alone that won me,
> Oh no! 'twas the truth in her eye ever dawning,
> That made me love Mary, the Rose of Tralee.

The audience applauded generously; they loved me. I remember crossing one leg over the other and taking a deep bow. A smile, wider than the River Mersey, illuminated my face. I think it was possibly the first time I had received such a public accolade!

But school was probably my greatest escape and mostly it was a happy place for me. However, there is one occasion that I still remember with embarrassment. It was a warm summer's day. I must have been around thirteen and had grown considerably.

The teacher pulled me to the front of the class and pointed out that my rather shabby dress was held together with a safety pin instead of a button. She said, 'There's no excuse for slovenliness, Annie,' then went on to lecture the whole class about tidiness and cleanliness being next to godliness!

I was mortified as the other kids laughed at me. I felt so ashamed. I determined then that I would never be put in such a position again: I would learn to sew. It was Dad's mum, Grandma Gidman, who taught me. Soon, not only could I sew on a button, but I also learnt to darn socks, sew hems and later in life, I even learnt to knit.

My final teacher at secondary school, Miss Hardcastle, was very keen for me to stay beyond the minimum leaving age. She said I had the potential to go on to higher education and even become a teacher myself. She encouraged me to work hard at my studies, which was not easy because there was no support at home. But I did try hard. I was well ahead of my year group and had to mark time by doing two years in Standard 7. In fact, I was so on top of my studies that I was often given the job of preparing tea and biscuits for the teachers at lunchtime. I enjoyed this immensely as it was a wonderful opportunity to help myself to a couple of biscuits while I was about it. I suppose it could have been interpreted as stealing, but back then I only thought about getting rid of the hunger pains that gnawed at me most days.

Towards the end of the school year in 1929, Miss Hardcastle said I should ask my parents about remaining at school with a view to going to teachers' college, so I went home to speak to Mum and Dad.

Dad was totally supportive. The contemporary thinking in 1929 was that education was a waste of time for girls as they would grow up and get married, but Dad had a different view. He said education was the key to change and that I should be given the opportunity.

Not surprisingly, Nellie thought otherwise. 'Harry, our Annie needs to leave school and start contributing to the family,' said Mum. 'She knows her letters and can add up. What use is geography or history?'

'But Nellie, if Annie went to teachers' college, she'd be a professional,' said Dad. 'She'd be on a good wage, more than she'd get going to work now.' Dad was always sensible, and he always looked ahead.

But Nellie was like a dog with a bone. 'Harry, you left school at nine and you've done all right for yourself. I left at thirteen and so did our Louie and our Alice. Why do you want to treat Annie any different?'

''Cos Annie will go places, Nellie, if you just let her. There's a determined streak in that girl and we should give her this chance.'

'No, she needs to earn her keep like the rest of us,' said Nellie, as obstinate and unreasonable as ever, and with that she stormed out.

Dad brooded on it for a day or so and I went back to school to say my parents were thinking about me staying on.

A few days later, Miss Hardcastle visited us at home. I remember opening the door and being extremely surprised to see her there. Hope reignited in my heart.

'Are your Mum and Dad in, Annie?' she asked.

I invited her into the front room. For once, Nellie was actually home, while Dad was fast asleep upstairs in readiness for the night shift – an unfortunate coincidence. I was sent into the kitchen, but I listened intently at the door.

'Your Annie is a bright girl, Mrs Gidman. It's my belief that she could go on at school and get herself a position at college. Please give her this opportunity. I don't think you would ever regret it,' said Miss Hardcastle.

'But why should she go to college when she can earn a perfectly good wage right now?' said Mum. 'It's all right for the likes of you, but we need her wages. Anyway, what right do you have to come here and tell us how to bring up our girl? We know what's best for her. I'd like you to leave now, Miss Hardcastle, and don't raise this subject again,' said Nellie sternly. And with that, Miss Hardcastle was shown the door.

I was mortified at the treatment Miss Hardcastle had received from Nellie. I was devastated by Nellie's hard-headedness and simply could not comprehend why my mother did not care about my future. I really thought Miss Hardcastle would have persuaded Mother. I had dreamed about going to college and becoming an educated lady. There was a moment when I truly wondered what I had done so wrong that would make Nellie so mean to me. I was frustrated, angry and impotent against Nellie's obstinate attitude.

But my dream was not to be. Therefore, when I turned fourteen in the June of 1929, I left school. I often think about sliding doors and wonder what my life would have been like had I stayed on at school and gone on to higher education. But it is no use looking back, since I cannot change history.

10

Mum and Dad

The tension between Louie and Nellie grew over the years. This tension was compounded every time Nellie, with a few drinks inside her, turned into another person. Now that I am older, I can see that alcohol took the edge off the treadmill of her life. Sadly, we did not think so kindly of her circumstances when we were kids, and I remember as a young person Louie pledged never to drink because it was partly Nellie's drinking that kept us so poor. Then an opportunity presented itself.

Mr Brierly used to leave his daily paper for Dad to read; one day we saw in the paper an advertisement offering a cure for alcoholism. The advertisement claimed that 'one teaspoon of this special powder in a cup of tea will cure people from the demon drink'.

So we decided to pool our pocket money and run messages for Mrs Dale and Mrs Goodyear to raise the sixpence we needed to buy the special powder. We sent away for the product and even arranged for it to be delivered to the Brierly household as Amy was my best friend and I knew she would not tell her parents what we were doing. In due course, the parcel arrived, and Amy brought it round.

When Nellie arrived home from work, we offered to make her a cup of tea and we discreetly put a teaspoon of the special powder into her cup.

'Here you are, Mum, drink this up. It will do you good,' Louie said.

'Well, this is a nice surprise. What do you girls want?' said Nellie.

'Nothing, Mum,' we answered in unison.

As she sipped her tea, three pairs of eyes were on the alert for some miracle. Goodness knows what we expected, but it certainly was not what happened.

She stood up and grabbing her overcoat and bag, said, with great flourish, 'I'm off up to the Waterloo for a refreshment before dinner.'

Well, you could have knocked us over with a feather. When she had left, we all looked at each other and decided that she probably needed more than one cuppa for it to work.

So the next day we made her another cuppa after work and again laced it with the special powder but again it was the same story. For a whole week, we kept this up until eventually all the powder was gone. It made not one scrap of difference to Nellie's drinking, but it was a salutary lesson to the three of us about the power of false advertising.

*

How fortunate we were, though, to have such a loving father. When Dad came home from the bakery around six a.m., he would light the fire, start the breakfast, and sometimes, if he could afford it, give us tuppence to buy oatcakes from Mrs Bishop up the entry. They were a treat for us. He would potter around the house in the morning, and when we came home from school or work at lunchtime, our meal would be on the table. If money was tight, we had porridge with sugar for lunch. Funnily enough, I remember that the only person in the house permitted to have cheese was Dad.

He told me once that he always tried to keep a little bit of money back from his wages each week, and sometimes he would buy sixpenny-worth of gravy beef and stew it up for lunch. However, if Nellie had got into debt and Dad had to bail her out, it meant there was no money for beef; nevertheless, he would still make us a nice gravy to dip our bread into. Occasionally, Mrs Wilkinson would give us vegetables, so he would add them to the gravy. But he never brought home bread from the bakery because he viewed that as stealing. My darling Dad was as honest as the day is long.

I also remember how he looked after our shoes. He would buy rubber soles and heels and repair our footwear on a last he had at home. Dad knew a fellow who worked at the shoe factory and he would often cadge pieces of leather and patch the shoe top. Sometimes he would repair the top using pieces of leather from the belts used to drive machinery in the factories. Dad was a genius at creating something from nothing.

In my heart, I felt Dad was perfect. He was always looking out for us. His whole demeanour exuded a calmness and we all felt safe in his presence. I recall him getting angry only once and that happened at work.

He had chastised one of the bakery employees, Percy Michaels, for not weighing the dough properly. Percy became angry and threw a knife at Dad, missing him by inches. Dad had to sack him. It was the sacking that got to him, because Percy had a family to support and he knew there would be no income until Percy found another job. It was typical of Dad to worry about others, but then he was a gentleman.

11

Work and Home Life

Thanks to Nellie, I left school in 1929 and started my working life as an apprentice hairdresser. The salon was called Hairdressers of Macclesfield and it was owned by a young married woman called Sally Brocklebank, who lived with her husband in the flat above the shop. I started work at seven-thirty each morning and I remember those early days so well.

Tom Jolliffe was the 'knocker-up' man who tapped his metal-tipped pole on the bedroom windows of the terraced cottages around six each morning. Soon afterwards, the factory hooters would call the people to work and the whole street would come alive. Mrs Dale would be producing her hot oatcakes and often as I left for work, the rag and bone man would be shouting out for donations. I would often race out of the door with little more than a sugar butty in my hand.

I worked until six p.m., six days a week, for the princely salary of seven shillings and sixpence. Mrs Brocklebank was having a baby when I joined the salon, but I did not think much about it at the time. My first weeks consisted of shampooing and sweeping up hair. It was repetitive work but the other girl in the salon was nice and it was a happy place.

A couple of months after I started, Mrs Brocklebank had her baby – a gorgeous little thing she called Gwyneth. Mrs Brocklebank was not off work long because she was the main hairdresser, so she would bring young Gwyneth downstairs with her to the salon. Then my working day changed and so did the nature of my work.

'Annie, would you take Gwyneth for a walk in the pram,' I was asked. Then it was, 'Oh, Annie, can you please give Gwyneth her bottle…or change her nappy…or burp her…or rock her to sleep.' After that, it was, 'Annie, could you make the tea and sweep the flat,' and soon I was spending more time child-minding and housekeeping than I was learning anything about hairdressing. At seven shillings and sixpence a week, I was turning into a very cheap childminder and housekeeper.

About this time, my friend Ethel Newton told me that there was work going at Peter Devonport's mill, where the pay was better and the hours shorter; so after twelve months at Hairdressers of Macclesfield, I decided to go for an interview at Devonport's.

I thought I could get there and back in my half-hour lunch break but the walk to the mill was longer than I had reckoned, which, with my short interview, meant I was away for almost an hour. That week, when the pays were made up, Mrs Brocklebank docked me sixpence for 'missing' half an hour. Considering I was putting in a ten-and-a-half-hour day, six days a week, for seven shillings and sixpence, the sixpence penalty seemed very unfair.

Anyway, I won the job at Devonport's, so I handed in my notice. Mrs Brocklebank seemed genuinely surprised at my wanting to leave. Dad had always instilled in me that any parting should be on good terms, so tempted though I was to truthfully explain my reasons for going, I kept my mouth shut, said my goodbyes on the last day, and looked forward to starting my training as a weaver.

Peter Devonport's specialised in 'small wear' weaving and my friend Ethel trained me up. I learnt very quickly and there was a wonderful sense of camaraderie among the girls on the mill floor. Better still, I was earning eight shillings a week for fewer hours and there was opportunity for promotion once I had learnt the ropes.

*

Life at home continued in much the same way. We three girls kept the house clean, with every Tuesday and Thursday being 'bucket' nights.

Upstairs was done on a Tuesday and downstairs on a Thursday. We took it in turns to scrub the lino floor on our hands and knees. One week, Louie would do the front bedroom; Alice, the back; and I would dust and tidy up. Over the next two weeks, we rotated the work, so we all got a turn at the hard and easier jobs. It was the same downstairs. We were poor, but we kept our house clean. Nellie always stayed well away on bucket nights, and frankly we preferred it that way, as it meant she would not criticise what we were doing.

Washday was Sunday, and this was a huge palaver. Firstly, the boiler was stoked, and we filled three tubs with water using a bucket. In the first tub, there was soft soap where we washed using a ponser (a wooden shaft with a wooden cross piece) that we rotated in the water to provide a form of agitation. In the second tub, there was clear water for rinsing and in the third tub, there was starch. All the wringing-out was done by hand and in the winter our hands chapped very easily. We only changed our top clothes on a Friday and our undies every fourth day. The bottom bed sheet was changed once a fortnight and we alternated changing the bed so that there was only ever one sheet per week to wash. This might seem a lot of work for young folk, but we were capable at a very early age. Well, it was either that or we got a belting from Nellie!

*

When we washed and changed ourselves, we heated the kettle and filled the kitchen sink. Whoever's turn it was to wash had full run of the kitchen, with everyone else banned from entering. We started face first, and worked our way down. Cleaning our teeth was something else again. I did not even have a toothbrush as a kid. I used to take soot from the back of the chimney and rub it on my teeth. This created friction which helped remove the plaque. I then washed my mouth with soap and water and finally rinsed out. The soap tasted so foul that we only cleaned our teeth every couple of days.

I remember two little luxuries that came from working and earning my own money. One was buying a toothbrush and some Gibbs dentifrice, which was a pink paste that came in a little round tin. We three girls shared the same tin and we would rub our toothbrush on the paste to make a small lather then scrub our teeth. It was hardly the most hygienic practice and the toothpaste did not taste very nice, but it was a huge improvement on soot and soapy water. It led to us all brushing our teeth daily.

My other luxury was going with our Louie and Alice on a Friday night to the public baths in Devonport Street and paying sixpence for a bath. That was just wonderful. We girls loved to soak in the warm soapy tubs, easily taking an hour, and coming out with fingers that looked like scrunched-up crêpe paper. 'Old Man's hands', we used to call them. We would take a jar of lanolin to rub over our skin after bathing. I thought I was the Queen of England, bathing every week. Nellie, however, thought bathing every week was a total waste of her beer or snuff money, so she only took a bath once a year, just before going off for Wakes week, though in truth I do not remember that she smelled.

*

But back to my job. As I became more proficient, my wages went up. Nellie could see that my skills were growing and regularly asked whether I had received a rise. Every time my pay rose, Nellie put up my board. She also had an uncanny way of getting extra money out of us. She would tell us that we could have some luxury item if we contributed a bit more. I remember we all loved our music and one day she said, 'Girls, you could have a gramophone if you paid me a bit more money each week.' So she increased our board by a shilling. It took us five weeks to pay off the gramophone; however, she did not reduce our board once it was paid for.

Nellie was a devious woman and it was risky to leave money in the house, because she always found it. I met Harry Kirk when I was fifteen and, although we did not start courting for a long time, we were friends.

He was having trouble at home, which I will tell you about later, so each week he gave me a little of his apprentice pay, as he needed eight shillings to buy some special signwriting books for his job. As we girls all had a drawer of our own for personal things, I put the money Harry gave me at the back of my drawer. On the final week when I was about to add the last sixpence to the savings, I felt in the drawer and all the money was gone. I checked with Dad first to see whether he might have borrowed it and then with our Louie and Alice, who both swore black and blue that they had not taken the money, so I confronted Nellie about it.

'Mum, have you taken the money from my drawer?' I accused.

'Why would I do that?' she said. 'I wouldn't take your money.'

'Well, I know that Dad, Louie and Alice have definitely not taken it, so it only leaves you.'

'How can you say that about your own mother!'

'Easy,' I said, 'because it wouldn't be the first time.'

Dad walked in at that point and frowned at me, telling me I should not speak to my mother like that, but he knew in his heart of hearts I was right.

Nellie continued to deny that she had taken the money but, as a sweetener, she told me to go up the street to Mrs Bradbury and ask her to lend me the eight shillings. Nellie then volunteered to pay it off at threepence a week. I know my mother would never have paid off the debt had she been innocent of taking the money in the first place.

She also stole money off Dad. He used to save his low-value coins in a dimple whisky bottle on the top shelf in the kitchen. One day, Nellie 'accidentally' dropped the bottle and the coins fell out. While she returned some of the money, she never repaid the full amount, and she still pleaded innocence.

I became very secretive about money as I grew older. When I was putting together my glory box, I bought a tea cosy in the shape of a black cat. It had a red lining and quite thick padding, so I decided to unpick a few stitches at the side, squirrel away my notes, then stitch the cat up again. It was sad that I needed to be so secretive, but I am pleased to say Nellie never found my stash.

*

Apart from being very partial to the amber liquid and her snuff, Nellie's other vice was betting on the horses. Often, she used Sykes, the SP bookie who operated out of Waterloo Street. When I was a kid, she would send me to Sykes's with instructions to back sixpence each way on three or four horses. I was always reminded to use the back door.

'Annie, just remember that Police Officer Simms lives over the road from Sykes' place and if he sees you gambling, it'll be you that'll be summonsed to court,' warned my mother.

I was terrified of being arrested but it was not me who was breaking the law. It was Nellie, who sent me to do her bidding.

Another little deception that mother indulged in related to lighting the house. Once Dad had gone to work and we girls might be playing in the street, she always left the house lights on if she went out for the evening.

When I asked her why, she used to say, 'The lights will warm up the room, our Annie,' but the truth was that she did not want people to know she was out drinking.

She also used to put slippers on when she went out so that Grandma Gidman did not hear her footsteps through the thin wall that joined our two houses. Nellie was cunningly devious, like a caged animal looking for escape, but for all her wiles, I do not believe that she tricked Grandma Gidman.

12

Life As a Young Woman

We girls did most things together, from bathing, to working, to going dancing. Louie and Alice were wonderful dancers, especially Alice, who was not only really pretty but light on her feet and graceful in her movement. Alice had been working a lot longer than me and she used to buy herself lovely clothes. By the time I had paid my board, paid for my bath and put a bit aside for savings, there was not a lot left. Alice never worried about saving; at twenty years of age, her priority was looking good, and she spent everything she had on clothes and make-up. But, oh, she always looked so beautiful! Also, to retain her slim figure, she would regularly choose to have a couple of cigarettes for lunch instead of anything wholesome.

I remember that I had just started going out with a good-looking boy called Andy Robinson. He invited me to a dance at the Stanley Hall, but I had nothing to wear. Alice and Louie were going off somewhere else that Saturday night, so I opened Alice's cupboard and saw her pink floral skirt and lacy cream top. I had always envied her looking so glamorous in those clothes and I thought they would suit me too.

'She won't mind if I borrow these,' I said to myself, so I had a washdown and put on Alice's beautiful skirt and top. I felt like a princess. Andy Robinson said I was the prettiest girl in the room and he partnered me in the first three dances. Then when he went outside for a smoke, Mickey Blake came up and asked me to dance with him too. Oh, what a wonderful night I was having, until around nine o'clock when I looked up and saw Alice and Dad at the dance hall door. Immediately, a wave of guilt washed over me and I could feel my colour rising from the tip of my toes to the crown of my head. Dad gave me his most disapproving look and beckoned me over with his finger. Reluctantly, I left the Stanley Hall.

Dad said not a single word all the way home but once we were inside the door, he looked at me disappointedly and said, 'Our Annie, do you know why I've brought you home?'

'Yes, Dad,' I said very quietly, 'it's because I borrowed our Alice's skirt and top.'

'And did you ask her permission to borrow those clothes, Annie?'

'No, Dad, I didn't think she'd mind.'

'Did you really think that, Annie, or did you just think you wouldn't be found out?'

I remember looking shamefacedly at the floor.

'Now go upstairs, hang our Alice's clothes up and put on that skirt Mrs Isherwood gave you last week. You must tell Alice how sorry you are, and only then can you go back to the dance.'

I did go back dressed in the hand-me-down from Mrs Isherwood, but no one asked me to dance. I felt deflated, but most of all Dad had made me feel ashamed of myself for being so dishonest.

*

Coming back to my young life, I stayed on at Devonport's for a couple of years. When I was around seventeen, our Louie talked me into moving to Smail's with her, Alice and Nellie as the mill specialised in jacquard weaving which, although hard and intricate work, paid really well. I remember earning fourteen shillings and we only had to work five days a week.

In jacquard weaving, there are lots of cards on wires with the pattern that is being woven. The wires have to be carried up the gantry and great care has to be taken that nothing becomes caught in the wires. Girls with long hair were required to wear a hairnet but it was not always well monitored.

Martha Westrop was a beautiful young woman with bright red hair that everyone admired. She was running up the gantry with her cards one Thursday morning when her hair became caught in the wires. She screamed for the loom to be stopped but it was almost impossible to hear her cries over the machinery noise. She screamed louder and a few of us nearby shut down our looms, but by then Martha had been totally scalped. In such a few seconds, this stunning-looking young woman changed. The trauma of scalping distorted her facial features and I remember looking at her in shocked disbelief, and thinking – just for a second – that she resembled a goblin. I chastised myself for having such an awful thought.

The factory owner told Martha it was her fault for not wearing a hairnet and she received no compensation. She was very ill for a long time and off work for a couple of months. I remember that the foreman, a nice older man with a lovely smile, suggested that we all chip in to help her out, so he organised a whip-round and we raised quite a bit of money. Martha did eventually recover, and her facial features returned to normal, but she had to wear a wig for the rest of her life. It was a poignant reminder for all of us to wear a hairnet while we worked.

It was while I was at Smail's that Louie and Alice, who were then twenty-three and twenty-two, encouraged me to enter the Miss Silk Queen competition. This was a grand event and the idea was to promote silk across the country, in the same way that the Cotton Queens of Lancashire promoted cotton. The award was made at a local carnival. I wanted to enter but did not have nice clothes, so our Alice said I could borrow some of hers. As usual Nellie was not supportive, but Louie and Alice egged me on.

I cannot recall who the judges were, but they were certainly local bigwigs. Anyway, carnival time came around. There were about twenty girls vying for the title of Miss Silk Queen. Some of them came from the wealthier families of Macclesfield and their dresses were exquisite. We were all interviewed by the judges and then we strutted our stuff. I was not really expecting to win but surprise, surprise, I was nominated runner-up to Ms Brenda Goodwin, Macclesfield Silk Queen of 1932.

*

I saved quite well when I was at Smail's. Over the summer of 1932, my lovely friend Marjory Finlow suggested that rather than going to Blackpool for Wakes week, I might like to go to the Potteries and stay with her mother.

The Potteries encompass six towns: Turnstall, Burslem, Hanley, Stoke, Fenton and Longton, which now make up the city of Stoke-on-Trent in Staffordshire. Two key commodities were abundant in the region: a local reddish clay or marl, ideal for making pots, and a huge seam of readily accessible coal to fire the furnaces. So plentiful was the coal that householders met their own heating needs by digging coal from their own cellars.

In 1720, a potter named John Astbury discovered that by adding heated and ground flint powder to the local marl, he could create a more palatable white or cream product. Unfortunately, the ground flint produced a fine dust which resulted in many pottery workers suffering from silicosis. By the early 1900s, ground-up bone replaced the flint, hence the term bone china, but while it led to a lighter, more attractive product, the incidence of silicosis did not diminish.

Staffordshire became officially recognised as the world capital of ceramics, with the famous Wedgwood pottery being made there.

Marjory's mother operated a bed and breakfast to supplement her income, and Marjory was very keen that I go. I was not sure at first, but then our Louie said she would come too, so that settled it. What a good choice we made. because I finished up having an amazing adventure!

Let me tell you about Mrs Finlow's house. I was in awe from the moment I saw it. It was a picture straight from the top of a chocolate box, painted white, with a small picket fence, and a garden filled with stunning roses. I can still smell their perfume, which was heady in the summer sunshine. We stepped into the vestibule with its floor of small black-and-white tiles. Once we had removed our hats and coats, we were invited into the lounge. It had the thickest carpet I had ever seen, with a lovely swirl pattern; cream curtains were swept to one side and held back with a tassel; and the furniture was so elegant. Mrs Finlow made our Louie and me feel most welcome. Our meals were served in the dining room on the rosewood table. It was paradise compared to the row of industrial houses where I lived.

While staying in the Potteries, Louie and I decided we would each spend sixpence and visit the local fortune-teller. I was not so sure, but Louie said it would be fun. She was a game girl and would have a go at anything. She went in first and the fortune-teller said she would meet someone tall, dark and handsome but to me she simply said she could see me on a beach with golden sand and beautiful blue waters and that I would find peace and calm there. I actually hoped she would tell me that I too would meet someone tall, dark and handsome, but that did not happen.

There were four other guests staying at Mrs Finlow's and we all chattered over breakfast. On the second day we were there, I met an Indian prince. His name was Swashanaswah Mokojay and he was from Hyderabad in the south-eastern part of India. He was tall, with flashing brown eyes and the whitest teeth I had ever seen. He spoke precise English, having been educated at the best school in Hyderabad and having then gone to university in London. He was very gracious and engaged in conversation with the guests, including our Louie and me.

When he introduced himself, we struggled to get our lips around his name, but he made it easy for us by saying 'Call me Smasha.'

On our third day there, he invited me out. 'Annie, I would consider it a great honour if you would do me the courtesy of accompanying me to dinner this evening,' he said.

Now you must remember that in 1932 black people were not commonly seen in England, and it was most definitely frowned upon for a white girl to be seen with a black boy. So I said I could not go out with him. He too must have been conscious of colour, but I knew he liked me. So the next day, after breakfast, he told me that he had bought the best seats for the pictures that evening and that I simply could not refuse.

I was nervous, but Louie said not to worry about what other people thought, so I went. She also said, 'I don't know why he isn't taking me out, as the fortune-teller told me I'd be the one to meet someone tall, dark and handsome – and dark he is.'

I had to pinch myself because here was I, a mill girl from Macclesfield, going to the pictures with a prince – even if he was black! Smasha was a perfect gentleman. He did not try to hold my hand or touch me in any way, and after the pictures he took me to supper. But the oddest thing happened. He kept waving his handkerchief over his face. Just picture it – he took one bite of his supper, flashed the hankie as though he was waving a flag, then took another bite, and this happened right through the meal. It was as though he was trying to wave away his colour – I mean, as if he could! It was really disconcerting.

Over breakfast the next day, he asked me out again, but I did not want people to think I was a loose woman going out with a darkie, so I said I had already made arrangements to go out with our Louie. And that was that, but I can truly say that I once went out with a prince!

Another funny thing happened while we were at Mrs Finlow's. She had a brother called Bernie, who was a real trickster.

I was in the bath one night before Louie and I went out dancing. I was humming a tune to myself while I had a nice soak in the warm water when all of a sudden, I heard Bernie yell, 'So, who's my beauty lying in the bath?'

I half shot out of the water and grabbed the flannel to try and hide my nakedness because I thought Bernie had come into the bathroom, as his voice sounded so close.

'What are you doing in the bathroom, you cheeky perve,' I remember yelling out.

But Bernie was not in the bathroom at all. He had tapped on the wastepipe that ran up outside the bathroom wall and the sound of his voice had reverberated, so for all the world it sounded as though he was in the room. Mrs Finlow told me later that he often did that to scare the young ladies. When I was dressed afterwards, I gave him short shrift for being such a cheeky bugger.

13

My Business Start-up and Nellie's Antics

Very early in my life, I took Dad's advice to heart about keeping quiet on how much money I had. I paid my board and the extras that Nellie dreamed up, but I was careful with the rest and slowly but surely built up a small nest egg and started my first little business when I was about eighteen years old.

I used to go to Manchester on a Saturday and buy items such as tablecloths, towels, sheets, blouses, skirts and pretty underwear. I would sell them to the girls on the factory floor on the basis of a shilling down and a shilling a week, or whatever they could afford, until the item was paid off. We called it lay-away. I saved an initial stake of ten pounds to buy my first lot of stock, adding a small margin when I sold. Bit by bit, I replenished stock and it became a profitable sideline.

Nellie also ran a John Noble club. Dressy clothes were advertised in the John Noble catalogue and the factory girls would again select an item and pay if off over several weeks.

Nellie had been talking for some time about the fact that she could not afford to go away at Barnaby. I think she was expecting me to stump up the money. Anyway, all of a sudden, quite out of the blue, she was cashed-up and went off with Dad. Then I discovered the source of her wealth.

My friend Amy Brierly had been paying two shillings a week into John Noble for a new dress and coat. She was up to week sixteen and only had another four weeks to go before taking delivery of her new outfit. Sadly, Nellie had never placed the order. Week seventeen came and still Nellie took the payment, but by week nineteen she became very anxious.

'Annie, I have a confession to make,' said Nellie. 'I've misplaced Amy's money for the John Noble club and she's expecting to get her dress and coat next week.'

'Mother, you've spent that money, haven't you?' I accused.

'Not exactly. I think I've put it somewhere safe, but I can't find it,' Nellie answered.

'Mum, you know Amy Brierly is my best friend. How could you have done this?' I said, feeling the anger rising within me. 'You used her money to go away, didn't you?'

'No, no,' she replied, 'I've just misplaced it.'

It simply had not occurred to me that she would be so dishonest with the John Noble money. It was one thing to steal from within the family but, although that was unacceptable, it was quite another thing to use the money other people had entrusted to her, so she could take a holiday.

There was nothing for it really: I had to loan my mother the cash. My friendship with Amy Brierly was important and I had no intention of allowing Nellie's dishonesty and complete disregard for proper behaviour to jeopardise that friendship. I also marvelled at how Nellie could look me straight in the eye and come up with the lie about misplacing the cash. I was furious and had no intention of just coughing up the money, without extracting from Nellie, in writing, a commitment to pay back every penny.

Nellie placed the order and on the twentieth week Amy received her new outfit. It was a close call.

14

Harry Kirk

I want to step back a little now to 1930 and tell you how I met Harry Kirk. I was fifteen years old and taught Sunday school at St Michael's Church in Market Place next to the town centre.

I loved the elegance of this old building, which is recorded in England's National Heritage List as a Grade II building. It had been built as a chapel sometime around 1220, soon after the borough of Macclesfield was established. Some fifty years later, Queen Eleanor, wife of Edward I, extended the church and renamed it All Saints. There have been many changes since the thirteenth century but finally in 1740 the church was totally rebuilt and rededicated to St Michael.

But I am digressing. Coming back to Harry, after Sunday school I would often go for a walk in the country with Elsie and Emma Bradshaw. The countryside around Macclesfield is truly beautiful in every season. We would walk over fields, uphill and down dale, and in the spring, there was absolute joy in seeing the tiny snowdrops popping their delicate heads through the snow that cloaked the hillside. As the weather warmed, wild violets, primroses and swathes of wild garlic provided a feast for the eyes and nose. In summer vivid deeply coloured bluebells carpeted the woods. We would tramp over bridges and stiles, muddy paths, pockmarked with horses' hooves, all the while seeing wonderful racehorses, cows and sheep grazing lazily in the fields.

Harry Kirk would also tramp around the hills with his mates. During one of these walks, Harry made a point of catching up with me and walking alongside. He was not a bad-looking chap – quite tall, fair hair, blue eyes, eighteen years old and an apprentice signwriter at the Hovis. He had the same name as my darling Dad, so that was something in his favour, but sadly, he was a bit too quiet for me. Harry pestered me to go out with him, but I was not keen. In fact, I tried to match him up with my friend Amy Brierly, who was really sweet on him.

'Hey, Harry, why don't you ask Amy Brierly out? She's a lovely girl and I know she has an eye for you.'

'Oh, Annie, Amy isn't my type. I like girls with a bit of spirit about them, girls who know their own mind,' he said. 'Amy is sweet enough, but she's not for me.'

'I'm not sure why you're keen on me, Harry,' I said, fishing for a compliment.

'Well, Annie, you have good spirit and a sense of drive about you. I like that. I think you'll go places one day and I'd like to go with you,' he said as a charming smile spread across his face.

His comment did not convince me, but I did like the flattery. After our second or third walk, he asked me to meet him on my own, and reluctantly I agreed. I arranged to meet him under the Buxton Road Bridge the following Wednesday at six p.m. When I arrived there, I could see him in the distance, pacing up and down but, being a fickle fifteen-year-old, I decided I did not really like him after all, so I changed my mind and went back home. I would never have done that sort of thing as an adult. I would have told him to his face that there was no future for us, but at fifteen, I did not have the courage.

The following Sunday after church, Harry and his mates came walking with us again and, clearly, he was very hurt, so I had to lie and tell him that mother would not let me go out and I did not know how to get the message to him. Oh dear, perhaps I was picking up my mother's habit of glossing over the truth when it suited.

One thing I will say for Harry, he was persistent. If he suggested a date to meet and I said I was busy, he would suggest another. He brought me tiny gifts: a posy of flowers, a wonderful drawing of a horse, and a small brooch in the shape of a heart. He never gave up. I did like the attention, I did like that he cared so much about me, and, over time, I guess he grew on me.

He was in my life a good three years before we became serious. During those three years, he came to know all my family. He was good mates with Charlie Steele, who had married our Louie in 1931. He knew Alice, and while he thought she was a beauty, he recognised that she was the softie in the family. Louie, Charlie and Harry got on really well and that turned out to be an absolute blessing when Harry had a run-in with his father.

*

Let me tell you about Harry Kirk's family. His father, Frank Kirk, was a difficult man who had grown up on a farm under the strict eye of a quite cruel father. Harry's mother, Ruth Ethel Baguley, known as Ethel, was a softly spoken, gentle girl who came from a reasonably wealthy family of cattle breeders. It was often whispered that in marrying Frank she had married beneath her. There is no doubt that Frank could be charming when he chose, and he wove his magic on Ethel and her parents until eventually Ethel's father agreed that she and Frank could marry. Ethel's Dad even took Frank into his business.

Ethel and Frank had two sons: Harry, born 18 November 1912, and Arthur, born two years later in 1914. After school, the boys would work on the farm with their dad, tending the cattle and the pigs. Cattle sales, which Frank attended, were held every Monday and after his business was done, he would have a pint or two with the other farmers. However, alcohol made him a nasty drunk and when he arrived home, he would find fault with the slightest thing and direct his nastiness at Ethel. If the house was not perfect, he would say she was slovenly. If she had prepared a cold lunch, he would demand a hot one. And, worst of all, he would accuse her of being unfaithful, simply because she was friendly with the baker and the milkman. He was both jealous and spiteful.

Harry told me that he became a King's Scout in 1928, which was a wonderful honour. He had worked very hard to obtain all his badges and his mother was very proud of him. When the King's representative came to Macclesfield to present the award to Harry, his father would not permit him to attend, instead making him clean out the pigsties. Harry was devastated. He had worked like a trojan for two years to attain the highest possible recognition in the scouting world. For his father to then deny Harry the opportunity to stand with his scoutmaster and fellow scouts and be recognised for his commitment, competence and dedication, was, in my view, unpardonable.

Ethel tried to persuade Frank to let Harry go, but it was no use.

'The boy's wasted enough time on his rope-tying and whatever else he does at scouts. He needs to focus on his apprenticeship and the farm and not be messing around with scouts,' said Frank.

Both Ethel and Harry knew it was no use arguing, because if Frank did not get his own way by authoritative rule, then he got his own way with his fists. Harry never did get to see the King's representative, but he did receive his King's Scout badge through the mail.

Harry served his seven-year apprenticeship in signwriting at the Hovis bread factory, where my own dad baked the bread. As an apprentice, Harry earned very low wages, so he lived at home. He did, however, manage to save up enough to buy special signwriting brushes. After Harry had done his farm chores, he would often practise his signwriting at home. When he finished with his brushes, he would wash them out and leave them to dry on the shelf near the back door. He came home from the Hovis factory at lunchtime one day and found that his father had taken the biggest brush and was using it to creosote the fence.

'What on earth are you doing, Dad? That's one of my signwriting brushes. You can't use it for creosote,' said Harry in total disbelief.

'That brush is in my house. I can use it for whatever I like,' retorted Frank.

'But I won't be able to use it for my signwriting again, Dad. You know that. The creosote will seep into the bristles. Why did you do it?' asked Harry.

'Don't give me any of your lip, boy. I'll use what I want, when I want,' replied Frank as unreasonable as ever.

Ethel could sense that an argument was brewing, so she encouraged Harry to come inside for his lunch. Harry was furious and was stewing over what his father had done when Frank walked in.

'You want your brush back, lad. Well, here it is,' said Frank, with which he raised his arm and stuffed the brush with the creosote into Harry's mouth, then turned on his heel and began walking away slowly.

Harry removed the brush, stood up, took a deep breath, walked to his father, turned him round and, raising his right arm, hit him hard right in the face, knocking Frank out cold. He then looked at his mother and said, 'I'm going back to work. Don't let him touch any other brushes.'

After work that night when Harry went home, his father told him to pack his bags and get out. Given that he was only earning ten shillings a week, he was not in a position to rent a place or even pay board anywhere. But he packed his clothes, gathered his brushes, kissed his Mum goodbye and left home. Where was he to go? He walked the streets for a while and, as it was getting dark, somehow his feet took him to our Louie's doorstep.

'I've been thrown out by the old man, Louie, and I've nowhere to go,' he said.

'Well, you'd better come in then,' she said. 'You can spend a few nights here while you get yourself sorted out.'

Those few nights led to a few weeks, the few weeks to a few months and the months to years. It worked out really well for all three of them. Charlie had a drinking companion and Louie said she would not charge Harry any board as long as he painted and decorated the living room for her. That suited Harry, because it was just his labour, and as time rolled on, he gradually redecorated the whole house.

Of course, with Harry living at Louie and Charlie's place, I saw more and more of him and over time I became quite fond of him. But that is in the future. First, I need to tell you more about my sisters.

15

Louie

With Dad needing his daytime sleep, we were always sent out of the house on a weekend. If we did not fancy walking the beautiful countryside around Macclesfield, then we would visit Granelli's ice creamery up in Chestergate.

Granelli's was a magic place. It was started by Angelo Granelli in 1890. He came from a small Italian village called Santa Maria del Taro in the Ligurian Mountains, near the Port of Genoa. Angelo brought with him the knowledge of making ice cream, which he had learnt in the mountain villages. He produced the very first ice cream available for sale to the public in Macclesfield. Given that refrigeration as it is today did not exist then, Angelo Granelli used to freeze that delicious mixture of cream, sugar and vanilla by packing wooden tubs with ice and salt around a zinc cylindrical container. Sometimes in the summer we would buy ice cream from Granelli's handcart, but in the winter, we stayed inside their café, as they always had a roaring fire. We would buy tuppence-worth of ice cream with three spoons and we would try to make it last as long as possible.

One afternoon, Charlie Steele came to Granelli's and started chatting to us. He had his eye on our Louie, who with her petite figure, dark hair and icy-blue eyes, was quite a striking-looking girl. Boys always fussed around Louie because she was small, and they thought she was helpless, but how wrong they were! I remember one day when Charlie really blotted his copybook. Louie was coming back to our table to sit down when Charlie pulled the chair out from under her and she crashed to the floor, hurting her back quite badly. Well, there was nothing helpless and dainty about Louie then.

'You silly bloody fool, Charlie Steele,' Louie yelled. 'I've met some idiots in my time but none as stupid as you. Fancy pulling a chair out from a girl. I suppose you thought it was funny. Well, it's not. You're a stupid silly sod,' she finished off.

Charlie scuttled out of the place quick sharp and Louie hobbled home, with Alice and me helping. She really was in pain with her back, but Nellie, with her typical no-care attitude, said Louie should not make such a fuss, so it was never checked out by the doctor. It will come as no surprise to learn that Louie suffered from a bad back for the rest of her life and many a time cursed Charlie Steele for his stupidity.

But Charlie was not deterred. He thought Louie had pluck; he liked her fighting spirit and so he would find out where she was going and go there too. He turned up in the oddest places: dances, church, picnic spots; he seemed almost to stalk her. Eventually she said she would go out with him, but I think it was Nellie who pushed the relationship.

'You know, our Louie, that Charlie Steele would be a good catch for any girl. He's a trained mechanic. You could do a lot worse,' said Nellie.

'I know, Mum, but it's my life and I'll decide when and whom I marry,' replied Louie.

'Well, you're not getting any younger and it's time you left home,' Nellie said in her blunt, no punches pulled manner. That sort of harshness was so typical of Nellie. There is no doubt that our mother wanted us all gone from home, and the sooner, the better!

Charlie was persistent; he really loved our Louie, and eventually Louie weakened and went out with him. He charmed her, and over the months his affections were reciprocated, and so it came to pass that in 1931 Louisa Gidman married Charlie Steele.

*

Like Nellie, Louie was totally irresponsible with money. When Charlie Steele's father died, Charlie and Louie inherited a thousand pounds, which was an absolute fortune in those days. But rather than buy a house or save it, they went on a big spending-spree, which lasted about three years. Charlie bought Louie a six-stranded pearl necklace and a fur coat, and they went on several holidays to Great Yarmouth, Brighton and Morecombe. They regularly went up to Manchester for the night, taking in the latest stage show that had come up from London. Louie once bought me a new dress but mainly Louie and Charlie spent the inheritance on the high life.

The sad thing was that over those three years, Alice and I saw little of our Louie. It was as though she had moved on from us, and I must say that at the time it upset us both. We had been the Aramis, D'Artagnan and Athos of Macclesfield – the Gidman Girl musketeers – but now Louie seemed to have little time for us, and it hurt Alice and me.

But nothing lasts forever and nor did their money. It was almost all spent when Louie fell pregnant. It was not an easy pregnancy, with Louie's chronically bad back and permanent cough. Therefore, I suppose, as much as anything, she needed the support of the two people she could trust who had been there for her all her life: Alice and me.

*

Charles Michael Steele (known as Michael) was born on 6 April 1934. Louie had a long and very difficult labour, and when Michael popped out he had a head shaped like an ice cream cone. I remember looking at him and trying to think of something positive to say – 'Oh, Louie, he's lovely' – but Louie looked at him and said, 'He's an ugly little sod. He's the first and he'll be the last, I can tell you that, our Annie.'

The ugly little sod turned into the most beautiful child once the trauma of his birth had passed. He had dark eyes and a cherubic face, and I absolutely loved him. I made any excuse to go round to our Louie's to see the baby. On a Sunday, I would put him in his pram and

Harry and I would take Michael out for a walk. If I met someone I did not know, I used to pretend he was mine.

When Michael was about twelve months old, Louie came down with tonsillitis, which turned into quinsies, and she was very sick. With quinsies, an abscess develops beside the tonsils, there is fever, headache and a distortion of vowels, often leading to a 'hot potato voice'. Other symptoms include neck pain and swollen lymph nodes.

Poor Louie was sick for months, as there were no antibiotics available then; we just treated the swelling with poultices. She became so ill that she could not keep her balance, so I offered to take Michael. Harry and I were newly married and we both adored the little boy, who stayed with us for almost a year.

I recall the railway track at the back of the house; as a toddler Michael would hear a train coming and say to Harry, 'Puppachain, Uncle Harry, puppachain,' with which Harry would scoop up Michael, race upstairs and look out of the back-bedroom window to see the train racing by.

I have only the nicest of memories of young Michael, and throughout his life I held him close in my heart. I often wished he was my son, so strong was the love I felt for him.

16

Alice

Alice was as different from Louie as chalk is from cheese. With her tall, slim figure and her long, flowing locks our Alice made heads turn. She was very conscious of her looks and would not even go to the corner shop without wearing full make-up. As I have told you, she was also a very beautiful dancer. She met Jack Unwin at the Stanley Hall in the early 1930s. He was handsome and danced like a professional. In fact, they made the perfect dancing pair.

Jack worked in the local laundry. It was quite common practice in the 1920s and 1930s for people to take their weekly wash to the laundry for others to do. A bagful of washing cost one shilling and ten pence and it certainly saved a whole day's labour for those who could afford it.

He always liked to look smart and would place his trousers between two pieces of paper and put them under a rug so the pleats down the front were always crisp. Louie and I thought he was rather self-opinionated, but the women seemed to like him. When he and Alice stepped onto the dance floor, people would applaud, so glamorous and elegant did they look. They glided over the dance floor as gracefully as swans glide over water. They were the Fred Astaire and Ginger Rogers of Macclesfield.

Alice and Jack married in 1934 and initially it was a very happy relationship. They would work in the day and go dancing three or four nights a week. Then around 1938 things started to go awry. On the evenings they did not go dancing, Alice would do her housework and shopping or go out with Louie and me, while Jack went bowling. It was there that he met another woman who took a real shine to him. One of Alice's mates at work told her that Jack was having an affair. But Alice would have none of it. She had lived with everyone telling her that they were the perfect couple and she wanted to believe in the fairy tale. They were the peaches and cream of the dancing world, but now there was a crack appearing in the façade.

The next bowling night when Jack came late home, Alice asked him where he had been. 'I thought bowling finished at eight o'clock, Jack, but it's close to midnight. Where've you been?'

'One of the chaps wanted to have a bit of a chat, so I stayed on for a beer,' replied Jack.

'But the pub closes at ten-thirty,' responded Alice, 'and it's almost eleven forty-five.'

'Oh, is it?' said Jack vaguely. 'I must have lost track of the time.'

The seed was sown, and Alice was suspicious. 'Annie,' she said to me, 'I need to know whether Jack's having an affair and I want you to come and check things out with me.'

The bowling green was close to Fence Street, at the southern end of Victoria Park, and there was a small wall around the clubhouse that was relatively easy to climb, so we took to scrambling up the wall and watching the goings on in the club. We noticed that as soon as Jack finished his game of bowls, he would nod to a woman who had been knitting. She would put her knitting away and the two of them would leave the club together. At first, we were not sure that we had interpreted the situation correctly, so a couple of nights later we repeated our surveillance. Again, we saw the nod after the game and the two of them disappearing together. Alice could not believe it and it took a further two visits to persuade her that Jack was cheating on her.

Interestingly, Jack was jealous of Alice and he regularly accused her of having affairs with other men, even if she was just going out with Louie and me. Effectively, he was accusing her of something he was doing himself.

I think he would have liked children, but Alice was not sure whether that was wise. She just felt she could not trust him. Then in 1939, after war was declared, Jack came home and announced that he had joined the army. He headed for Aldershot, where he undertook his basic training. As they say, 'when the cat's away, the mice will play', but more on that later.

17

Harry and I

When Harry finished his apprenticeship in 1934, he asked me to marry him. I really was not that keen. He was a pleasant enough man and I was definitely fond of him, but I cannot say I was truly in love. Nellie had been at me for a while to get married. She pointed out that the Kirks came from a better class than we did as they were cattle breeders and given that Harry had a trade and was fully qualified, I would be making a good match. Also, life at home with Nellie was stressful. I did not trust her; I was anxious about my secret savings and her tendency to search and seize, and by 1934, I was the only one left at home, so there was no one else to moan to about her spitefulness.

I recall one night when Harry and I were courting, we went to the pictures. Nellie had told me to be home by nine-thirty, but the picture ran longer than we had thought, making me late getting back.

'It will be all right, Annie,' Harry said. 'Your mother won't mind you being a bit late. She knows you're out with me and I'll look after you.'

We started to run and just as we arrived under the Buxton Road Bridge there was Nellie with a look of thunder on her face.

'What have you two been up to? It's ten o'clock and I told you to be home by nine-thirty, Annie.'

'Sorry, Mum,' I said, 'but the picture ran longer than we thought, and we've come straight from there.'

'That's not good enough,' said Nellie. 'When I say nine-thirty, I mean nine-thirty and no later,' she said, grabbing me by the shoulders.

She then kicked me all the way home: up East Gate, into Waterloo Street, Wellington Street and then into Fence Street.

I was mortified and was waiting for Harry to defend me, but he said nothing because he was used to parental violence in his own home. I certainly did not deserve to be treated like that and I was resentful towards Nellie for humiliating me in this way. I was also disappointed that Harry did not speak up.

But in so many other ways he was a good man. He had a sense of humour, he got on well with my sisters and my dad, and so I eventually agreed to marry him. A few weeks before the wedding, we rented a house in Hope Street. Harry moved from our Louie's into the rental property while I stayed at home. We painted and decorated the Hope Street house, and Mrs Brierly, Amy's mother, came around to look at the place when it was finished, and she said she had never seen such a lovely home.

We were married on 8 June 1935. I remember the morning well. Nellie, Louie and Alice had left for the church. Dad and I were about to leave when Dad took me to one side and said, 'Annie, are you happy to be getting married today?' He was so totally tuned in to me that he knew I had reservations.

'Well, Dad,' I said, 'I can hardly back out now. Everyone will be at the church; people have delivered presents, and the reception is paid for.'

'Annie, you do know this is a lifetime commitment and once you go, there's no coming back. Marriage is for life.'

'I know, Dad. I'll make it work,' and on that note, we left for the church.

The day itself was actually a very happy one. My dress was white silk with ragamuffin sleeves and I carried orange blossom in my bouquet. I had a coronet of organza flowers with the train attached and Harry later told me that when I walked up the aisle on Dad's arm, a tear came to his eye, because he could not believe that he was marrying such a beautiful woman.

The service was held at St Michael's Church and I had four bridesmaids – Louie, Alice, my best friend Amy Brierly, and Marjory Finlow, my workmate who came from the Potteries. Harry had his brother Arthur as his best man, plus Charlie Steele and Jack Unwin for his groomsmen. Because Harry had fallen out with his father, neither of his parents were invited. The reception was at the Co-op. It was a proper do, not a homespun affair as my sisters had had. We had sandwiches with the crust removed as we thought it was very posh; we had cheese on little cracker biscuits; there was a lovely sponge cake with jam and cream in the middle; and we had an iced wedding cake. We served beer, sherry and orange juice. It was quite a grand affair. We then delayed our honeymoon for a couple of weeks so that it aligned with the Barnaby holidays.

*

Virtually everything shut down during Barnaby as residents from Macclesfield travelled to Blackpool, Morecombe or one of the many Butlin's holiday camps on specially arranged buses and trains. Blackpool was such a popular destination for weavers that the *Macclesfield Express* was sent to Blackpool so that Maxonians could keep up with the news from home. Many an *Express* photographer would travel to the seaside resort to catch pictures of Maxonians sporting kiss-me-quick hats while clutching sticks of Blackpool rock.

But the Barnaby holiday of 1935 was a little different for us because we decided to go to Great Yarmouth. We stayed at a very upmarket bed-and-breakfast and we had the most glorious weather. It was so sunny that Harry finished up with first-degree sunburn on his face. He came back with puffy cheeks and peeling skin, looking like a pickled beetroot.

On our return from Great Yarmouth, we bought ourselves a tandem bicycle and we used to cycle out to Prestbury, which is about two miles north of Macclesfield. It is a beautiful town and we often talked of buying our dream home there.

I continued working at the mill after I was married and became a very good weaver. Over time, I graduated onto piecework, whereby I was paid for every item produced. I wove complex pieces such as coats of arms, heraldry items, university colours, and the fabric for naval ties. Though it makes me sound boastful, I can in all honesty say that my work was beautiful.

*

Harry was a very skilled sign-writer and the Macclesfield Council ran a competition for someone to paint the city's coat of arms. Harry decided to give the competition a go and he worked for weeks on his entry. Eventually it was completed, and he submitted it for judging. He had done a beautiful job and I was immensely proud of him. When the judges gave their verdict, it turned out that Harry was runner-up. His boss, who had taught him his trade, was the winner, so Harry was happy with that.

Harry always handed over his pay packet to me and I organised everything. We always saved for something we wanted such as a new lounge suite or a bedroom suite, never buying anything on credit. Harry would often ask me how much we had in the bank and in the beginning, I used to tell him the exact sum. However, every time we got ahead a bit, he would think of something else to buy. I desperately wanted to buy a house, but it wasn't on Harry's radar. Soon our tandem bicycle was replaced with a Norton motorbike and sidecar, which years later was replaced with a motor car. In those days, cars were started with a crank handle located at the front of the vehicle under the radiator. Harry would turn the handle until the motor spluttered into life, then leap into the driver's seat, release the brake and off we would roar.

Overall, they were pretty good years, although my husband did have a cruel streak which manifested itself very occasionally. I remember just one month after we were married, I was knitting a complex fair isle-patterned jumper. It required considerable concentration because there were numerous balls of wool that had to be knitted into the design.

Right in the middle of a row, Harry would come into the sitting room and turn off the overhead light, saying that we were wasting electricity. I would then lose my place and have to take the row back to the beginning and start again. It is often said that how a person is treated as a child is reflected in how they behave as an adult, and this cruel streak, which only showed itself from time to time, perhaps reflected on how his father had treated him.

*

In early 1937, we moved into a different rental house at 72 Waterloo Street, just around the corner from Fence Street, where I had grown up. It had two decent-sized bedrooms and a tiny box room. Although it was a rental property, Harry and I decided to turn the box room into a little bathroom. Harry did most of the work and the landlord went 50/50 on the cost. Oh, the luxury of indoor plumbing!

Soon after we moved, I fell pregnant with our first child. Both Harry and I were thrilled. I was about six months into the pregnancy and spent most of my evenings knitting gorgeous clothes for this baby: beautiful matinee jackets, booties and shawls. A friend of mine gave me some lovely soft cotton fabric and I decided to make some cot sheets and nighties for the new arrival. My mother offered me the family sewing machine and I went round the corner to Fence Street to pick it up.

'I'll carry it for you, Annie. It's rather heavy,' Nellie said.

'No, I'll be right, Mum,' I replied.

But she was right. It was very heavy, and although I only had about three hundred yards to carry it home, I should not have done so. No sooner had I arrived home than I felt a really sharp pain in my stomach, and I decided to lie down. Things seemed to settle but a few days later I realised that the baby was not moving. I waited about five days, each day hoping I would feel movement, but there was an awful stillness.

Lovely Dr Sommerville had retired by then and Dr Gillies had taken over the practice. So, heavy of heart, I paid Dr Gillies a visit.

He confirmed my worst fears, 'I'm very sorry, Mrs Kirk, but your baby is dead.'

His words pounded in my head like an unrelenting drum: 'Your baby's dead, your baby's dead.' I was devastated. It was all my fault. I had killed my own child.

Dr Gillies felt that the cord must have caught around the baby's neck and it had choked. In those days, babies were not induced, they just came when they were ready. I carried that child for several weeks until one morning I woke up to find that I was bleeding. Harry took me to the infirmary and I went into labour. The really distressing thing was that the baby had putrefied inside me, and when it was born the skin was almost black and the smell was indescribable. It was a little boy – my precious son. I was not asked whether I wanted to hold him; he was whisked away like some kind of unwanted garbage to be disposed of.

We had planned to call any son we might have Stephen. My heart was broken; he was so wanted and through my stubbornness, he was dead. The guilt, the loss and the sadness overwhelmed me. I was inconsolable. In my head, I kept thinking of all the 'what ifs': what if I had bought cot sheets instead of making them; what if I had let my mother carry the sewing machine; what if I had bought a sewing machine of my own? I tortured myself in my grief.

'Harry, I'm sorry I've let you down. I'm sorry this has happened. It was all my fault, I should never have picked up the sewing machine.'

'Don't you worry, lass. There will be other babies. This little fellow was just not meant for us,' said Harry kindly.

I remember crying my heart out. I cried and grieved for that child, and somehow did not have the strength to move forward, to put it behind me. It was my little boy – I wanted him so much and he was dead. Although I am now in my eighties, the memory of Stephen's death can still bring me to tears.

I was in the infirmary for about two weeks and was very ill. I was not allowed any visitors other than Harry but we Gidman Girls had stuck together through thick and thin, so when Louie learnt that she was not allowed to visit, she cooked up an idea. She rolled up at the infirmary door, telling the staff that it was critical that I sign some insurance papers and she had to see me, if only for a few minutes. They relented, and Louie sneaked in. She did not have any papers, but she had baked some lemon cheese tarts, which to my lips at that time tasted like heaven. She knew how much I wanted Stephen.

I remember she put her arms around me and rocked me like a baby while I sobbed my heart out. In so many ways, Louie was my soulmate and she understood my pain. 'Don't cry, our Annie,' she soothed. 'You have your own little angel watching over you now.'

In due course, I went home to the beautiful little nursery that Harry and I had decorated. It had bright yellow walls, and a crisp white cot, with a tiny bear propped in the corner. I had drawers full of baby clothes but I had no baby.

I remember Amy Brierly came around to visit me and I showed her all my beautiful knitting.

'Wouldn't this baby have been well dressed?' said Amy and she turned to me and cradled me in her arms while we both cried.

I can hardly describe the heartache. But there was worse to come.

The smell of the dead child stayed with me for months. No matter how often I washed and bathed, I could still smell the putrefication. I even used to put disinfectant in the chamber pot under the bed and when the smell overwhelmed me, I would pull the chamber pot out and smell the Dettol. The weeks went by, but my grieving did not stop. The weight dropped off me and at five feet eight inches tall, I weighed only six stone twelve pounds. I was a walking skeleton.

Dr Gillies told me that I would never carry another child. He did not explain why but said only that having lost this first child I would be unlikely to carry another. He was worried about my loss of weight and put me on Sanatogen to build up my strength. It took months, but slowly, slowly I regained my weight and in mid-1938 I fell pregnant again. Unfortunately, I only carried the child for about two months, then towards the end of 1938 again I conceived but again the baby would not stay put. I was bitterly disappointed. I felt incomplete. I felt hollow. My whole psyche wanted to carry and nurture a child, but my body let me down.

In so many ways, 1937 and 1938 were overwhelmingly sad years; not only did I lose my baby son and have two miscarriages, but I also lost my mother-in-law, Ethel Kirk. She was a fine lady, and her passing only added to my chasm of despair.

18

Frank and Ethel Kirk

Frank Kirk had always been a tough taskmaster, with both his sons and with his wife. One Monday in May 1938, Frank had gone to the cattle auctions. It had rained most of the day, so sales had been slow, and he had taken himself off to the pub. When he walked into the house around five p.m., he demanded his tea, but Ethel told him that it would be an hour before it was ready. That was all it took for him to decide she needed teaching a lesson, so he belted her. He then insisted that she go outside and stand in the pouring rain. She was a timid woman and did everything her husband demanded but making her stand in the rain was unconscionable. I doubt that any Western woman in today's world would tolerate such treatment, but Ethel lived in fear of Frank and always tried to defuse his anger by complying. The rain was unrelenting and only days later, she suffered the first of three strokes. She was in her early forties.

Much as I disliked Frank Kirk, I was very fond of my mother-in-law. She was a kindly soul, quite genteel, but I think whatever spirit she might have had as a young woman had been beaten out of her. Ethel had led a miserable life with Frank, always placating his anger, or cowering to his violence. She tried to protect her sons when they were small and, as they grew, I know they stuck up for her, but once they had left home, she bore the full brunt of Frank's cruelty.

When Ethel had her stroke, I looked after her and as she became sicker, I would often stay over at the Kirks house then go to work from there the following day. I cared for Ethel, washing her, changing her sheets, and tempting her to eat with easily digested food. Over the weeks, we developed a lovely bond and she would often tell me how glad she was that I had married Harry because he deserved someone kind to look after him. Even Nellie was quite fond of Ethel and sometimes she would stay overnight at the Kirks to give me a break.

I remember it was a Thursday night and Ethel had been struggling to breathe all day. I had stayed over the previous two nights, having worked during the day.

Nellie came around as she knew I had been keeping a vigil at Ethel's bedside. 'Go home, our Annie, you look done in. I'll keep an eye on Ethel tonight and you can see her on your way to work in the morning,' mother said, most uncharacteristically, but I guess even Nellie had a heart sometimes.

'I can't leave her, Mum. She seems to draw strength from my being here.'

'Annie, don't argue with me. You've been through a lot yourself in recent times so go home and get a good night's sleep,' she insisted.

So I kissed Ethel on the forehead and told her I would be back the next day.

It was six a.m. when Mother knocked on my door. 'Ethel's gone,' she said, and she put her arms around me, something she had not done since I was a very little girl.

It was as though Ethel stayed because I willed her to, but when I left, she let go. It was another loss; it was another death of a person that I loved; but I used to think of her in heaven with Stephen – a silly thought really but somehow it gave me comfort.

19

Frank Kirk and Emmie Collins

Ethel had not been buried six months when Frank Kirk began to court Emmie Collins. It was something of a scandal within the family at the time.

'Mum's not six months in the grave and he's out there rutting,' Harry said to me. 'I hate him.'

Emmie came from a strong Catholic family and had attended the local Catholic school run by the nuns. As a young schoolgirl, she was gossiping in class one day. She had been warned by the nun to behave. However, Emmie then passed a note to her friend. The nun spied this and threw the cane at Emmie. She tried to duck but failed to get out of the way quickly enough and the cane took Emmie's eye completely out of its socket. Emmie was sent home.

When she told her mother what had happened at school, her mother reacted in the same way as Nellie would have done. 'You must have deserved it,' said Emmie's mother. 'The nuns would not chastise you unless you had tested them beyond the limit.'

In those days, enormous respect was rendered to the Church and ordinary folk did not challenge the authority that the Church represented. As a result, no complaint was ever made about the nun's actions. It is impossible to imagine this happening today, but this is fact, not fiction.

Emmie was fitted with a glass eye, and I would try my hardest not to stare, but the rigidity of the eye fascinated me because when the good eye moved to the right or left, the artificial one stayed still.

Emmie was a chubby but quite pretty girl who thought her chances of marriage had passed her by. When Frank began courting her, and to her amazement asked for her hand in marriage, she instantly agreed.

Unfortunately, before long he slipped into his old ways, picking on Emmie for the slightest thing. One night, in an intoxicated state, he hit Emmie across the face, leaving a red welt and bruising around her eye. She fled the house, returning to her parents' home. The next day, Emmie's three brothers paid Frank Kirk a visit.

Alf Collins accused him of cowardice, hitting a defenceless woman without provocation of any sort. 'Only spineless creatures do that,' said Alf.

'Well, she should do as I tell her,' was Frank's cocky retort.

'Not in our world,' said Barnie, Emmie's older brother. 'We respect our womenfolk.'

With that, Frank lunged forward and took a swipe at Alf. Alf ducked, raised his fists and punched Frank in the face, knocking him to the ground and busting his lip open.

Alf leaned over and said, 'Frank, if you touch our Emmie again, I'll bloody kill you. Let this be a lesson. There'll be no second chance.'

I did not see a great deal of Frank and Emmie after they married. I did learn, however, that after Frank died, Emmie was worried that Harry or Arthur would make a claim on the family home, so within a couple of weeks of Frank's death, fearing homelessness, Emmie sold up the farm and bought herself a bungalow in her own name on Congleton Road. When I asked Harry whether he would have made a claim on his father's estate, he said it had not even crossed his mind.

20

Harry, the Baby and the Early Months of the War

War broke out on 3 September 1939 and it was around this time that I fell pregnant again. I was determined to carry this child to full term, despite what the doctor had said.

Very quickly, fit young men were being called up, the single fellows first, and we knew it would not be long before the married men would go too. Harry said he did not want to go into the army and he knew that if he waited, he would not be given a choice on what branch of the military he joined. I begged him to stay until the baby was born. He waited a while but at work his mates were receiving their call-up papers almost by the day. So one Friday night after work and a visit to the pub, Harry went down to the recruitment office and signed on for the navy. I was really angry with him. I thought he could have waited until the baby was born, or at least discussed his plan with me. I almost lost my life with Stephen, and I just wanted him to stay until the birth; however, he was anxious to go, so he signed on the dotted line, then left for his basic training in February 1940.

Dr Gillies told me that I needed to be very careful if I was to see the pregnancy through. I must say that this time I was cautious in carrying anything. If there were lots of cards to put on the rack at the mill, I always got the fellas to carry them for me. I barely picked up a mop bucket for fear that something would happen. I remember Dad was very supportive. He would come around on a weekend and help lift or move anything I needed.

The beginning of the war was almost an anticlimax. We had all received our instructions on the right way to wear a gas mask and told to go quickly and quietly to the air-raid shelters as soon as the sirens went off. But for several months, life just went on as normal in our part of the world. The only visible difference was the tape over all the windows and the need for blackout curtains.

Then around March 1940, I was woken in the night by the sound of sirens. Our Louie and young Michael were staying with me, so I went to wake them.

'Louie, the Germans are coming. I can hear the sirens. We've got to get to the shelters,' I yelled.

'Don't be daft, you're imagining things,' replied Louie in her half-asleep/half-awake state.

'No, I'm not. We've got to move. Hurry up,' I urged.

It took Louie a few moments to shake herself properly awake before she registered that the sirens were real. Years later, we would often laugh, as Louie thought that the pregnancy was making me imagine the long, mournful wail of those air-raid warnings.

The months quickly slipped by and I kept working. I had not washed any of the baby things for fear that I would somehow put a hex on the new infant.

When I only had about two weeks to go, Louie bullied me into getting things ready. 'Do you want this baby to sleep in a drawer or are you actually going to put up the cot, Annie,' she inquired. And so, hesitantly, Louie helped me make the room ready and then we waited.

On the evening of Thursday 20 June 1940, I went into labour. Faithful as ever, our Louie stayed with me through the night and around six a.m. she sent for the midwife. My beautiful son was born at seven-thirty a.m. on Friday 21 June. I cradled him in my arms and my chest swelled with affection. I was in love with this child from the moment I saw him. I had carried this baby full term; he was perfect, and I, at long last, was a mother.

Unfortunately, the midwife delayed informing Dr Gillies that I had delivered, and it was midday before he arrived to stitch me up, by which time I had regained considerable feeling, so the repair process was extremely painful. But the joy of having delivered a healthy son mitigated the pain and I snuggled him to me like a proud lioness with a precious cub.

We called him Rodney Beaconsfield Kirk: Rodney for HMS *Rodney* on which Harry was serving and Beaconsfield after Benjamin Disraeli, the Earl of Beaconsfield, who was not only a very successful politician in the mid-1800s but also a prolific author.

'Congratulations, Annie, this is the biggest surprise ever. I never thought you'd carry a child to full term. I'm delighted for you,' said Dr Gillies.

As a smile crept over my lips, I said, 'Well, it shows what a bit of determination can do, Dr Gillies.'

Harry managed to get some leave soon after Rodney was born. When he arrived, he made me a table with a steel top, which meant that when the sirens went off, rather than having to dive into the filthy air-raid shelters, I could scoop Rodney up and we would huddle under the table together. When the raids were on, I used to send up a silent prayer, asking that if 1 was killed, then the baby would die also because I knew no one could love our Rodney as much as I did.

I clearly remember December 1940 when Rodney was six months old, and I was woken by the demanding wail of the sirens. The German Luftwaffe had begun its relentless raids on the north west of England. Manchester, which was only a few miles from Macclesfield, was an important inland port and industrial city, while Trafford Park in neighbouring Stretford was a major centre of war production. Over a four-day period, the Germans dropped 470 tonnes of high explosive and more than 30,000 incendiary bombs in a bid to stymie the British war effort. As we were so close by, we took our share of hits.

During the nights of 22–24 December 1940, Manchester Cathedral, the Royal Exchange and the Free Trade hall were all hit, and it was estimated that over 680 people were killed with a further 2,000 injured.

When the screeching sirens woke me on Christmas Eve, I pulled the eiderdown and pillow off the bed, ran into the nursery and gently lifted Rod from his cot. I padded downstairs and crawled under the table. With Rod cradled in the crook of my arm, we snuggled together under the cover. The bombing was unrelenting, with incendiaries dropping everywhere. I heard engines overhead and I was certain that a plane was right above us. I held my breath. I squeezed Rodney to me tightly, and in that instant, I prayed that we might both be spared.

Then BOOM, the most massive explosion pounded in my ears. The bomb had hit Teg's Nose, a small hill right behind 72 Waterloo Street.

Rodney screamed in fright as glass shattered everywhere. It was horrific. Shards of glass, like jagged daggers, covered everything. All the windows in the house were broken, and all the plates on my dresser crashed to the floor and lay there in a million pieces, like pottery confetti. But we were alive.

I had to put cardboard up at the windows and it took weeks before a glazier came to repair them.

Looking back on that time, I remember so clearly how the screeching wail of the sirens engendered fear and panic. We were frightened that we might not reach shelter before the bombs were dropped, or that our homes might not be standing when the all clear sounded. There is no doubt in my mind that the war went some way towards breaking down the class structure in Britain as the bombs did not discriminate between the wealthy and the poor. There was a sense that we were all in it together.

I will never forget the fear I felt on the night of the Teg's Nose drop. Another few yards in our direction and it would all have been over. But I guess it was not my time. I still had a home but, best of all, I had my son, so there was much to be grateful for.

21

Alice and Norman Rodman

With her marriage on the rocks and Jack Unwin away in the army, Alice started walking out with Norman Rodman, whom she had met at the Bulls Head. He came from Stockport, about ten miles north of Macclesfield. Most evenings, Norman would pick up Alice after work and they would go for a drink or to the pictures. Although they did not see each other every night, they dated pretty regularly. They soon became very close and Alice fell head over heels in love.

About six months into the relationship, I was at the Bulls Head with our Louie when we bumped into Benny Irwin and he asked me if he could have a word in private.

'What is it, Benny?' I asked.

'Annie, do you know your Alice is going out with Norman Rodman and he's a married man,' said Benny.

'He can't be,' I replied. 'He sees our Alice almost every night and there's no way he could do that if he was married.'

'Well, he can get out at night because he drives taxis,' responded Benny. 'He does shifts in the day for wages and then tells his wife that he's working extra shifts at night.'

The very next day, I saw Alice at the mill and told her that Norman Rodman was married. Alice was totally in denial and wanted to know who had spread such lies. When I told her it was Benny Irwin, whose opinion we all valued, she still did not want to confront the issue. So life carried on for Alice and Norman, with Alice not saying one word. She was such a silly girl.

Then in August 1941 Alice fell pregnant. 'Norman, I have some wonderful news,' she said to him. 'We're going to have a baby.'

'Oh, my God!' was Norman's response. 'My wife is having our fourth child.'

Alice was dumbfounded. 'Do you mean you're already married, and you're cheating on your wife?' said Alice in a disbelieving voice. 'You're a real cad.' She was devastated. First Jack Unwin had cheated on her and now Norman was also a liar and a cheat.

Dad was very disappointed in Alice, because he could hardly believe that his little princess would shame the family in this way.

Alice came to tell me, and I remember her lowering her head into her hands and sobbing. 'What am I going to do, Annie? What will people say?'

'Well, it's no use worrying what people will say, let's just worry about you,' I said as kindly as I could. I immediately thought about Benny Irwin's warning, but it was no use bringing that up again now.

Abortion was out of the question so, with a positive tone in my voice, I said, 'There's nothing for it but to all chip in together and get you through this.'

Norman's wife decided to sue for divorce and she cited Alice as the co-respondent.

Alice was summonsed to court as a witness and she was stricken with embarrassment. 'I can't face all those people in court looking at me, Annie. You must come with me. I can't go on my own,' she pleaded and so we sat, side by side, as the intimacies between Norman and Alice were aired for all to hear.

It was humiliating for Alice and, at the time, quite an embarrassment for the rest of the family. Mrs Rodman was granted her divorce; Norman disappeared from the scene and Alice – beautiful but gullible Alice – was literally left carrying the baby.

*

Life was tough financially during the war years. Harry earned thirty-seven shillings as a rating in the navy and out of that I paid seventeen shillings and sixpence in rent. Ten shillings a week went on Rodney's nursery fees, leaving me with nine shillings and sixpence to cover food, transport, gas, electricity, coal, clothing and medicines. My two sisters were in similar positions, so with Charlie Steele working as a staff sergeant in the army, Harry away in the navy, and Jack Unwin estranged from Alice, we girls made a decision to move in together at my place. We were company for each other, but the arrangement was a financial saving for us all with only one electricity bill, one gas bill, one rent bill and one coal bill to split three ways. Also, this set-up allowed Louie and me to help out our Alice as her confinement approached. I only had two bedrooms, so Louie and I shared the double bed in the front room and we had two small folding beds for Michael, who was eight, and Rodney, almost two. I set up the back room for Alice with a bed and a cot.

Late on Tuesday night, 19 May 1942, Alice went into labour. I raced up to the telephone box on the corner and phoned for a taxi. The taxi firm was reluctant to send a driver. With the blackout, it was hard for vehicles to see in the dark, but I pleaded with them.

'My sister's in labour,' I told them. 'We don't have a car and the buses stopped running two hours ago. I can't phone the midwife because with all this bloomin' rationing, we don't have the coupons we need for the linens.'

Eventually I sweet-talked someone into coming. Louie stayed home with the children and Alice and I took the taxi to West Park infirmary. I stayed there, dozing in the waiting room right through the night. Around nine. the next morning, the midwife came out to say Alice had been delivered of a little girl. She was a bonny child and her mother decided to call her Loraine.

I remember seeing Loraine for the first time. She had a topknot of blonde hair, big blue eyes and a very square jawline, just like Norman Rodman. There could be no doubt that this baby was Norman's. The thing was she had not written to Jack Unwin to tell him of the pregnancy as, despite being estranged, she still benefited from his army pay and she did not want that to stop. He was certainly in for a surprise when he came back from the war, but I will tell you about that later. Although Dad was disappointed in our Alice, he soon came around and fell in love with Loraine, as he always had a soft spot for the girls.

In those days, it was normal for women to stay in hospital for around ten days, but Alice developed abscesses in the breast and started running a fever. As a consequence, Loraine was discharged into my care, while Alice had to stay put for another two weeks until her fever came down and she was back on her feet. Between Louie, Dad and me, we juggled work and cared for Loraine, as no nursery would accept her until she was six weeks old. I can tell you, it was a very long six weeks for everyone: Alice was fretting after the baby, Dad was exhausted as he took the brunt of the daytime care then put in the hours at the bakery at night, while Louie and I worked in the day, then shared the night-time bottles. But we survived.

Eventually Alice came home, and she stayed with Louie and me for quite a few months. When Loraine started to crawl and assert her independence, however, the house suddenly seemed super-full, so Alice decided to get a place of her own.

'Annie, you know Mr Wardle who owns most of the houses around here,' said Alice. 'Do you think you could put in a good word for me to see if I could get the Harrises' house over the road which is coming empty next week?' she asked.

Accommodation was very difficult to secure as so many houses had been bombed but I had always been a good tenant for Mr Wardle – the rent was paid on time and I looked after the house well. 65 Waterloo Street was right opposite me. It was a two-up and two-down, with a sash window and a coal cellar beneath the kitchen at the back. The back door opened on to the Big Yard, as it was called, which housed all the toilets for the terrace. It was perfect for Alice's needs. I braced myself and paid Mr Wardle a visit.

'Mr Wardle, I've come to seek your help. As you know, our Alice has just had a baby and there isn't enough space at my place for us all. I see that 65 Waterloo Street is coming empty. Would you let our Alice have it?' I asked.

'Oh, I couldn't do that, Annie. I know Alice is on her own with a new baby. How's a single mother going to pay the rent? There are many families out there who would be more reliable than your Alice,' he replied.

'But Mr Wardle, Alice still has an army allowance from Jack and she'll be back at work in another fortnight. Also, we'll decorate the place for you at no charge, and I'll help her with the rent,' I promised, keeping my fingers crossed behind my back. I could barely afford my own living expenses, but I knew Alice would be a good tenant if only she could get the place.

Mr Wardle rubbed his chin, tilted his head to one side and took what seemed to be an absolute age, but eventually he said yes, she could have the house.

I was as good as my word and as soon as we had the keys, we worked like a hive of bees. We stripped off the old wallpaper in the front room and the two bedrooms and papered them. Harry had taught me how to decorate and I was quite skilled at it. It took us nearly two weeks working nights and weekends, but it was summer and light until late, so we managed to get the place looking good quite quickly. Alice begged and borrowed furniture and set up a nice little nest for Loraine and herself. The beauty of it was that she was just over the road from Louie and me.

Of course, when Jack Unwin returned from the war, he was in for a big surprise. While he was away, he had written talking of a reconciliation, so you can imagine his face when he arrived home and found out that his wife had had a baby by another man. Jack moved faster than a bullet from a Sten gun, in divorcing Alice on the grounds of her adultery. Again, she was in the spotlight for the wrong reasons, but as always Louie and I helped her through.

*

I often did wallpapering for friends as I found it quite relaxing. It is amazing what a bit of wallpaper can do to brighten up a room. I had a really good friend from the mill, Marion Lewis, who wanted her front room papered. I told Marion to move all her furniture to the middle of the room, so we could get a good start, but Marion told me that the furniture was too heavy to move and the wallpaper too expensive to hide behind furniture and that I should just paper around it. Well, what a business that turned out to be! I had to tuck the wallpaper ends behind the large settee and chairs. I can tell you that it was quite a tricky job, but I managed it. However, when Marion came to move to a new house a few years later and the furniture was shifted, the walls were a terrible sight. Still, I earned a bit extra, which all helped during the war years.

22

The War Years

Money was so tight during the war years that I had little choice but to return to work when Rodney was only six weeks old. It broke my heart to put him into nursery so young and if ever I was at work when the sirens wailed, I use to pray that Rod would stay safe. They were tough years in so many ways but there was also great camaraderie.

Blood donation was a huge issue, as massive quantities were needed for the military and those civilians injured in air raids. The Red Cross set up a national blood-donor program and called on all civilians over the age of seventeen to donate. Until the war, direct transfusion from donor to patient had been the common practice, but it was clear that civilians could not go out to the front line to donate, so blood banks came into existence, with one in every major town being set up for easy donor access.

My sisters and I all became donors and at one point during the war, I recall being asked to donate every fortnight. I did this for a little while but collapsed one day walking home from work. I remember Dr Gillies sitting me down and pointing out that I was raising my son single-handedly, working full-time, running a house and helping my sisters. His view was that I was doing enough. So that put an end to my blood-donor days.

Everything was rationed during the war and nothing could be acquired without coupons. We often swapped our coupons to suit our needs. For example, Annie Beard, my father's sister, married to Jim Beard, was a huge tea drinker and she liked her tea so strong that you could almost stand a spoon up in it. So we swapped our tea coupons for her clothing ones. In that way, as he grew, I could keep our Rodney dressed in reasonable clothes.

We recycled as much as we could and 'make do and mend' was the order of the day. Old sheets were made into pillowcases. Old curtains were made into a skirt, or short pants or cushion covers. Flour sacks were boiled, pressed and made into clothes. Worn-out jumpers were roved and reknitted. I recall that around 1936 I had knitted a long-sleeved jumper for Harry. It lasted about three years and when he wore the elbows out, I roved the jumper and knitted a sleeveless vest for him. When the front of the vest became thin, I roved the garment and knitted a long-sleeved jumper for Rodney, and when he wore the elbows out, I roved it again and knitted him a sleeveless vest. When, finally, that wore thin at the front, which I might add did not take very long, I roved it one final time and knitted a pair of socks. I was the queen of recycling!

At the factory, we began to weave silk for parachutes. It was the preferred fabric because it was tough. Alice, Louie, Nellie and I all wove parachute silk on a piecework basis, and we were a good team. The first one in each morning would clock in for the other three, get their own loom going and then get the looms of the others set up and operating. If anyone wanted to leave early, those remaining would keep the looms going until clocking-off time. If there had been an air raid overnight, it was often difficult to get through the debris on the way to the factory. At other times, I might be running late after taking Rodney to the nursery or our Louie might want to leave early to take in a show at Manchester or Stockport, so we pulled together and helped each other out. We were 'one for all, and all for one'.

A parachute took 129 yards of fabric, and once that was cut off the run, there would be pieces left over. There was virtually nothing to buy in the shops in the way of clothing and even if I had the money, there were insufficient coupons, so we would snaffle the remnants of the parachute silk and take them home to make undies and blouses. It was never sanctioned by the bosses, but neither were we punished for taking the offcuts. I remember wearing a blouse I had made to work one day, and the foreman looked at me good-humouredly, and with a glint of recognition in his eye, said, 'Nice fabric.'

Make-up was another thing in short supply, so we relied on cooking ingredients for our beauty rituals. Egg white and lemon juice became a face pack. One Saturday night, when we decided to have a girls' night in, we mixed beetroot juice with Vaseline to make lipstick. It had the weirdest taste, but our lips were a glorious juicy red colour.

*

Dad's sister, Selena, or Lena as we called her, had a pretty difficult time during the war. She was married to Harry Fisher and they had one child, Ernie. Lena was a quill-winder at the factory and her pay was quite low. One day, Harry Fisher went to the bank and took out all the money they had in their joint bank account and he left Lena for another woman. Lena was devastated. She had been a loyal wife and a good mother, while Harry was just driven by 'the middle leg'. We all loved our Auntie Lena, so we decided to chip in and make up a parcel of goodies for her. I took it round.

It was the winter of 1941 and it had been snowing heavily. Lena had gone to the toilet up the backyard; as she returned to the house, she saw footprints in the snow leading to her backdoor. 'Oh! my goodness, someone's in the house,' she said to herself and her heart began racing. Cautiously, she stepped inside and there on the table was our parcel.

I had hidden in the front room, but I peeked around the door and watched a disbelieving look creep across her face as she unpacked the goodies. We had cobbled together a cup of sugar, a small tin of Spam, a little block of cheese, some milk, a loaf of bread, some hand-me-down clothes for Ernie and a blouse that I had run up on the machine from the parachute silk. And on the card, we had written, 'With love from your favourite nieces, Louie, Alice and Annie.' Poor Auntie Lena was overwhelmed and burst into tears, so I popped in and put my arms around her. We had so little, but we shared what we had.

Auntie Lena never forgot our generosity. She struggled for years raising Ernie by herself and then one day, out of the blue, Harry Fisher knocked on the door. He was full of apologies for running off with someone else and begged to come back home. Whether Lena was motivated by duty, loneliness – or madness, as Louie and I surmised – she took Harry back. As our Louie said, 'Cheating on a good person such as Lena and going off with another woman is like throwing away a diamond and picking up a rock.'

*

As the war ground on and the German U-boats attacked our Atlantic merchant fleet, everything in England became scarce. The coupons were just not enough for what we needed but most things could be bought on the black market if you had enough money. So, to supplement my earnings from the mill, I worked a couple of hours three or four nights a week at the Waterloo Tavern on the corner of Waterloo Street. The back gate of my house used to face the back gate of the pub, so once I put our Rodney to bed at night, I would slip out of the gate and into the pub to work. Often, if Louie was out and I had to leave Rodney and Michael by themselves, I would pop back home every half hour or so just to check they were OK.

I met a lot of American GIs at the pub and being a good-looker in those days I was often propositioned. I never hid the fact that I was married and had a young son; in fact, many of the GIs were married themselves and were lonely and missed their families. One American I befriended was called Hank Grossman and he worked in the kitchen at the army base. He was married with children at home and in civilian life he worked in a funeral parlour. I used to flutter my eyes at him and always strike up a conversation when he called in.

One day I said to him, 'Hank, can you get any supplies from the base?'

'Sure,' he replied. 'I can get anything. What do you want, Annie?'

'I dream of sugar, soap, margarine, nylon stockings and fruit, but we're short of everything, so whatever you could bring would be wonderful,' I said.

Well, was I in for a surprise! The very next day, he arrived with a one-pound bag of sugar which, at the time, was as precious as a bag of gold dust. Another day, he produced two ounces of real butter. We had been surviving on butchers' lard and I had not seen real butter in over two years, so this was luxury beyond description. But, best of all, I recall one particular night he brought in a commercial-sized tin of fruit which he must have pinched from the kitchen supplies.

I took it to Rodney's nursery and said to the matron, 'Look what I've brought you.'

The matron asked, 'Where on earth did that come from, Annie?'

'Ask me no questions and I'll tell you no lies,' I replied.

So the matron decided to give a party for the children and she divided the fruit among forty children and four staff. When I picked up Rodney that night, the matron said, 'You should have seen the looks on the children's faces when the fruit was produced, Mrs Kirk. They were beside themselves with excitement. Thank you so much.'

The next time I saw Hank, I told him what I had done with the fruit, and in his Yankee accent he said, 'Way to go, Annie.' He was a good guy.

Bill Smith, our local bookie, was also really good to me. He seemed to be able to lay his hand on any number of rare items. In some ways, he was the genie with the lamp. I only had to ask, and he could deliver. He once gave me a banana and I took it home for Rodney to eat.

Rodney had never even seen a banana in his short life. Tentatively, he raised it to his mouth and then said, 'Mummy, I don't like this, it tastes funny.'

'Oh, darling,' I replied, 'you need to take the skin off before you eat it.'

Once the skin was off, Rod devoured the banana and said it was the best thing he had ever tasted. Bananas are so plentiful in today's world, but back then fresh tropical fruit was virtually impossible to come by.

I also managed to snaffle extra vegetables from people I knew at the allotments. I would cadge an onion off Mr Brocklehurst, or a carrot off Mr Wainwright, and at the Co-op I would always chat up Walter, who would sell me a bag of bones for soup. Some days, I would look in the cupboard and wonder what on earth I could make from the little there was, but, somehow, we always seemed to manage.

*

There was seldom any money left over to go out and have a drink, but we Gidman girls used our looks and our company as currency. As we all lived together, we would take it in turns to childmind – one would babysit while the other two went out. We would have a ball but there was often an expectation from the American servicemen that we would spend the night with them. However, I had it all worked out.

At the end of an evening, I would say that I needed to use the bathroom. Louie would say that she needed to go too.

Our drinking companions would say something like, 'What are you going to do, slip out the back door?'

'No,' I would reply, 'I'm not going to slip away and to show you I mean it, you hold on to my white gloves.' They were only cheap cotton gloves, but it showed I was serious.

Then, Louie and I would go out the back, into the entry, over the wall and head for home. During the war, I literally left dozens of pairs of white gloves with American servicemen. Macclesfield must have been peppered with white gloves. In fact, I used to buy them by the boxful! We would then avoid that pub for a couple of weeks in the hope that the GIs had left town. We really were quite naughty. We were good girls…seldom!

Sometimes, the GIs would arrive with nylon stockings and I would say, 'I can't possibly accept those,' but the boys would insist so, never backwards in coming forwards, I would accept them with grateful thanks. If stockings were not available, our Louie and I would get an eyebrow pencil and draw lines up the back of our legs.

I guess in many ways Louie and I were 'takers' but it was really our means of survival, and we certainly were not the only ones to take advantage of the GIs' generosity. I can truly say that I never became sexually involved with any of our dates and I am pretty confident I could say the same for our Louie. As much as anything, we were terrified of catching VD, which was very prevalent during the war.

Another night, I went out with Marge Chifley, who was also married with a young son. We met two fellows and were having a lovely evening. As the night was drawing to a close, they suggested that they come home with us. We said we had a babysitter looking after the children and that if we arrived home with men, we would become the talk of the street. The boys had a car and said they would drive us home, so I told them that I lived in Fence Avenue, which was on the other side of Victoria Park from Waterloo Street. They drove us to Fence Avenue and we said we would go in, pay off the babysitter and come back for them.

'Where exactly do you live?' asked one of the young men.

'Just three houses around the corner but wait here and we'll be back. Here you are, hang on to my white gloves,' I said.

As soon as we turned the corner, we both took off our shoes, hoisted up our skirts and ran like a pair of gazelles in flight, right across the park, into Waterloo Street and home. Once inside, we collapsed laughing.

'I wonder how long they'll wait,' said Marge.

'I don't know,' I said, 'but there goes another pair of white gloves!'

*

Not all the girls were as careful as we were. We grew to know Sally Jones, who came from London. She considered herself a cut above the Macclesfield girls as she had a more educated voice and prized herself on attracting the best-looking fellas in the pub. When some girl went to the toilet, Sally would criticise her dress or make fun of the painted lines up the back of her legs. Sally said she knew how to catch any man she wanted, and that Marge and I should watch and learn. This went on for some months, but one night Sally arrived at our local. She was very subdued and started crying.

'Are you ill, Sally?' I asked.

'Not ill exactly, but do you know anyone who could shift a baby?'

'What do you mean?' I questioned.

'Well, I'm pregnant,' she responded, 'and I can't go back to London all banged-up.'

I should have been more sympathetic, I suppose, but she had been very scathing of us so, rather brutally, I said, 'Well, you've got yourself into this, girly, so you get yourself out of it.' As it happens, I did not know anyone then who could have helped.

While there is no doubt we were flighty, you have to remember that we were lonely, supplies were scarce, and we lived with the threat of death every day.

I can recall one winter's night I was walking home from work. I had just collected our Rodney when the sirens went off. With no time to get home, we headed for the nearest shelter. There was an elderly fellow heading for the shelter at the same time and we reached the entrance together. Right at the last minute, he realised that his faithful old dog had not followed him, so he turned back to find him. Five minutes later, a huge bomb was dropped.

Rod and I huddled together in the shelter for hours like a pair of Siamese twins. I was afraid that if I let go of him, somehow, in some crazy way, he would not be protected. I would sing to him and we would play I Spy to pass the time.

When the all-clear sounded and people left the shelter, we found the old man. He had been cut in half, his legs were on the lamp pole and his body on a nearby hedge. It was a macabre sight and I quickly diverted Rod's attention to the dog which, strangely enough, had survived the blast. Rod was keen to take the dog home, but it was hard enough feeding the two of us, never mind a pet. I did hear on the grapevine sometime later that the old fellow's son took the dog in. The point is: you just never knew when your number was up.

23

Harry and the Navy

Harry came home on leave every chance he got. Sometime around February 1941, when Rod was just eight months old, Harry managed to get a week's leave. Manchester and Salford had been under heavy bombing for some months and we were all on edge.

When Harry's week was over, I said I would see him off at the local railway station, but on the way the air-raid sirens went off and we headed for the shelters. We must have been down there about two hours, and when we came up, we discovered that the railway station had been blown up. We headed for the Exchange station but that had been bombed too. The statue of Queen Victoria, standing aloof and regal outside the station, was still erect and in one piece but she was riddled with so many shrapnel holes that she looked like a piece of Swiss cheese.

'I'm not too sure what to do now, Annie,' Harry exclaimed. 'I think I'll go to the RTO' — Recruitment and Training Office – 'and let them know I can't get back to base.'

I remember the RTO took all of Harry's details, and as it was getting late, we went back home.

Next morning, Harry was up early, and I walked with him to Manchester Road, where he thumbed a lorry which was heading south. Eventually, he arrived back at base but was in trouble, accused of being absent without leave. The navy stopped both his pay and my allowance for a whole week. I was outraged. Here he was, doing his bit for King and country; he had made every effort to get back; he had registered his inability to travel with the RTO; but nonetheless we were fined. That really hurt.

On another visit, around the time of Rodney's second birthday in June 1942, Harry got a week off. Rodney was talking very well then and he and I had a lovely bond. He did not really know his father, so when Harry came home, Rodney in his childlike way, told me that a 'man was eating the food from our cupboard'.

When I told him that the man was his father, Rodney said something to the effect of 'No, my daddy is the man on the mantelpiece', pointing to a photo of Harry in his navy uniform.

Sadly, even after the war, when Harry was demobbed, there was never really a close bond between Rodney and his father.

I noticed each time Harry came home on leave he seemed to drink excessively, but as he was only home for a short while, I tried not to say too much. One visit, when he had a forty-eight-hour pass, he brought home a mate, Bert Arbuckle. The moment they arrived home they started boozing and they stayed drunk for the whole forty-eight hours. When the leave was over, I remember grabbing my hat and coat.

'Oh,' said Harry, 'are you coming to see me off?'

'No,' I replied. 'I'm coming to see you bloody well go.' It was not the happiest of partings.

*

Harry was on the HMS *Avenger* when it was torpedoed in 1942. The *Avenger* was an escort aircraft carrier and along with HMS *Biter* and HMS *Victorious*, it left Scapa Flow for Greenock on 16 October 1942. *Avenger* had two Sea Hurricane squadrons on board, as well as two new aircraft armed with twenty-millimetre cannons. It was tasked with providing air cover for one of the convoys carrying the British assault force for an operation in North Africa. Once there, *Avenger* joined forces with three cruisers and five destroyers. Between 8 and 10 November 1942, *Avenger* flew sixty fighter missions but was then directed to sail for home. On 15 November, a German U-boat torpedoed *Avenger*, which sank quickly just west of Gibraltar. Initially we were told that the whole crew had perished. I recall the news was splashed all over the front page of the *Macclesfield Express*.

I truly thought I was a widow, but a telegram arrived around three weeks later to say that Harry had been rescued and was in a sanitarium somewhere in Scotland. I later learnt that he had been in the water for about fifteen hours, clinging to debris. He was one of only twelve survivors from a crew of 528. As he was very badly affected mentally by this ordeal, I was not permitted to visit him for several months. When I did see him, he was very nervous and still in shock. I cannot even begin to imagine the fear that must have welled up during his time in the water. He told me often that he thought he would die and there were times in the fifteen hours when part of him wanted to surrender to the sea but somehow, some inner strength kept him going. He said he had thought about me and our Rodney, about the home we had created, about his life, and he just hung on. There is no doubt in my mind that the experience had a profound effect on him, but in good old British tradition, he hid his feelings, put on a brave face and was returned to active service.

*

The Normandy landings began on 6 June 1944. Harry by then had been posted to the battleship HMS *Warspite*, which was the first ship to open fire on D-Day, bombarding the German battery at Villerville from a position 26,000 yards offshore. *Warspite*'s mission was to support landings by the British 3rd Division on Sword Beach.

Warspite continued bombardment duties on 7 June, but after firing over three hundred shells she had to rearm so raced back to Portsmouth, returning to Normandy on 9 June to support American forces at Utah Beach. On 11 June, she took up position off Gold Beach and supported the British 69th Infantry Brigade near Cristot.

On 12 June, she returned to Portsmouth, but her guns were worn out, so she was ordered to sail to Rosyth in Scotland via the Straits of Dover, the first British battleship to have done so since the war began. Harry fell and broke his leg on the trip to Portsmouth and was hospitalised, then sent to a sanitarium once more. I still laugh when I think of the story he told.

'Bloody nurses, bloody hospitals, and bloody rules,' he exclaimed. 'The nurses told me that before I went to surgery, they needed to shave me. Well, fair enough, I thought, they can shave my leg. But, oh no, it was not just my leg they wanted to denude, but my privates too. I mean, seriously, my leg was broken below the knee, but the hospital rules said that I needed to have my pubic hair removed as hair was a great conductor of bacteria. Well, that's a right rum thing, I can tell you. And it was so embarrassing. I recall saying to the nurse as she went about her business, "Well, my dear, I don't mind you removing the undergrowth so long as you leave the tall timbers standing."'

It was three months before Harry's leg healed but at least this time I was able to see him.

Victory in Europe was declared on 8 May 1945 and Harry was demobbed in July that year. The war had definitely changed him. He was no longer the carefree, earnest young man I had married.

But the war had also changed me. I did the work of two men at the mill; I ran a household; I managed money; I was a single parent; and, with all that, I also had freedom.

When I look back on my marriage, I can honestly say that the best years were the six years Harry was away at the war. I should never have married him, but unrelenting pressure from Nellie and a fervent desire to get away from her, together with Harry's persistence, took me down a path that was difficult to change. It was like stepping onto a conveyor belt that carried me along, and once on, I did not know how to get off.

Eastern aspect, Adlington Hall, Macclesfield, Cheshire. Mary Elizabeth Hayes was in service here.

Back row, far right: Harry Gidman at Hovis bread factory, circa 1912.

Alice aged 2 and Louisa aged 3, 1913.

*Back row, far left: Annie.
Front row, far left: Louie.
Factory outing, circa 1931.*

Annie aged about 16, circa 1931.

Alice aged about 20, circa 1931.

Louie aged about 21, circa 1931.

Louie and Charlie Steele on honeymoon, 1931.

Alice and Jack Unwin on their wedding day, 1934.

Louie and Charlie Steele with son Michael, circa 1934.

Annie and Harry Kirk on their wedding day, 6 June 1936.
Back row: second from left, Harry Gidman (Annie's father); fourth from left, Charlie Steele (Louie's husband); fifth from left, Louie. Front row: second from left, Alice; third from left, Michael Steele aged 2.

Annie and Harry on their honeymoon in Great Yarmouth,

Harry Gidman, Nellie Gidman and Charlie Steele on beach holiday, circa 1938.

Harry Kirk in navy uniform, circa 1941.

Harry Kirk with his Auntie Lil, circa 1941.

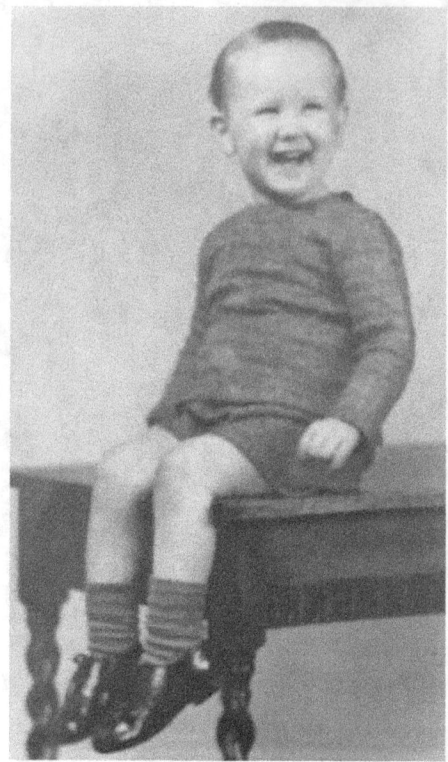

Rod aged 3, 1943.

Life in the war, circa 1944. Second from left, Charlie Steele. Third from left, Louie. Far right: Alice.

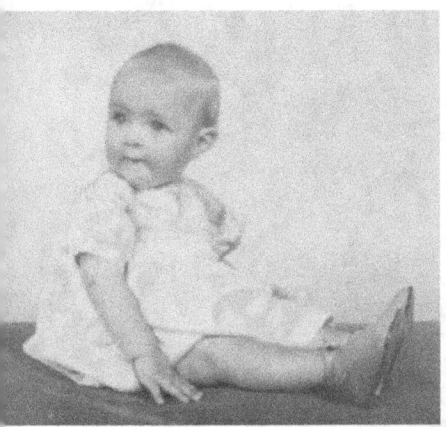

Jenni aged 10 months, 1947.

Freddie Thornicroft, Annie's friend, mentor and financier, circa 1948.

Far right: Nellie, circa 1959.

Louie, Nellie and Annie, circa 1959.

Louie, circa 1959.

Loraine aged 18, 1960.

Benny Wallbank, Maureen Bamford, Annie and Charlie Bullen, circa 1960.

Annie aged about 45, circa 1960.

Annie with her accountant Clifford Hodgson, circa 1961.

Rod, graduating from University of Liverpool, 1961.

Clifford Hodgson, Annie and Rod, circa 1962.

Rod, before he left for Australia, 1962.

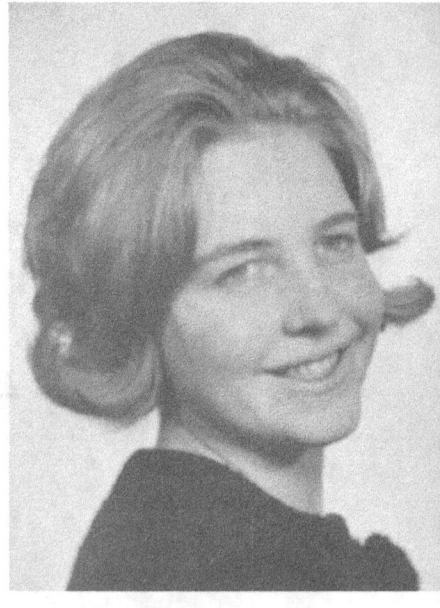

Jenni aged 16, 1962

Harry Kirk aged 53, circa 1965.

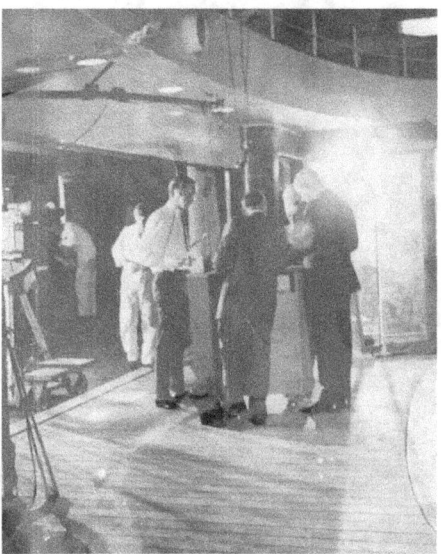

Rod as TV director and producer, ATN Channel 7, circa 1966.

Loraine's children Dawn aged 2, and twins Aaron and Simon aged 6 months, 1967.

Annie and Jenni on Jenni's wedding day, 5 December 1969.

Rod, who gave Jenni away.

Brian McMullan and Jenni on their wedding day.

Phil and Annie, circa 1979.

Kathryn aged 3, and Elizabeth aged 9, 1982.

Loraine, visiting Australia, April 1982, with Kathryn and Elizabeth.

Mary Robinson and Annie, July 1994.

Last gathering of Annie and the children she raised, May 2002. Loraine came from England to say her goodbyes. L to R: Jenni, Rod, Annie, Loraine and Michael.

Jenni and Annie, May 2002.

24

Harry Gidman

Through the latter part of the war, I noticed how thin my father was becoming. But still he went to work as he had a great commitment to his job, plus a strong sense of doing the right thing. Sometimes, in the early evening, he would go out with one of us girls when Nellie was off doing her own thing, and I remember a really funny incident. I decided to take Dad for a meal to the Old Millstone Hotel on Waters Green. Dad was frail, and the walk took all the breath out of him. A friend of Nellie's saw Dad on the arm of a young woman and, not recognising it was me, assumed that Dad had a fancy woman and told Nellie that Dad must have been having an affair.

When Nellie confronted Dad, he said, 'Yes, there was another woman. It was our Annie, you daft bugger.'

I was at Dr Gillies's one day with our Rodney and I asked him why he had not hospitalised my father, as clearly Dad was unwell. Dr Gillies said it was because Dad had told him that he had to keep working because the 'littlies' depended on him.

'But I'm the youngest, Dr Gillies. The only littlies are the grandchildren,' I said.

And then it dawned on me. Dad was treating his Hovis loaves like little children. The dough had to be kneaded every night and popped into tins, just like putting little children into bed. He nurtured his bread in the same loving way he nurtured his family. Like any hopeful father, he wanted his littlies to turn out well.

Dr Gillies agreed that Dad was indeed ill. He confided that Dad had advanced silicosis from over forty years of working with flour, and together with his weak heart, a legacy from the rheumatic fever he suffered as a child, Dad was in a poor state.

That very day, I went around to Mum and Dad's, and while Dad was sleeping, I removed the bakery keys from his coat. I took them to Jack Livney and asked him to open the bakery and to be sure to put the Hovis in first.

Dad rose for work around six p.m. but I told him he was too ill to go.

'But I have to get the Hovis out,' he replied.

'No, Dad,' I responded. 'I've given the keys to Jack Livney and told him what to do. You must rest until you're well and then you can go back.'

Over the next few weeks, his brother-in-law, Jim Beard, would pop in to see him and of course his mother and sisters, but no one from the Hovis visited. He had been so dedicated to the bakery and gave it so much of his life yet once he was sick, the management seemed to put my father out of their minds. They discarded him, like a worn-out pair of shoes. It made me really angry.

A couple of weeks after Dad stopped work, I was worried, so I asked our Louie and Alice to keep my looms going while I ducked home to see how he was faring. I found him trying to swallow soup Nellie had made, but it was floating in so much fat that it was making him sick. I took it from Dad's hands and threw it on the ash pit. I was spitting chips with Nellie. She was selfish and thoughtless. Dad had stood by her through thick and thin, but where was her loyalty? She had given him a bowl of floating fat globules. She knew how ill Dad was, and that was the best she could do? I went home, made him a ham and tomato sandwich, brewed him a cuppa and took it back.

'Oh, Annie, you're a blessing,' he said as he gratefully ate his sandwich and sipped his tea.

I remember he said then, 'Girl, you'll go a long way in life because you're determined.'

I was close to tears to see this frail man I loved so much still giving me support. Again, I told him that when I was rich, I would arrive at his front door and take him for a drive in my very own motor car.

'Yes, I know you will,' Dad replied but in his heart of hearts he knew that his time was limited. His breathing became more laboured, he hardly had the energy to walk to the toilet, and to see him struggle like that broke my heart.

Eventually, Dad was moved to the infirmary and he was there for several weeks. As his illness progressed, there was less and less that he was able to eat. But egg was one thing he could still swallow. Rationing was still in place and we only received one fresh egg every six weeks, but I wanted to do something really nice for my father. Ever so carefully, I carried our one egg to the infirmary and gently labelled it with his name.

'I'll keep this for my breakfast tomorrow, Annie,' he said. 'You're a good girl and I love you.'

'And I love you, Dad,' I replied. 'Sleep well and I'll be back tomorrow.'

There is nothing more heart-rending than watching life slip away from someone you love. If I could have given ten years of my own life to him, I would have done so in the blink of an eye, so precious was he to me.

My father died overnight. The hospital returned the egg and on the night of Dad's funeral I soft-boiled it, and Rodney and I shared it between us. We made toast and cut it into soldiers and as we dipped them into the egg yolk, we both had tears streaming down our cheeks.

After Dad passed away, his body was transferred back to Fence Street where he lay in his coffin under the window for a full week. All the mirrors were turned to the wall and the neighbours came in to pay their respects.

Despite displaying little compassion for us girls, Mum was upset about Dad dying, so I offered to stay with her during this time. As Dad's body began to decay, the gases escaped, and it sounded as though he was breaking wind. I remember saying to Mum that Dad must still be alive, and I even took his pulse to check. I can still recall him lying in the satin-lined coffin in his best Sunday suit, his beautiful face ashen but peaceful. I lifted his wrist to check for signs of life, half-willing to feel a beat, but half-knowing there would be none.

The funeral was held on the first Saturday in February 1945 and fellows from the Macclesfield Equitable Provident Society were the pallbearers. It was a cold, bleak day, as it had snowed overnight. Dad's brothers, sisters and their partners all attended. I felt particularly sorry for Dad's sister, Annie, as her husband, Jimmy Beard, had passed away in December 1944, so in the space of two months she had lost her partner in life and her much-loved brother.

To this day, I still have a picture engraved in my mind of Nellie, Louie, Alice and me, huddled around Dad's coffin as it was lowered into the ground. You often hear the expression 'a broken heart' and while that is physically not possible, I can tell you that the sense of loss and overwhelming sadness literally weighed on my chest until it felt as though I was being crushed. Dad was my guide, my mentor, my hero and my friend and he was gone.

Nine months after Dad passed away, the bakery sent an envelope to Mum containing forty pounds and a message that said, 'Forty pounds for forty years of faithful service.' I was insulted. All those years of effort he had put in, yet while he lay on his sick bed at home no one from the Hovis had called to see how he was and only the bakery manager, Mr Harrison, attended his funeral. It struck me that big business uses its people and discards them like rags when they are no longer of use.

I was disgusted and told Mum to send the money back, but Nellie, as canny as ever, would not let pride get in her way. 'No, Annie, the money's mine and I'm going to keep it.'

25

Freddie Thornicroft

One of my greatest supporters, mentors and friends in life was a chap called Freddie Thornicroft. He was about thirty years older than me, married, but separated from his wife. I met him through a friend of mine, Alice Wall. Alice and her husband Frank kept house for Freddie.

It was a very strange set-up because Alice and Freddie conducted a long-term affair with Frank's knowledge. I am not sure whether it was a *ménage à trois*, but I do know that every so often Frank would become jealous of the relationship and insist that Alice end the affair, or they would leave Freddie's house. The problem with that idea was that they had nowhere else to go. Housing was at a premium and besides Alice quite liked the idea of a husband and a lover under one roof. However, whenever the pressure from Frank got too much, Alice would cool things with her lover and it was then that Freddie would start paying more attention to me.

Freddie owned a chain of butcher's shops in Manchester and Macclesfield. I would often put in a Saturday afternoon for him, especially around Christmas or Easter, when things were really busy. We got on like a house on fire, and when he and Alice were going through one of their 'separations', he would take me out. Our friendship started off around 1938, went right through the war and for years after, but I never made a secret of it with Harry. I told Harry that Freddie thought of me as a daughter, but in truth Freddie often used to muse that if Harry was killed in the war, he would marry me.

Freddie took me to Scotland for Hogmanay and he regularly showered me with gifts. He used to say that he enjoyed having a good-looking woman on his arm. He bought me a Siberian squirrel fur coat with a sway back which I absolutely loved. The cuffs were so large that they formed a muff when I snuggled my hands up the sleeves. He bought me shoes and on one special occasion he bought a six-carat Brazilian straw diamond ring. It is absolutely stunning, with a high degree of clarity, and I have cherished that ring all my life. It cost him sixty-eight pounds and was the last item to be sold to close an old lady's trust.

Freddie also bought me a fur stole with fox tails on it, very fashionable in the 1940s. I recall being out with Louie one evening wearing my fur stole when a black American GI started to chat us up. He bought me a brandy and ginger ale, and Louie a rum and coke. Neither of us really liked him, however. He was not a gentleman like my friend Smasha Mokojay; in fact, he was rather a nuisance. He kept pestering me to go outside with him for a kiss and I kept saying no. So he whipped out a penknife and cut off one of the fox tails from my stole. I was furious; I slapped him across the face and left him – and my brandy and ginger – and raced home.

Although my outings with Freddie would wax and wane depending on how things were with Alice, I really did not mind because he was a true friend.

Our Louie asked me once whether I was having an affair with Freddie, given his generosity towards me, but I assured her that was not the case.

'Well, I know what Charlie Steele would say if I arrived home with a fur coat and a six-carat diamond ring. He'd want to know what price I'd paid for it,' said our Louie.

In so many ways, Freddie was my sugar daddy, but without the intimacy. Although our relationship did not sit easily with Harry, he did trust me, which was a good thing because in later life Freddie financed me into the business that would change my fortunes.

26

A Second Child

With the war over and life returning to some form of normality, I was keen to have a second child. I had always thought how lonely it would have been if I had been an only child, for much as Louie, Alice and I had our disagreements, we did have each other, and I know we would have sworn through a yard of Bibles in defence of one another.

Within a few months, I was pregnant and because of the difficulty in getting sufficient linen, I booked into the infirmary to have the baby. I had decided that if it was a girl, I would call her Jennifer, after Gertie Cawley's daughter Jennifer, who was such a beautiful child. The pregnancy was trouble-free, and right on the due date, 29 November, Jennifer Ann arrived in my life. I bonded with her immediately; she was such a darling baby, with skin as silky as satin, hair the colour of golden flax and deep blue eyes, like two beautiful pools, dominating her tiny face. She was everything I could have wished for.

Unfortunately, at the time of her birth, there was an outbreak of gastroenteritis in the hospital and Jennifer picked up the bug.

I was in the maternity ward with a fifteen-year-old girl who had just given birth and much attention was devoted to this young lass by the female doctor. As a result, I was left largely to cope with my sick baby. The doctor seemed to feel that Jennifer would get better in her own time and that I should not make a fuss. But, instinctively, I knew things were not right. Jennifer vomited continuously and began to lose weight. She was six pounds and twelve ounces at birth but a week later she only weighed five pounds and six ounces and was not thriving. I was discharged from the infirmary and sent home without my baby. I went in every day, but Jennifer showed no signs of improvement. She just lay lethargically in her cot and when I tried to feed her, she brought it all back up immediately. Her weight dropped even further and at three weeks she only weighed five pounds. I felt I had to do something drastic, so a few days before Christmas I made the call. I decided to take my baby home.

'Mrs Kirk, you're putting that child at great risk to take her out of the hospital now,' the doctor told me.

'Well, she's going to die if I leave her here,' I replied.

So I bundled her up tightly in her lovely hand-knitted clothes and a big shawl I had made and I asked the nurse to phone for a taxi. It was snowing outside and so bitterly cold that doubt set in, and I wondered if I was doing the right thing.

The nurse, sensing my dilemma, was very kind. 'Annie, always wear a hanky over your mouth when you handle the baby and don't let any visitors near the child until she stops vomiting. Give her one and a half ounces of milk every one and a half hours. Be sure you disinfect your hands before touching her, as gastroenteritis is highly contagious.'

My heart was thumping as I swaddled this precious baby to my chest in the taxi on the way home. I told Rodney that his baby sister was very sick and that he could not touch her, even once, without thoroughly washing his hands with the special lotion on the kitchen sink. I told Harry the same thing.

I knew I had acted rashly, and I was scared. My head told me that I might have made the wrong decision, but my heart told me the opposite, so I followed the nurse's instructions to the letter. Day followed night and the days dragged into weeks. I made up the one-and-a-half-ounce bottles of baby formula but invariably Jennifer vomited most of it back. Her weight dropped to four pounds and ten ounces on my kitchen scales and I was terrified she would die. Harry and I hardly slept, and even he took a turn at night feeding to give me a break.

Family and friends came to visit but I refused to let anyone near

Jennifer. Rumours began to circulate that she was handicapped, and I was hiding her because she was deformed. Hard as I tried, I could not persuade people that Jennifer was perfectly normal, just very sick.

Without antibiotics, there was little I could do. I simply persevered with the regular formula and slowly but surely the vomiting became less and less. Then one day in late January, Jennifer kept the whole feed down. It seemed like a miracle, so little by little I built up the amount of formula she received. Gradually, she began to gain weight, and slowly but surely, my anxiety lessened. However, it took until the end of March, a whole four months, before she regained her birth weight.

When Jennifer was around five months and thriving, I had to slip into town and left the baby with Harry. I bumped into Sister Thompson from the Macclesfield Infirmary and she said, 'I'm so sorry your baby died, Annie, but you do know she was very ill. I hope you're coping OK.'

'She didn't die, sister,' I replied. 'When I took her home, I followed the duty nurse's advice to the letter, and fed her one and a half ounces of formula every one and a half hours for over a month and eventually she came good. She's at home with Harry at the moment and doing really well.'

'Oh, my goodness,' said Sister Thompson. 'I was off duty and when I came back the next day, Jennifer was gone, so I thought she'd passed away. I'll tell you something, Annie, it was only mother love that kept your daughter alive. God bless you!'

Jennifer went on to thrive and in no time at all became a chubby, happy little baby and the apple of our eye. To Rodney, she was always 'his baby'. Although only a young child himself when I brought Jennifer home, he knew that he had to treat her with great care. I can still see him, in my mind's eye, sitting on the sofa with a mask across his face, cradling the baby in his arms and humming to her. He was her protector then and it was a role he adopted throughout his whole life.

At her christening around June 1947, I asked Freddie Thornicroft to stand as godfather and Alice Wall as godmother.

27

Rodney and the King's School

The most prestigious school in Macclesfield was the King's School on Cumberland Street. It had been established in the sixteenth century by John Percyvale, who left Macclesfield to make his fortune. He succeeded beyond his wildest dreams, acquiring a knighthood, a rich wife, powerful friends and a spell as lord mayor of London. At the end of his life, his thoughts turned to immortality and he decided to endow a chantry school in his home town. It was established in the Savage Chapel of Macclesfield Parish Church shortly after Sir John's death. The year was 1502.

It survived Henry VIII's reign, only to be threatened by the Duke of Northumberland's closure of chantries under Edward VI. However, through the influence of key players, it survived. One of its teachers during the seventeenth century was John Brownswerde, a famous classical scholar and poet. It is rumoured that he taught the young William Shakespeare in Stratford-upon-Avon before taking up a position at King's.

In 1745, Bonnie Prince Charlie commandeered the school premises for a short period when he was en route to Scotland.

The school had an excellent reputation, but the fees were high. A glimmer of hope lay with the limited number of scholarships offered each year. Advertisements appeared in the local paper each March inviting students to apply for a scholarship by sitting a public exam. I was very keen for Rodney to try. Charlie Steele's brother Fred had a son called Howard, and on the Saturday morning of the public exam I bumped into Fred.

'What are you doing here, Annie?' Fred asked me in an incredulous voice.

'The same as you,' I replied.

'But my son is going to sit the scholarship exam,' responded Fred.

'And so is mine,' I said with a smile.

As Rodney went into the exam, I crouched down to him and said, 'All the best, our Rodney. Just try your hardest. I can't ask you to do any more than that.'

The school said that parents would receive a letter the following Friday morning if their child had been successful. There were over one hundred children sitting the exam, with only fifteen scholarships on offer.

The early post came on that Friday and it turned out that our Rodney had come seventh in the exam and was offered a place with full fees paid.

'Oh, our Rodney, what a wonderful opportunity this is. I am so proud of you,' I said, hugging him to me and smiling through my tears of joy.

I went off to work with a huge grin on my face and a lively spring in my step. My son had won a scholarship to the most prestigious school in the county! I felt so proud. As I was passing the Co-op in Sunderland Street, I bumped into Fred Steele and his wife Fanny.

'Did you get your letter this morning, Fred?' I queried.

'No, the post hasn't been delivered yet,' he replied.

'Oh, yes it has,' I said, proudly producing my letter, 'and our Rodney came seventh out of all the students sitting the exam. He has a scholarship!'

'There will be a letter for us when we get home,' said Fred, a little too self-assuredly, and with that he and Fanny beat a hasty retreat.

As it turned out, Howard sat the King's School scholarship exam three times, but he never gained admission.

Just because we were poor, just because we came from humble circumstances, it did not stop me from aspiring to better things for my children.

In many ways, Harry was proud of his son's achievements but in other ways he was intimidated by Rodney's intelligence. When Rod was a teenager and Harry came home after work, he used to say, 'Is the professor home yet?' which really demeaned our son's capabilities. It also did not help that Rod was very quick with his tongue and could be quite sarcastic. But that was when he grew older.

Rod was always very close to Jennifer and he would regularly play with her when he arrived home from school. Hide and seek was a popular game and the shrieks of laughter that emanated from the living room when Rod discovered the hiding spot was a delight to hear. If he had homework, then play time either did not happen or was very short. One day when Jenni was about two, Rodney arrived home and while he was getting something to eat, she took all his books out of his bag and hid them. When Rodney went to get them, his bag was empty.

'Where have you put my books, Jennifer?' he asked in a pleading tone, but she said nothing.

'Where are they?' I said, and still she said nothing. 'Have you done something with them? Look at me now! I know when you tell a lie you have a green light in your eye,' I taunted.

She believed me because she refused to give me eye contact. We searched all over the house, but the books were nowhere to be found. Eventually we gave up and I went to prepare tea. I turned the oven on and within ten minutes there was an extraordinary smell. Burnt pages!

'You're a very naughty girl, Jennifer Ann, and I'm going to smack you,' but Rodney butted in. 'No, Mum, she's only a baby, she doesn't know what she's done.'

'She knows very well what she's done, and she needs to be chastised. She needs to learn right from wrong,' I retorted.

'No, you can't hit her, Mum,' with which he scooped Jennifer up, ran upstairs and pushed her under his bed out of my reach.

I could hear him whispering to her. 'You stay quiet, Jennifer, and I'll make sure you don't get a spanking.'

While I was cross, it actually warmed my heart to see the love he had for her.

28

New Beginnings

Harry went back to signwriting for the Hovis when he was discharged from the navy, but he did not settle. In his six years away, he had seen so much death and destruction; he had spent hours in the water fighting for his life; he had spent months in the sanatorium trying to regain both physical and mental strength; and he came home to a wife who had gained an immense amount of independence. He was depressed. I suppose today we would call it post-traumatic stress syndrome but then it was just depression. I wanted things to be different; I wanted him to feel his old self again. He drank a lot and I was at a loss to know what to do.

Early in 1948 we went away to Blackpool for a long weekend and I spotted an advertisement in *The Blackpool Gazette* inviting submissions for the leasehold on the Wyre Dock Café in Fleetwood.

Founded in the Middle Ages, Fleetwood is located on the southern side of Morecambe Bay. It acquired its modern character in the 1830s when Peter Hesketh-Fleetwood MP conceived an ambitious plan to redevelop the town into a seaport and railway spur. Hesketh-Fleetwood commissioned the design for a number of substantial civic buildings, plus two lighthouses.

Construction of the North Euston Hotel was completed in 1841. It is an elegant, semicircular building overlooking the bay and is situated on the estuary of the River Wyre. The hotel was a popular stopover for guests taking the train from Euston Station in London to Fleetwood, as steamers to Scotland departed from a wharf near the hotel. Queen Victoria herself made the journey in 1847.

The town expanded greatly in the first half of the twentieth century with the growth of the fishing industry and the establishment of a passenger ferry terminal to the Isle of Man.

With the seas not fished in any serious way for the six years of the war, the business on the docks seemed a perfect opportunity. I made some inquiries through the Wyre Dock management office and learnt that the Sweeney family, who had held the licence for twenty years, were looking to retire.

Harry and I visited the café. It was enormous. There were three dining areas. The First Class Bar, which provided dining services to the fish buyers and the trawler owners, seated about fifty people. The Second Class Bar was frequented by the skippers, leading hands and other middle managers working at the power station. It accommodated about sixty people. But by far the largest was the Third Class Bar, which seated around a hundred. This was where all the workers took their meals.

The whole place was sad, tired and uninviting. The tables and chairs needed replacing, the walls had not been painted in years and the windows were filthy. All the bars and the kitchen needed a thoroughly good clean, but I could see the potential of the café. We talked with the management office and they advised that they were looking for two thousand pounds for a ten-year lease, plus four hundred pounds a year as a share of profits.

Harry and I talked it over and wondered how we could raise the money. Harry said we should make a bold offer but in so doing try and bargain them down and discuss a payment plan. It was a big ask, but he headed off to the management office sounding very confident. He pointed out the poor condition of the property, the additional money required for refurbishment, but on the plus side, if they awarded the lease to us, they would get two young, very committed people. And he pulled it off! We were offered Sweeney's for a total of fifteen hundred pounds, one thousand down with the remaining five hundred pounds to be paid over the first six months. But we still did not have the money. We decided to approach the bank, but with no real collateral, the bank manager said the most he could let us have was three hundred pounds. It was a start, but still not enough.

Freddie Thornicroft crept into my mind and how generous he had always been to me. I decided to pay him a visit. 'Freddie, you know how hard things have been for Harry since he came home. Well, I think we need to make a change in our life. So I've come up with an idea and I'm wondering whether you might be interested.'

I told him about the Wyre Dock Café and the cost involved. It was a huge amount of money – at least it was to us. 'I'm happy to offer you a twenty per cent share in the business, Freddie, in return for a loan of two thousand pounds,' I said in as confident a voice as I could muster, but he was not interested.

'No, lass, I wouldn't do that, you need this to be your business. However, I'll tell you what I'll do. I'll loan you two thousand pounds at bank interest rates, to be paid back over five years. This will allow you to pay the one thousand deposit, upgrade the property, purchase the furniture, crockery and cutlery you need and still have some working capital. Don't touch the bank's three hundred pounds. Have the one debt and pay me back as you can.'

What an amazing offer. His generosity brought a lump to my throat. I was delighted, but also felt quite humbled that he had such faith in me. I suggested we have our agreement drawn up legally but as Freddie shook my hand, I will always remember what he said.

'Annie, you know I've always been very fond of you. I've seen you battle through some tough times. I've seen you stand by your sister. I know the woman that you are, and you won't let me down.'

He wrote out a cheque there and then to the Wyre Dock management for a thousand pounds. Then my biggest surprise came when he gave me a further one thousand in cash.

This was definitely a sliding door moment in my life. We would never have afforded the café without Freddie's help. He was a true friend and his faith in me empowered me. It also allowed me to make a huge change in my life.

29

Café Life and Staff

Harry and I resigned from our jobs and passed up the lease on 72 Waterloo Street in Macclesfield, where we had lived for eleven years. It was a risky decision to move, as we were taking on a big job and a big debt. Harry was terrific, and the fresh challenge gave him a new lease on life.

I interviewed the existing staff who had worked for Sweeney's and retained all four of them: Mary Ebdell, who worked in the bakehouse; Flora Fitzgerald, a gentle but slow-witted soul who, to be honest, was about as useful as a chocolate teapot; Maureen Bamford, who ran the First Class Bar; and Mavis Harris, who manned the Second Class Bar.

We closed the café for a month and Harry and I worked like navvies in a coal mine. All four staff came to labour for us and they began by cleaning the place while Harry and I started painting each of the bars. He and I worked twelve-hour days. I made expeditions to the Manchester warehouses and bought chairs, crockery and cutlery – quite a lot of it second-hand – and then I set about recruiting two more staff. I needed a good cook, and someone for the Third Class Bar. As it turned out, Maureen suggested her mother Brenda Wright as the cook and her sister Sheila, who at fourteen had just left school, as someone good for the Third Class Bar. I took them on a trial basis and they turned out to be salt-of-the-earth, hard-working troopers.

The café was hard work. Even with eight of us, it was tough-going. Typical breakfasts were bacon, eggs and toast or beans on toast or bacon sandwiches. Literally hundreds of these meals were sold every day. Forty loaves of bread were delivered daily. Milk arrived in an eight-gallon churn which I diluted with about a gallon of water to make it go further. Tea was often sold by the huge kettleful, containing as much as a gallon of liquid. I used to get up at four-thirty every morning and start in the bakehouse, making batches of scones, rock cakes, custard cakes, sponges and Eccles cakes for morning and afternoon teas. Mary Edbell would arrive around eight and begin work on the pies for lunches: steak and potato, steak and vegies, or pepper pies – all served with chips or mash plus mushy peas.

Within six months, the café was a roaring success and I paid off the five-hundred-pound balance to the Wyre Dock management committee. I also met my four-hundred-pound yearly commitment with ease at the end of the first twelve months. I then set about reducing the debt to Freddie. It took me another two years, but I repaid every penny plus interest. It would have been impossible without the support of the staff. They were ordinary, everyday characters who worked their socks off for me, and I grew to love them as an extension of my family. I must say, though, a couple of them lived quite extraordinary lives.

Let me tell you about them. Brenda Wright had fallen pregnant and was married at seventeen to a fellow called Archie Sanderson, a cook on one of the trawlers out of Fleetwood. Typically, the boats would go out fishing for anywhere up to two weeks, returning for five to seven days before heading out again. Brenda was a plain woman; she worked hard, and I had no complaints. However, she did have a very high libido, which got her into trouble now and then. While Archie was at sea, it was not uncommon for her to get dolled up and hop on the tram to Blackpool, where she would pick up a fellow for the night. While Brenda did not confide in me, she did talk to Mary Edbell from the bakehouse.

Conversations covered her adventures in detail: 'Mary, I had such a good night last night. I met this fella in the bar at the Imperial. He was quite a toff. He bought me four rum and cokes and we had a bit of a dance, then he invited me to his room. I've never seen such a huge pecker in my life and he gave it to me good and proper.'

Another time,, she told Mary in graphic detail about her night with an Italian who 'had so much energy to burn that he fucked me all night'.

'Brenda,' said Mary, 'you should watch yourself. What if Archie finds out you've been having a bit on the side? He'll bloody kill you!'

'No, he won't find out 'cos I never go with a bloke from Fleetwood.'

Brenda had five children all up but if any child other than the first one was Archie's, I would be surprised. Archie used to turn a blind eye to Brenda's philanderings, but it eroded the relationship and after about twenty years it broke up. Twelve months later, Brenda took up with a fellow fifteen years younger than herself by the name of Ernie Wright and they were married at the local registry office. However, she never bothered to get a divorce from Archie; although the police knew she was a bigamist, they never did anything about it.

Brenda was very keen for her youngest daughter Sheila to marry well and kept creating opportunities for her and one of the assistant skippers, Malcolm Burns, to get together. Malcolm was really sweet on Sheila, but Sheila had her eye on Ginger, who was a filleter for Ward's fisheries.

'Malcolm has a much better job than Ginger,' Brenda told Sheila. 'He'll be a better provider.'

'But I don't love him, Mum,' was the response.

'Well, it's time you moved out of the house, and anyway, you'll grow to love him eventually,' insisted her mother.

And so, with Brenda's constant heckling, Sheila and Malcolm were married. Oh, how this situation reminded me of my relationship with Nellie and how she had hassled me to marry and leave home.

Within a year, Shelia's first baby arrived but she could not stop thinking about Ginger. When Malcolm was away at sea, she began meeting Ginger secretly. Very quickly, she knew she had made a mistake in listening to her mother; so, while still breastfeeding her baby, she packed up her bags and moved in with her first love. Baby number two arrived the following year; baby number three the year after; then baby number four twelve months later; and finally, baby number five. Malcolm sued for divorce, citing her adultery.

About six months later, Sheila visited me at the café with her brood in tow and with great aplomb announced, 'I'm getting married.'

'Oh,' I said, 'and will it be a white wedding?' at which point Sheila burst out laughing and said, 'Mrs Kirk, you are a cheeky bugger.'

Another of Brenda Wright's children was Sean. His wife Elsie ran the local dry cleaners shop. Sean crewed on the *Ella Hewitt* and did the usual two weeks at sea with one week home. Elsie was very keen to have a baby, but in twelve years of marriage nothing had happened. So, she set her cap for Malcolm Burns, her ex-brother-in-law, who was still smarting over Sheila's departure. When Sean was at sea, Elsie would meet Malcolm for a drink at the County Hotel in Blackpool, so avoiding being seen together. One thing led to another and Elsie fell pregnant. She was very excited but chose not to tell Malcolm. She simply broke off the affair, then when her husband was next home from sea, she passed on the good news that they were to become parents. After twelve years of marriage and no pregnancy, most men would suspect something, but Sean never wised up to the fact that the child was not his. What treacherous lives people lead!

Flora Fitzgerald was a different kettle of fish. She had been adopted as a baby and was something of a disappointment to her mother. She did her job satisfactorily, but instructions had to be simple and clear. She was well into her forties but had the intellectual capacity of a ten-year-old. One of the very specific instructions I gave was that she was never to sign for deliveries. My rule was that all deliveries should be signed for either by me or by Maureen, my second-in-charge.

One day, a delivery fellow arrived with a one-hundred-pound-weight bag of custard powder. He pushed the delivery docket under Flora's nose for a signature.

'Only Mrs Kirk can sign for deliveries,' said Flora in a flustered state.

'Well, I don't have time for you to be finding her,' he said.

So reluctantly Flora signed the docket and asked where the custard powder was. 'It's at the bottom of the stairs,' said the delivery man.

'Oh, I don't think Mrs Kirk will want that. She'll want it brought up to the kitchen,' Flora responded.

'Well, I'm in a hurry,' and with that he snatched the docket out of Flora's hand and started down the stairs.

Flora quickly ran to find me to explain what had happened. I raced after him and caught up with him just as he climbed into his truck.

'I see you've brought the custard powder,' I said. 'Could you please take it upstairs.'

'Well,' he said, 'it's three flights. You carry it up.'

I took a deep breath, braced my shoulders and said, 'Delivery means delivery to the kitchen. I can't carry a hundred-pound bag up three flights.'

'But I'm in a hurry,' he replied.

'As far as I'm concerned, there's no delivery until it's in the kitchen and I will telephone your firm and let them know that I have not accepted delivery.'

'Oh, you can't do that. I'll lose my job,' he said.

'Well, it's up to you,' I replied.

Grumpily, he climbed down from his truck, stared at the hundred-pound bag, let out a huge growl, then picked up the bag and hauled it upstairs. He then threw it right across the kitchen floor and as it slammed up against the cupboard, the bag burst wide open, spraying custard powder all over the kitchen. It looked like yellow snow shrouding everything in sight.

Dripping with sarcasm, I said, 'Well, that's bloody clever.'

The delivery guy panicked so I picked my moment.

'I'll tell you what we'll do. You'll sweep the powder up and put it into these containers. I will then sign for a damaged hundred-pound bag of custard powder for which I'll pay you half price.'

You should have seen the snarly, angry look he gave me. It would have scared the devil out of his den.

After he left, I turned to Maureen and commented that many men would try anything on with a female boss, but I am absolutely sure he learnt his lesson that day.

As everything remained rationed for a long time after the war, I used to get quite a few supplies off the black market. I had a couple of wonderful friends, Agnes and Brian Thorpe, who ran a pub called the Boot and Shoe in Huddersfield. I had met them during the war and we remained good friends even after I left Macclesfield. It never seemed any problem for them to acquire supplies that the rest of us only ever dreamed about.

In truth, I reckon they did a roaring trade with folk who walked on the shady side of the street. However, I never let that worry me. The point was that they could let me have fifty-pound bags of sugar and commercial-sized containers of jam, all without coupons. Harry and I would drive over to Huddersfield every couple of months and pick up what we needed.

The Thorpes had a talking budgerigar who absolutely fascinated me. Brian had taught him a wonderful rhyme and the bird would chatter away to anyone who passed by. His favourite rhyme was

> I'm Joey Thorpe from the Boot and Shoe
> All the way from Timbuctoo
> Will he walk it 'Oh, no fear'
> That's too far for Joey dear.

That bird was one in a million and Joey always made the trip to the Boot and Shoe a real pleasure.

I recall one Sunday night Harry and I were coming back from Huddersfield laden with black-market goodies when we had a flat tyre. We had a Commer van and the spare was in the back. There was no option but to pull out our contraband and pile it on the pavement while Harry changed the tyre. I was really anxious, as we had nothing to cover our loot up with. Just as he finished the job and was loading the last of the goodies back into the van, a police car drew up beside us and asked if they could be of any help. My heart was in my mouth. *Fleetwood Chronicle* headlines flashed before my eyes: 'Kirks support black-market racket'.

I took a deep breath and walked quickly to the police car, 'Oh, thank you, officer, for your assistance, but my husband has just managed to change the tyre and we're about to leave.'

'And what cargo have you got aboard?' they inquired.

Without stopping to even think, I astounded myself, when out of my lips came my reply, 'Oh, we have some old tins of paint and a large bag of woodchips from our friend's allotment,' I said without hesitation. 'Do you want to have a look?'

'Ah, no thanks,' said the constable, 'so long as you're all right then.'

And off they went. I was still trembling half an hour later. Much later, it did cross my mind that they might have been a bit like the dock police, in that a small bribe would have got us off the hook. But you never know. We could have finished up in court!

30

Alice and Loraine

As I have mentioned, Alice was on her own with Loraine through the war. She continued working at the mill, and while she loved Loraine dearly, her first priority was ensuring that she and Loraine were well dressed; this came at the cost of good, nourishing food. It was not unusual for Alice to skip breakfast and lunch, making do with a couple of cigarettes and a cuppa. Loraine grew up on a diet of oatcakes bought from the houses up the back entry, takeaway fish and chips at teatime and lollies. Every payday, Alice would buy piles of lollies and put them in the cupboard for Loraine to snack on. There was never any bread and cheese or home-cooked food.

Loraine was five when Alice met Charlie Dutton at Jennifer's christening. He was quite a flash dash and certainly very charming. Alice was swept away by his good looks, and when he asked her to marry him, she accepted. Charlie officially adopted Loraine as he knew that Alice and Loraine came as a package deal, but in reality, he had little affection for the child.

When Alice was at work, our crusty old aunt, Annie Beard, looked after Loraine. Annie never had children of her own and in fact had little patience with them, but Alice's babysitting money was a bonus, so she put up with the child. Annie Beard was very strict, always insisting Loraine do exactly as she was told. She frequently hit Loraine if the child disobeyed.

One afternoon when Alice collected her daughter, she saw a large red welt across her face. 'Who did that, Loraine?' her mother asked.

'It was Auntie Annie,' Loraine replied.

Alice said not one single word to our aunt, but instead came to me to complain about her.

Wanting to do the right thing by the child, I went up to see Auntie Annie and said, 'Auntie Annie, if you ever hit our Loraine again, I'll make your life a misery.'

To be truthful, I was unsure what I would do, but I think the fact that she knew that I knew what she had done was enough. It was not long after, perhaps when Loraine was eight years old, that Alice allowed Loraine to go straight home from school and wait there until she came home. Effectively, she became a latchkey child.

Loraine was not a studious child, and instead of doing her homework, she would go to the park to play on the swings and generally muck around. Alice often had to go looking for Loraine when she got home from work and almost always found her hanging out with other kids, mainly boys.

Loraine had a pal, Pamela Moat, and the pair regularly hung out together. One Saturday, when Loraine was around nine, she and Pamela made arrangements to play with Tom and Michael Sanderson in the park, but her mother said she could not go and banished her to the bedroom. However, Loraine had other ideas. She heard her mother chatting to a neighbour and sneaked down the stairs. She slipped through the back door, climbed on the rubbish bin, and was pulling herself onto the roof of Jack Gaskill's greenhouse when the rubbish bin lid slid from under her. Loraine lost her footing, crashing her left arm through the roof of the greenhouse.

'Help, help,' she screamed as she hung there, blood streaming down her arm.

Mr Gaskill came out and was furious. 'How dare you climb on my greenhouse roof,' he yelled. 'Just you come down from there.'

'I can't move, I'm stuck on the glass, Mr Gaskill,' Loraine sobbed.

It was only then that he realised how serious it was. He told Pamela to run and find Alice while he fetched a stepladder. With a gentle tap of his hammer, he broke the glass away from Loraine's arm, and she spurted blood everywhere. He pulled her down and wrapped her arm in a towel. Alice called a taxi to take them to the infirmary.

Loraine had cut her left arm from the wrist to the elbow. The tendons and nerves to her fourth and fifth fingers had been severed. She was admitted to hospital and had over forty stitches. It took months for her to be able to use her arm again. In fact, she was never again able to fully extend the fourth and fifth fingers on her left hand. However, Loraine was very lucky she had not broken her neck.

Mr Gaskill was more angry about his damaged greenhouse roof than worried about Loraine and poor Alice had to pay for the roof to be repaired.

*

I used to visit Macclesfield quite regularly. It was about one-and-a-half hours by car. I always felt obliged to visit my mother, and once I was financially established, I used to pay her rent, six months in advance. I also used it as a good opportunity to catch up with our Louie and Alice.

Around Christmas 1950, I noticed Alice was looking quite ill. She was still working but her skin had a ghostly translucence and she was incredibly thin. I queried whether she was eating, and she assured me she was and that it was just the winter weather that was getting her down. Nonetheless, I was worried about her. I returned to the café with a heavy heart, then, one Wednesday morning late in January 1951, I received an urgent call from our Louie.

'Annie,' she said, 'our Alice is very poorly. She can hardly stand up and she's coughing her lungs out. I really don't like the look of it. Can you come home?'

I felt a wave of panic rise from my chest to my throat and it spurred me into immediate action. Within an hour, I was on the road, leaving Maureen and Harry to run the café.

It transpired that Alice had caught Asian flu. Charlie Dutton had no idea what to do, so he made himself scarce. I bunked in with Loraine and made hot toddy drinks for Alice. She barely had the strength to sip liquids. Dr Gillies came but said there was little he could do. He instructed me to keep her warm, keep her fluids up and pray. Antibiotics were in their infancy and he certainly did not prescribe any for her. She was significantly underweight and had little resistance to the infection. Wednesday drifted into Thursday and still Alice was no better.

By Thursday night, I was frightened that she would die. Louie came over and we took it in three-hour shifts to stay with Alice through the night. Her breathing became more and more shallow and around eight o'clock Friday morning she looked at both of us, smiled her beautiful smile, told us she loved us, closed her eyes and passed away. I loved my sister. We had fought through so much together and in a way, I was angry that she chose to leave us, and I was hurting. We had been the three musketeers, the three Gidman girls, and now one of us was gone.

As Louie said to me, 'Grief is the price we pay for love.'

Alice was just shy of her fortieth birthday.

*

Before she was even buried, Charlie Dutton asked me what I was going to do about Loraine. 'I only took her on because of Alice. What am I going to do with a nine-year-old?' he said.

Nellie said she was too old to take on a child, so I said to our Louie, 'What about you take Loraine? You live locally so she won't lose her friends and she'll be good company for you.'

'Annie, I've got my freedom now. Our Michael is almost an adult. I don't want to be tied down with another child. Why don't we put her in a home?' she said.

I already had two children, I was running a business with eight staff, I had a husband who gambled and drank, but I could not let Loraine go into an orphanage. I was Loraine's godmother and I remember making a solemn promise at her christening to watch over the child and look out for her spiritual welfare.

'Loraine, once your mother is buried, I want you to pack your things and come home with me.'

'But what about Dad?' Loraine asked.

'Oh, he'll be fine. Don't you worry,' I replied.

Charlie asked me about the insurance policy on Loraine's life. He suggested that he could continue to pay it and then when it matured, said he would send the money to Loraine.

'Oh, Charlie,' I replied, 'since I'm taking Loraine, I'll continue with the policy and use it for her when it matures.' She would never have seen the money if he had taken over. He chose not to argue.

Alice had not been buried a month before Charlie was sleeping with Polly Ratcliffe, a young single woman. He was still in the house at 65 Waterloo Street, racing Polly off in Alice's own bed. I felt sickened when I found out and thought he was a dirty old bugger who showed no respect for my sister. The affair lasted a short while, then he took up with a married woman, Maureen Appleby, who came from one of the scruffiest families in Macclesfield. Charlie gave Maureen all of Alice's beautiful clothes, never offering so much as a handkerchief to Louie or me. A few months later, Charlie and Maureen applied for emigration to Australia, sold everything up and departed, leaving a trail of debt behind them. Good riddance, I thought.

*

When I arrived home with Loraine after Alice's funeral, Harry said, 'So you've brought Loraine home for a holiday, have you?'

'No,' I said, 'I've brought her home for good.'

Harry was none too pleased initially but since he had little to do with running the household, things soon settled down.

As Loraine was such a skinny, pale child, I decided to take her to our family GP, Dr Yule, for a check-up. It came as no surprise to learn that the child was suffering from malnutrition. However, in an environment like the café, where food was plentiful, it was not too long before Loraine started to fill out and look really healthy. It did my heart good to see her tuck into meat and three vegies, then watch her polish off a custard tart. She became a porky little dumpling in no time.

About four weeks after her arrival, she came to me one day and said, 'I want to be like the other kids at school. They talk about their family, so would it be OK if I called you and Uncle Harry Mum and Dad?' I was really touched. I never formally adopted Loraine, but from the moment I took her home with me, she was my third child.

I recall another incident a few months after her arrival. We were sitting over the dinner table and Loraine relayed a joke everyone at school had been laughing at. It was the story of a man who bred and raced pigeons and he had sent his birds off in a race. As they were returning home, the man's wife was removing clean washing from the line – sheets, towels, underwear – while he was trying to get the birds back into their coop.

He turned to his wife and said, 'Quickly, get those knickers down so I can get my cock in.'

'Everyone laughed but I don't get it,' said Loraine innocently.

Harry almost had apoplexy. 'What sort of school is this child going to?'

'What's so funny? I don't understand,' the child muttered.

I must say, I fumbled a very poor reply.

31

Life at the Kings School

When we moved to Fleetwood, Rodney was still at the King's School on scholarship and I was not keen to move him, so Harry and I decided to have Rodney board with his housemaster, Mr Martin, and his wife, a rather mean-spirited woman. Mr Martin played the violin and he thought it would be a good idea if Rodney learnt as well. Lessons cost two shillings and sixpence for one hour and Rod had a lesson each Wednesday after school. Sadly, he hated it. Each week was a torment. One school holiday, at home, I listened to him. He was awful; the screeching of the bow across the strings was like chalk scratching a blackboard. It was immensely painful to the ear. I was aware that the violin teacher was trying his best but somehow Rod never improved.

One Wednesday afternoon, instead of paying for his violin lesson, Rodney decided to buy an ice cream and some comics at the local newsagent, then he took himself off to the park. He had a lovely time, skimming stones across the pond and watching the swans glide gracefully by. The following week, he decided to do the same thing. No one seemed to know, and Rodney was very happy. Then on the Wednesday of the third week, he arrived back at the Martins and a very stern Mr Martin was waiting for him.

'Where have you been, Rodney?'

'To my violin class, Mr Martin.'

'And how was the lesson?'

'Oh, I'm not very good,' Rodney mumbled.

'Nor will you ever be, boy, especially as you're also a liar. The violin teacher phoned and asked where you've been for the last three weeks, so explain yourself, boy.'

'Well, sir,' he said matter of factly, 'no one ever asked me if I wanted to learn the violin and I really don't.'

Noting the increasing intensity of the thunderous scowl that darkened Mr Martin's face, Rod plucked up courage and continued. 'I know I did the wrong thing in going to the park, but I truly hate the lessons,' confessed a shamefaced Rodney.

'You're in serious trouble, boy. I'm going to telephone your mother and tell her of your deceitfulness.'

Mr Martin phoned me in high dudgeon. To say that I was furious with Rodney at the time would be an understatement. The housemaster and I had much discussion about Rod's punishment and in the end we agreed that he would mow Mr Martin's grass for three weeks and also write three hundred times, 'I will not be deceitful'.

It had simply never occurred to Rodney that the violin teacher would follow up on his absence. Such is the naivety of a nine-year-old boy.

Rodney was very homesick at the Martins and he used to write every week asking when he could come home. I could read his sadness between the lines and my heart ached for him. I was torn between him staying on or tossing in the scholarship and bringing him to Fleetwood, but he had only just over a year before high school. So I sat down with him and we talked it through. In the end he stayed, and I will always be thankful to our Louie, who stepped up to help, and also to Harry's cousin, Dorothy Darby, and her mother, Harry's Auntie Lil. They all pitched in to make life away from home a little less unbearable for my son.

Often on a weekend, Louie would sweet-talk Jimmy McMahon, who owned a taxi, to collect Rodney from the Martins and she would take him to the pictures and then the pub for tea. He thought that was terrific. She always got Jimmy to take Rodney back to the Martins on a Sunday night. Travel by taxi was quite a thrill in those days. Our Rod used to think that Louie actually owned the taxi as she was so bossy with Jimmy.

Sometimes, Rod stayed the weekend with Dorothy and Auntie Lil. Dorothy had married late in life so she had no children of her own. As a result, she took a real shine to our Rod. They lived on Congleton Road, adjacent to farmland and woodland. It was always pleasant to go for long walks through the meadows and into the woods, where the ground was thick with decades of beech and chestnut leaves. A good brisk walk was always followed by delicious tea and buttery scones with homemade jam. Auntie Lil had her own vegetable patch and was proud of her produce. She was forever wanting to feed Rodney, and the rest of us when we visited. Invariably, she would say, 'You must be hungry. Here, have a tomato.'

When Rod was eleven, he sat the eleven plus exam and won a place at Baines Grammar School at Poulton-Le-Fylde, a twenty-minute bus ride from Fleetwood. So in 1951 Rodney left Macclesfield and the Martins and came home to his family. My gorgeous boy had been living away from home for almost three years.

*

I used to take our Jennifer on my visits to Macclesfield while Rod was at the Kings School. I recall one incident when we were staying with Nellie and Louie popped over to see us. The front steps to our house had worn away with years of people traffic and the concrete had quite a dip in it. Jennifer was outside skipping and singing to herself when I called her inside for lunch. She would have been almost four years old. As she came up the front step, she slipped and hit her head on the concrete step. Blood flooded down her little face and I could see straightaway that a sticking plaster would not do the job. So I asked our Louie to nurse Jenni while I drove us all to the Macclesfield infirmary. Jenni was immediately placed on a gurney and the nurse cleaned up her face, ready for the doctor to examine the damage. I was holding Jenni's hand when he arrived. To my absolute astonishment, he was as black as the ace of spades.

'Would you please wait outside, Mrs Kirk, while I examine your daughter,' he said.

I joined our Louie just behind the curtain and could hear every word.

'Louie,' I whispered, 'I know she's going to say something to that doctor because I don't think she's ever seen a black person before.'

And sure enough, she did. I heard this little voice say, 'Have you been on your holidays?'

'No, I haven't been on my holidays,' he replied.

'Well, you're very suntanned,' she said with a note of challenge in her voice.

'I'm not suntanned,' was the reply. He continued, pointing to his hand, then his face. 'This is the colour that people are where I come from.'

'Oh,' she said with a sense of fascination in her voice…and then it happened.

She spat on her fingers and rubbed his skin. 'It's real,' she said, 'You're like chocolate.'

To which the doctor gave a hearty chuckle. 'I've been called many things in my time, but it's the first time I've been called chocolate.'

32

Café Life and Colourful Customers

I must now take you back to the café and fill you in on our life there.

Once the place had been totally painted through and was running smoothly, Harry was at a loose end. It was obvious to him that the staff and I could pretty much run the place ourselves, so he decided to open an SP bookie shop.

SP bookies are a colourful and interesting part of Britain's gambling history. In the days before the introduction of fully licensed high street bookmakers, and long before online betting services, SP bookies were about the only way to place a bet on the horses. SP stands for 'starting price'. Harry found premises in Dock Street and he opened Wednesday to Saturday each week.

Monday and Tuesday were his days off, when he would do the odd job around the place, and Sunday afternoon, we would go out to the farms around Poulton and buy twenty chickens for the week, our bacon supply and around forty dozen eggs. We would then have an early tea before returning home, where Harry would pluck the chickens, clean out the gizzards and prepare them for cooking on the Monday. There was very little relaxation time, but we were making a good living and I was saving hard.

The men who visited the café certainly provided the colour in our lives. By and large, the majority of those who worked on the docks and patronised the café were well-meaning, decent blue-collar workers. They had a variety of jobs: crewing as fishermen on the trawlers, sorting fish when it was landed, filleting fish, packaging and sending it to various towns. Others worked at the power station, which apart from the fishing, provided the second-largest employment opportunity in Fleetwood. Then there was our elite customer base: the trawler owners, the fish buyers and the various administrative assistants, some of whom were female, supporting the fishing industry.

My little girl, Jennifer, at four years old was a fantastic helper in the Third Class Bar, collecting the dirty cups from tables and taking them to be washed. She befriended a couple of the fellows, Ambrose and Stezzie, who were always very kind to her. They encouraged her to be precocious by having her get up on the tables and sing and dance for them, then they would give her a penny, which she thought was very special. I can recall her rendition of 'I'm a Little Teapot' with all the accompanying actions. She was super cute and always managed to put a smile on the men's faces. I rather suspect she loved the attention.

One of the regulars, a fellow called Bert Johnson, was not as friendly as Ambrose and Stezzie. Most days, Bert arrived at lunchtime and had his standard fare of two aspirins with a cup of coffee for lunch. He was a miserable bugger and I could not warm to him. Jenni always avoided him because she said he was scary.

One day, he touched her on the leg and she spat at him, so he smacked her. She came running to me and said that Mr Johnson had hit her. Well, that was like a red rag to a bull.

I stormed up to him and quietly, with menace in my voice, said, 'Don't you ever touch my child! If she's done something wrong, you tell me, and I'll chastise her. If you touch her again, I'll ban you from the café.'

I am pleased to say I did not see much of him after that. It is often said in life that 'you win some and you lose some' and he was one customer I was happy to see the back of.

*

I remember three other regulars from Robertson's Fishery who came into the Third Class Bar. They were also disagreeable types, always complaining and always trying to put me down. If there was a late fish landing and they had to work overtime, they would come to the café at the end of the working day to buy something for their tea. Our food turnover was very high and by closing time there was little on offer.

'Is that all the rubbish you have left?' they said to me one afternoon.

Dripping with sarcasm, I replied, 'Oh yes, we've saved this rubbish especially for you.'

That same afternoon, just after the Robertsons guys had been in, Harry went down to lock up and found that thick black grease – blech, I called it – had been smeared over the stairwell. Harry had only finished the painting the previous week. We were damned sure it was the Robertsons guys, but neither of us had seen them do it, so could not prove anything. However, my antenna was up, and each time they came in after that, I would have one of the staff follow them downstairs on some pretext or other, to make sure they did no further damage.

*

Another interesting character was Peter Sullivan, a middle-aged chap who worked as a roustabout on the docks. His problem was that he was a real gambler. This habit had led to a broken marriage and the loss of several jobs. He would often come into the Third Class Bar as I was closing up and ask if I had any leftover food I was going to throw out. I always gave him a meat pie and a cup of tea, and over the weeks he told me his story.

'I was happily married, we had a home and a little 'un and I was in regular work, but I went to the racetrack one day and it was as though another world opened up for me. At first, I did quite well but then I started to lose. I always thought that the next race would be it. I took out a bigger mortgage on the house without telling the wife, and then I started to steal from the wife's housekeeping jar. This led to tensions and I'm ashamed to say that at one point I emptied my little boy's savings account. My wife threw me out. I lost everything. Now I sleep rough, but I can't break the habit.'

I thought for a while about what he had said, and when I saw him next, I suggested that when he drew his pay, he should give it to me and I would give him a daily allowance. That way he would not be tempted to spend it all on the horses or dogs. The look on his face was humbling.

With tears in his eyes, he said, 'Mrs Kirk, would you do that for me? Would you help me out like that?'

I think everyone else had given up on him. I will say I was pretty strict with Peter. When I gave him his money, I told him to go straight to the seaman's shelter and pay for that night's dinner, bed and breakfast straight away. Sometimes, though, especially in the summer when the weather was kinder, he would gamble the money and sleep rough. I was never able to get him to quit. Even when his weekly money was gone, I always found a meal and a cuppa for him, or in winter I would loan him a few bob for the seaman's home. I suppose in today's world I would encourage him to go to Gamblers' Anonymous, but I am not sure that such organisations existed then.

*

Bill Ward was another patron who provided a few challenges. He was a misogynist and certainly had no sense of fairness or doing the right thing by a woman who was running a significant business. The café normally closed around four-thirty to five p.m., but if there was a late tide, around four p.m. Bill would send over a whole tray of filleted fish, with an order for the fish to be cooked plus served with chips and peas for his twenty staff. On the one hand, this was a good order for the business, but on the other, it was a real nuisance because the staff were ready for home and I would have to turn around, light up the chip pan and cook everything myself. Having started work at five a.m., I found it to be a big ask.

The really annoying thing, though, was Bill's tendency to avoid payment. I always had to chase him for his money.

Bill was a hoity-toity fellow and when I asked him for payment one time he said, 'Well, Mrs Kirk, we have to balance our income. You'll be paid when I'm ready.'

Sharp as a tack, I told him that I too had to balance my income and that there would be no dinners ready for him until the previous one was paid for. A cheque was couriered over the next day. Such is the magic of a monopoly service!

*

One day, sometime around 1953, a seaman arrived at the café with an African monkey that he had picked up from another ship. It was a fragile little animal, approximately seven inches in body length with a tail twice as long. It had been badly treated aboard ship, with the sailors regularly dangling it over the ship's rail to the water line, then watching it trying to scramble up a rope to safety.

'Mrs Kirk, will you look after this monkey for me because if I take it back to sea, I doubt whether it will survive.'

So we became proud owners of a monkey that we named Joey. Harry built him a cage from a couple of tea chests and we placed the cage beside the bakehouse oven. Joey slept there at night but in the day he was allowed out, whereupon he would scramble up the living room curtains and squawk loudly. Traps were regularly put out for mice at the café; one day I was about to bin a mouse that had been caught in a trap when Joey saw it, flew down the curtains, snatched it from my hand and scampered up the curtains to eat it. He gave us all quite a lot of pleasure, but it was hardly the healthiest of environments for what was essentially a wild animal. Sadly, Joey was found dead at the bottom of his tea chest cage about three months after he came to us. Quite what he died from is a mystery.

*

There was another incident with a coloured man a couple of years after Jenni's accident, but this time it was Loraine who made the gaffe. It was very rare to see black people in Fleetwood in the 1950s but one day a young African came into the café. Loraine, who was about fourteen, had been helping out in the Second Class Bar. She had only ever seen black people as illiterate itinerants or servants, as portrayed in movies.

She looked at this young fellow and said, as slowly and as distinctly as she could, in a rather loud voice, 'Do…you…want…a…cup…of…coffee?'

He nodded.

She then said, 'Do…you…want…sugar…with…that?'

Again, he nodded.

'Can…I…get…you…anything…else?' to which he replied in the most polished English accent, 'Yes, a bacon sandwich and an Eccles cake would be most appreciated.'

'Oh, you speak English!' was Loraine's shocked reply.

'Yes,' said the man, 'I'm studying for my doctorate in engineering but I'm working during the university vacation.'

Loraine blushed and rushed into the First Class Bar to tell me what she had done. 'Honestly, Mum, I was talking to him as though he'd just dropped out of a tree. I feel so embarrassed.'

33

Two Nasty Accidents

During our early years at the café, Jennifer had two catastrophic accidents. I put the first one down to my own carelessness. You see, living on the docks meant that we were a good couple of miles from anywhere, so if ever I wanted to go into Fleetwood proper, I would always take the car. Invariably, I would also take Jenni with me. As a consequence, I had not instilled any road sense in her.

During the Easter school holidays of 1951 Shelia Wright offered to take Jenni to the pictures to see *The Wizard of Oz*, which was showing at the local cinema in Poulton Road. Jenni was so excited as she had never seen the film and pleaded to be allowed to go. I gave Shelia six shillings, time off work and away they went. Shelia bought Jennifer an ice cream at the sweet shop opposite the picture house then, just as they were about to cross the road, Jenni saw the hoarding advertising the movie and immediately ran across, oblivious to traffic. At that very moment, a motorbike came charging down Poulton Road.

'Stop,' yelled Sheila, but it was too late.

Jennifer was hit smack in the middle of her little torso. The rider immediately pulled over and people appeared from everywhere. Jenni was unconscious, lying like a rag doll on the bitumen. Sheila was in panic mode. Someone called an ambulance, which I am told arrived promptly, and took her to hospital. I received the call that all parents dread.

'Mrs Kirk, I'm the matron at Fleetwood Infirmary. I'm afraid to tell you that there's been an accident and we have your little girl here.'

I went onto autopilot but stayed remarkably calm. I called Harry, collected him from the betting shop and we raced to the infirmary. It was only when I saw my little girl, unconscious on a gurney, that I burst into tears. Our baby looked like Sleeping Beauty, but with lacerations and bruises all over her body. The doctor said it was too early to tell the extent of the damage, but he was hopeful.

I sat beside her bed and kept repeating to myself, 'Please, God, let it be all right. Let my little girl wake up and come out of this all right.' I am not a religious person but, in those hours, as I sat there, watching and waiting, I prayed to some greater force. I remember thinking how she and I had fought for her life when she was just a baby, and now here we were again. I was just willing her to wake up.

The night dragged on. She lay in her own world while my head was in torment. I kept thinking that ir would not have happened if I had taken her to the pictures myself. I would have stopped her from crossing the road. I would not have let it happen. Then I stopped, and I thought of Shelia and the agonies she must be feeling.

She had met Harry and me at the hospital and kept repeating over and over, 'I'm so sorry, Mrs Kirk. She moved so quickly. I'm so sorry. It was horrible. The motorbike came from nowhere.'

I was cross with myself for judging Shelia so harshly because I do know how impulsive small children can be and how quickly they can move. The thoughts became all muddled in my head as Harry and I waited.

At around four a.m., as I was stroking her forehead and trying, in some unfathomable way, to project my energies into her, two little blue eyes blinked at me from a tiny face that was swollen and bloodied. I have never been so thankful for anything in all my life and I remember saying, 'Thank you, God, thank you. Thank you for answering my prayers.'

Jennifer simply looked up at me and said, 'Where am I, Mummy?

The second catastrophe occurred about eighteen months later when Jennifer was about six. It was towards the end of the working day and Maureen was mopping in the First Class Bar. She used to fill the mop bucket with boiling water and disinfectant. Jennifer was sitting up on the counter, chatting away to Maureen while she worked, but just as Maureen moved the bucket, Jenni jumped down from the counter, fell to the floor and knocked the bucket of boiling water all over legs.

She screamed the most piercing of anguished cries, yelling, 'Mummy… Mummy!'

I can still hear that scream resonating in my brain. It was sheer fear. I ran as fast as I could into the bar, along with three of the customers from the First Class, who came to help. I stripped the child naked and plunged her under running cold water and yelled to Maureen, 'Call Dr Yule quickly, Maureen, and get him to come right away.'

Jennifer was scalded from her bottom right down to her ankles.

I tried to calm my baby down, telling her she would be all right, but she sobbed and whimpered, crying, 'Mummy, it hurts so much.'

When your child is in pain, you are in pain too. I was hugging her; I had tears streaming down my face. The three white knights from the First Class Bar were wonderful, filling the bigger bar sink with cold water and plunging Jenni in. One of them kept filling an empty kettle with cold water and pouring it over her legs. She was such a gorgeous little girl with her blonde hair, big blue eyes and firm little body but her legs and bottom were as red raw as freshly butchered meat.

Dr Yule arrived within minutes, abandoning a surgery full of patients. He took one look and ordered an ambulance to take Jennifer to the infirmary. He gave her an injection which made her sleepy and we arrived at the hospital about fifteen minutes later.

Jenni was sedated in hospital while the burns were treated. The blistering was horrific, and the hospital staff kept her in a semi-conscious state for about three days. Certainly, the pain medication made my little girl much calmer. Harry and I barely left her side, napping in a chair beside the bed. She was in hospital for about ten days and I knew she was getting better when she started complaining that they treated her like a baby because she was in a bed with sides up. She kept calling it her cot.

When Jenni eventually came home, she still had huge blisters at the top of her legs. She told me, with all the seriousness that a six-year-old can muster, that she could never go into the First Class Bar again because the men had seen her bare bottom. Oh, for the modesty of a little girl!

34

The Police

Our local police on the docks were an interesting bunch of characters. Rationing was in place long after the war and the police would regularly arrive at the café, see the sweets on display and ask to buy them.

'Where's your ration book?' I would ask.

'Oh, the wife has it, but you'll let us have the sweets anyway, won't you, Mrs Kirk?' It was difficult to refuse as we relied on them for any problems in the café, but it did mean that I had to use my own family's coupons to make up the shortfall.

The café was very large and quite isolated, making it a relatively easy target to break and enter. Our main break-ins occurred in the week before Christmas and the week before Easter. Although the café did not sell alcohol, it had a large stock of cigarettes and sweets. Harry installed an alarm bell at the back of the main till which serviced the First and Second Class bars. It was switched off during the working day but always put on at night. I used to leave a five-pound float in the till in small change so that if a burglar opened the till, it would take them some time to remove all the coins and the bell would keep ringing in our flat.

In the week before the Easter of 1954, we woke one night to the sound of the till bell. 'Someone's broken in, Harry, go and have a look,' I said to him. Harry crept past the bakehouse with a cricket bat in his hand with me hot on his heels. We found a young kid stuffing his bag with cigarettes. I immediately recognised him as someone who had visited the café several times that same week.

'What are you up to?' yelled Harry. The young fellow produced a knife which I recognised as one of the dining room knives with a black handle, but he had sharpened the metal down to a thin blade. The young kid raised the knife and was poised to stab Harry.

I remember screaming at the top of my voice, 'Don't kill him, don't kill him!' The thief was distracted by my screams and Harry was able to wrestle him to the ground, at the same time yelling out to me to phone the police. I ran into the bakehouse where the phone was located and called the police at the dock gates.

'Come quickly! There's a burglar and he's pulled a knife on Harry.'

'We're on our way,' said Sergeant Collins.

I raced back to the fracas where Harry, being a much bigger and stronger man, was winning the fight. 'You bastard, you,' Harry yelled. 'Don't you pull a knife on me. I'll bloody kill you.'

I screamed at Harry, 'Don't kill him; he's some mother's son.' I looked at the lad, who would have been around seventeen and said, 'Sit down, sit down, or I'll hit you with this cricket bat.' The young fellow nodded his agreement, but the instant Harry released his grip, the burglar took off. He raced towards the living quarters, with Harry in close pursuit. My husband grabbed him by the hair but the young fellow twisted round and kneed Harry in the groin. The thief rushed into our living room, past the bathroom and into the bedroom ahead of him. This was Rodney's room and Rod was in bed, fast asleep. He jumped on to Rod's bed, rolled himself into a ball, and threw himself with great force at the plate-glass window, shattering it into a million pieces. It was like a rain shower of flying glass. The young chap landed on the roof of the offices below, rolled off that and on to the ground. Rod was terrified; woken suddenly from his deep sleep to find this unknown person leaping from his bed right through the bedroom window. It was a horrifying experience for our son.

The police arrived but by then the young fellow had scarpered. Harry and I were able to give a detailed description to the police, but we did not hold out much hope that he would ever be captured. One Sunday morning about three weeks later, however, as I was doing the washing, the police arrived to say they had someone in custody they were pretty sure had committed the robbery. They asked us to go down to the police station to identify him. He had been caught red-handed breaking into the local tobacconist shop which was right at the dock gates and he matched the description we had given to the police. I downed tools, quickly dressed in something a little more respectable than my house dress, whipped out my curlers, which was part of the Sunday morning routine, and went down to the police station.

As soon as I saw him, and without me saying one word, he blurted out: 'It wasn't me, it wasn't me Misses, I didn't break into your café.'

'Young fella,' I said, 'You've no idea how close you came to feeling the sharp end of that knife you filed down, so let this be a lesson to you.'

When he appeared in court, I learnt that he had been born in India of English parents and had come to Fleetwood to join a ship, but the ship had left Fleetwood the day before he arrived, so he was thieving to survive. He was found guilty of breaking and entering and of using a weapon with intent. His sentence was six months in gaol. I was terrified he would show up at the café when his sentence was up, but, thankfully, I never saw him again.

35

Rationing

With rationing still in place, all café owners were required to keep the government informed of the number of people they fed each month and the number of cups of tea or coffee they served. This information then allowed them to determine how much sugar and other supplies would be needed to run the business under a rationing quota.

One day in the early 1950s, a lady arrived from the Ministry of Food to conduct an audit of the supplies I was using. The lady sat on a stool positioned between the Second and Third Class Bars, which allowed her to see customers coming into all bars and hence gain an idea of the number of people being served and what they were buying. I agreed I would call out to the Ministry lady, to let her know what each customer ordered.

She sat poised with her pen and her record book to itemise every order. The first few customers came in.

'I'll have a cup of tea and a scone, Mrs Kirk,' said customer 1.

'That will be one tea and one scone,' I called out and the Ministry lady duly recorded the sale in her book.

Customer 2 came up to the counter. 'I'll have a cup of coffee and a meat pie, thanks, Mrs Kirk,' he said.

'That will be one coffee and one pie,' I echoed and again it was duly noted.

Then Ted Archer from the *Red Falcon* arrived with his large kettle from the ship and asked me to fill it with tea and add some sugar and milk. I did as I was asked and charged him for the kettle full.

'I'll also have a dozen scones, half-a-dozen Eccles cakes and three sponge cakes,' Ted said.

The Ministry lady said she needed to know specifically how many people would consume the purchase, so I asked Ted, 'How many are going to drink this tea and how many are going to eat these cakes?'

'How many what?' Ted queried with a puzzled look on his face.

'How many people are going to drink this tea and how many are going to eat these cakes?' I repeated.

'How the bloody hell do I know!' exclaimed Ted.

'What did he say?' asked the Ministry lady.

'He said, 'How the bloody hell do I know!' I replied.

The Ministry lady looked bamboozled.

The next customer was waiting with a huge tin pan and again asked me to fill it with tea. He too ordered Eccles cakes, pies and sponge cake.

'How many people will be drinking this and how many people will be eating the cake and pies?' I asked him, with a smile creeping across my lips.

'Are you bloody kidding me?' he said. 'I've got no bloody idea who's going to bloody drink this. It'll be first in, best dressed,' he replied.

'Well, what about the cakes and pies?' I said. 'How many people will be eating those?'

'I don't know who's going to eat one cake and who's going to eat two cakes or who'll have one pie or no pies. What a stupid bloody question! Don't be daft, woman!' he retorted.

I turned to the Ministry lady and when she asked me how many people would be getting drinks from the tin pan, I told her, 'Are you bloody kidding me? I've no bloody idea who's going to drink this. It will be first in, best dressed. And don't ask how many people will be eating the cakes and pies because he doesn't know whether people will have one or two.'

With that, the woman slapped her book shut and said, 'How do you manage to fill out your forms each month?'

'With the greatest of difficulty,' I replied.

The Ministry lady gave up in disgust, shook her head and said, 'I'll just have to make it up, then.'

'Well,' I said, 'would you like a cuppa before you go and perhaps a scone?'

She said, 'That would be lovely.'

'Well, just be sure to enter it in your book,' said I, grinning, at which point we both burst out laughing.

36

Nellie and Louie

I did well at the café and frequently helped out my mother, our Louie and, until she died, our Alice. But then something happened which made me think I was just being taken for granted.

Let me step back and tell you that when we started work, Nellie insured each of us girls for the 'penny burial'. This was managed by a friendly society, established with the express purpose of providing, through voluntary subscriptions, for the funeral expenses of a family member. When I moved to Fleetwood and the café was thriving, Nellie cashed in my policy, gave some of the money to Michael Steele, Louie's son, and some to Louie, who by then had spent her inheritance from her father-in-law but was keen to buy a house. Despite the insurance being on my life, Nellie did not offer me as much as one penny. Perhaps she decided I did not need any money; no doubt she thought she had a claim on it, but the point is, she did not even ask me.

With the money Louie received, she was one hundred pounds short on the deposit to buy a house, so she wrote to me in Fleetwood asking me to send her a hundred pounds by return post. I was furious because when Louie inherited, she and Charlie were pretty much the sole beneficiaries, and now she was virtually demanding that I make up the deposit difference. I wrote back saying that if I had received any benefit from the insurance policy on my own life, I might have one hundred pounds to lend, but since I had not, I was not in a position to help. This might sound mean as I was doing well, but it was the fact that they felt I was a money tree and it was their right to have a share of what I had worked for that really annoyed me. I know my response did not go down too well but I was angry, and at that point, did not care about what anyone thought.

Another thing I did once I was on my feet was to pay my mother's rent on Fence Street. I began by paying it six months in advance, but as I became more financially secure, I paid it a year ahead. At the subsidised rate of four shillings and ninepence a week, this came to twelve pounds seven shillings per annum. Stan Bartholomew was the rent collector who used to go round the weavers' houses every week collecting the cash. However, when I paid a year in advance, it was worth his time and effort to come to Fleetwood and collect Nellie's rent.

When he rolled up for the rent for 1953, I said to him, 'I'm sorry, Mr Bartholomew, but I won't be paying my mother's rent this year. She cashed in an insurance policy of mine so I'm sure she will have the money to pay you herself.' I must have sounded harsh, but I could sense that Stan Bartholomew was not judgemental and understood why I refused to pay Nellie's rent any longer.

Nellie never dared to question my decision.

This behaviour was typical of my mother. If I was up in Macclesfield and went out for a drink, Nellie always had a beer when it was her round, but as soon as it came to my turn, she would cough and say, 'Oh, our Annie, I think I need a brandy for me throat.' She was a manipulative woman. She saw me as a cash cow and I resented that.

37

Harry and I – the Roller-coaster Ride

Life with Harry was like a roller-coaster. When he was off the drink, he was kind and funny and very caring of me and the children. When he was drunk, he was angry and violent. He was the quintessential Dr Jekyll and Mr Hyde.

One incident I remember with mixed feelings, but mainly fondness, was when Jennifer fell ill. She was about eight years old and came down with a searing temperature and a vermilion-red rash over her whole body. Strangely, she looked like a little red Indian. Her skin felt like sandpaper. She complained of an awful headache and had enlarged lymph nodes.

I remember Harry being so caring of her as we drove to the doctors, saying, 'My Jenni Wren is a poorly little hen.'

It turned out that she had scarlet fever, which is caused by a toxin secreted by A streptococci. Untreated, it can lead to meningitis, pneumonia, rheumatic fever, and liver and kidney damage. Because it was highly contagious, Dr Yule made arrangements for our precious daughter to be admitted to the Deepdale Isolation Hospital in Blackpool Road, Preston. She was allocated a room on her own and we were only permitted to see her through a glass window. It is almost impossible for me to convey the anxiety I felt to have such a sick child and not be able to hold her.

I can still remember her crying and begging us not to leave. 'Don't leave me, Mummy, I'm frightened,' she sobbed, placing her little hands on the glass window.

I covered those precious little hands with mine, from the other side.

I pursed my lips against the glass to form a kiss and I can still see her small tear-streaked face come forward to kiss me back. I looked at Harry and he also had a tear rolling down his cheek.

'She's too little to leave by herself,' he said.

While I agreed, I had to emphasise to Harry how highly contagious she was. We were running a food business and I could not afford to have a disease such as this run rife. It would have meant the Health Department shutting us down.

Penicillin was becoming more available and, as far as I remember, that is what she was given. We both made a solemn promise to visit her every morning and every afternoon, and Harry promised to buy her a new doll. We were as good as our word, but it was heart-rending to leave our little girl behind. A mother is only ever as happy as her unhappiest child: my little girl was desperately unhappy, and scared, and so was I. Harry went every single morning and I recall one day when for some reason I was unable to go, he did the double shift. He loved his little 'hen'.

Another example of his incredible kindness was when I had been off colour for some weeks with what Dr Yule initially diagnosed as stomach flu. I experienced severe pains in the upper stomach, bloating and dreadful nausea. When the symptoms failed to settle, Dr Yule prescribed antacid tablets, but they were of no help. Then one morning I was serving in the Third Class Bar when I doubled over with pain. I had to retreat to our flat at the back of the café and go to bed. Harry kept checking on me during the morning but as the day wore on, I became progressively worse.

Eventually around one-thirty p.m. Harry called Dr Yule. He came around three after his lunchtime surgery and almost the moment he walked into the bedroom, I started to vomit. Dark blood, streaked with globules of tissue, poured out of my mouth, like suppurating lava from a volcano, and once I started, I could not stop. Dr Yule rescued the chamber pot from under the bed and, with Harry holding me up, I vomited and vomited. I remember Dr Yule saying I was doing well – as though I was winning some sort of bloody race – but I truly felt I was dying. Eventually, with a chamber pot about a quarter full of blood, mucus and tissue, the vomiting slowed. Dr Yule said that I had had a gastric ulcer which had ruptured and that I was very lucky to be alive. I stayed in bed most of the next week and Harry was nothing but kindness.

If only he could always have shown that side of himself. But I guess his own damaged childhood, his war experience, being an SP bookie and living with the tensions of potential losses made him turn to drink, and drink brought out the worst in him. When he was drunk, the slightest thing would set him off. Just as a match ignites gunpowder, so alcohol ignited Harry's temper.

*

I remember one night he came home from a race meeting and demanded his tea.

'I've worked all day. The children and I have had our meal but there's food in the fridge if you want something,' I said.

'I want that pork pie you made last week. There was still some in the fridge this morning,' slurred Harry.

'You can't eat that,' I replied. 'It was left out all day and it went off, so I threw it away. There's ham if you want it.'

'No, I want the pork pie,' he repeated stubbornly.

I could see where this was going and tried coaxing him, suggesting that he go to bed and sleep it off, but he turned nasty and hit me right across the face. I fell to the ground, he straddled me and pounded my chest until I lay still like a rag doll. Harry had trained as a boxer in the navy and I was no match for his strength. I remember he then took himself off to bed and left me lying on the living room floor.

The next morning, when he was sober, and he saw me, he asked me what I had done to have a black eye.

'You did this, Harry, and this,' I said, opening my blouse to show him the welts on my chest.

'Annie, I'm so sorry. I don't know what could have got into me. What have I done? When I've had a few, I don't know what comes over me. I have demons running about in my head and I don't feel in control. I think about how popular you are with the fellas who come into the café and I come over all jealous. Please forgive me, please, please. It won't happen again.'

'Harry, you've been drinking solidly for some time now. Will you please get some help? It was the bump on your head in the war that has made you like you are. Go and see a psychiatrist, if not for your own sake, then at least for me and the children.'

'OK, I'll go,' he would say, but somehow, he never quite got round to it.

For anywhere from three to six months, he would be as good as gold. We would be a normal family with lovely outings to Lytham St Anne's or to Blackpool on Sunday afternoons in the Ford Prefect, with the children piled in the back.

'The first to see Blackpool Tower will get a bob off me Dad,' Rod would say and he, Loraine and Jenni would peer out of the window, craning to be the first to spot the tower. Often, we would drop the kids off at the penny arcade and give them ten shillings to play there and at the putt-putt golf while Harry and I would sit on the seafront, read the Sunday papers and have a snooze. We would then collect the children and drive to the farms in Poulton to buy our supplies for the week. We always finished off with tea out. I used to laugh at our Jennifer because at our café she had the pick of anything we had, so when we went out to tea, she invariably asked for Welsh rarebit, which is only glorified cheese on toast, while the rest of us tucked into a roast, or a steak and chips. I enjoyed those times so much. Harry in his good times was wonderful, but when the demons arrived, he was the devil incarnate.

The worst of it was facing the customers after Harry had belted me. I used to lie and say, 'Oh, this. Yes, I hit my head on the cupboard,' but people knew what he was up to. I remember one chap actually offered to give Harry a taste of his own medicine for me, but I never followed this through. However, the anxiety was never far from the surface. I was always wondering what mood he would be in when he came home, and it did get to me. The staff knew what was happening and a couple of nights when I could see trouble brewing, I would collect the children and stay at Maureen's house in Mount Street.

Saturday nights were always times of anxiety even if we were out together, as it would depend on what he had drunk and whether I had talked with other people. His seething jealousy knew no bounds.

If I so much as chatted socially to anyone, he would say, 'Who's that, and how do you know them?'

If I said I did not know them, and I was just being friendly, he would get all huffy and have another drink.

One Sunday morning after a particularly bad session with Harry the previous night, I got in the car and drove myself to Blackpool. I remember it was winter and I put on the fur coat Freddie had given me. I was depressed and at the time could see no end to the cycle of violence. Depression and fear eroded my confidence and I was at my lowest ebb. I remember parking the car and found myself, inexplicably, drawn to the water. In that moment, I decided to put an end to it all and I waded into the sea. My coat became heavy and I could feel it dragging me down. My head slipped under the water; a calm tranquillity washed over me, and suddenly I was at peace. No more fights, no more slaps across the face, no more excuses, just a quiet emptiness. All anxiety was washed away; I was blissfully numb.

I learnt later that there were two young fellows walking along the beach with their dog and they had seen what was happening, so they raced into the water to pull me out. Suddenly the peace was gone; I was jerked back to reality.

I heard a voice saying, 'Hey, lady, look at me, look at me. It's OK, you're going to be all right.'

The next I knew, an ambulance officer was removing my coat and putting a warm blanket around my shivering shoulders. He gave me some hot tea and talked to me for a very long time.

I have no idea what he said, I just recall that he was comforting. His kindness opened the floodgates and I remember sobbing and sobbing. I was shocked at myself for trying to take my own life as I had three children totally dependent on me. But I had hit a wall; my spirit was broken, and I had no idea what to do.

So I went to see Dr Yule. He had treated me several times after Harry's violent episodes, including once when he broke two of my ribs, and the doctor knew my situation.

'Annie,' Dr Yule said to me, 'you need to leave Harry because if you don't, he'll be the death of you.'

He was right; I knew it in my head, but somehow, I could not take the next step. I kept telling myself that things would get better. I also remembered my darling dad telling me that marriage was for life. I had promised to be there 'in sickness and in health', and I took my marriage vows seriously.

38

Café Life, Staff Dramas and Unwanted Pregnancies

Life at the café continued with its many ups and downs.

Every Thursday afternoon, I drove down to Blackpool to visit my accountant, Clifford Hodgson, a wily old bugger who walked a very fine line in terms of a legal accounting practice. Computers did not exist in the 1950s and as a consequence Clifford could be very creative with the books. We had a set of white accounts, which were the ones submitted to the taxation office each year, and a set of black accounts which recorded the real revenue and expenditure.

I was only thirty-eight when I first met Clifford and he would have been close to sixty then, but we got on like a house on fire. Clifford was married to his second wife, quite a charming lady who had been a nurse in her early life. Clifford used to say he was fond of her but did not really love her as he had loved wife number one, who had died around 1912 giving birth to their second child. He had been left with two girls, a two-year-old and a newborn baby, so he hired a nurse to care for them. The neighbours were soon chinwagging about this nurse living in and Clifford felt he should do the right thing, so he asked her to marry him. She did a great job raising the girls, who were more or less around my age, and he and his new wife settled into a comfortable relationship. In fact, she became ill in her later years and he tended to her with a great deal of dignity. But I am digressing.

It was through Clifford that I met Jean Fish, and the three of us often went out for a drink together after Clifford had done the books each Thursday. Jean had been a nurse herself during the war and had knocked around with an American doctor. There were many unwanted pregnancies during wartime and this American doctor became highly skilled at undertaking terminations. Jean often assisted. Abortions were illegal and highly dangerous, but the American doctor had never lost a patient. Jean learnt well from the doctor, but he told her that under no circumstances should she conduct any abortions herself.

Then one Monday morning, Mary Ebdell, my wonderful pastry cook, came to see me in a highly agitated state because she had just found out she was pregnant. She was married to a fellow called Chub, who was a snotty-nosed rabbit, always considering himself a cut above those around him. He was known locally as the 'Monarch of all Arse Bay'. Mary was a great worker and good bakers were hard to come by. In fact, I was so keen to keep Mary that a couple of years before this, I bought an investment property in Manor Road and allowed Mary, Chub and their son Ivor to live there at a discounted rent.

When I visited Clifford the following Thursday, I asked him whether Jean would be willing to shift a baby. So we visited her and reluctantly she agreed. The next day, I told Mary that I knew someone who could help, and the fee was twenty pounds. She said she would talk it over with Chub before she finally decided. The following Monday, she came in and said that Chub was not keen for another child, so we made arrangements for Jean to come to Fleetwood to do the abortion at Mary's house. It was all over in thirty minutes and I took Jean back to the bus stop.

'Abortion might not be legal,' Jean said, 'but women should be able to have a say in how many children they bring into the world.'

Some months later, Maureen Bamford also found herself pregnant. Her husband Charlie was a very strong Catholic and given that they only had one daughter, Kathleen, he was very excited. However, Maureen was beside herself. She had come from a very poor background as one of Brenda Wright's five children and she was just getting on her feet. Another child would have set them back years. So she took to having extremely hot baths, drinking gin and having more sex in the hope that it would shift the baby. She woke one morning to find she was bleeding; pains started, and a little foetus was passed. It was about eight weeks old. Maureen quickly put it into a brown paper bag and burnt it. Charlie was most disappointed that she had lost the baby and Maureen pretended that she was too. However, Maureen's cycle did not return to normal and she continued to feel sick, so she visited Dr Yule who confirmed that she was still pregnant.

'How can that be, doctor? I passed a little foetus about four weeks ago.'

'You must have been carrying twins, Mrs Bamford,' was his response, 'and isn't it good news that you still have a wee one on the way? I would reckon you are about three and a half months gone.'

'Mummm,' muttered Maureen. This was catastrophic for her. I still remember her coming to me and crying. 'I can't have a baby. We don't have our own place and the landlord has asked us to vacate our rental as his daughter is getting married and he wants to put her into our place. What am I going to do, Annie?'

So, again, I made contact with Jean Fish. Jean was not keen to undertake a termination at almost four months, but I pleaded with her.

'Annie, I'm trying to stop doing this work. I'm very mindful of the danger it puts me in,' said Jean.

'Just this once, please, Jean. You've met Maureen. She'd never dob you in. Please help,' I begged.

So, reluctantly, Jean helped. I drove Maureen to Jean's house and waited. Again, it was over in about half-an-hour and I drove Maureen home. She went straight to bed and the foetus passed the next day.

Jean was a bit of a soft touch for a sob story.

One day, a young woman in her late thirties arrived on Jean doorstep and told her that her fifteen-year-old daughter was pregnant.

'You have to help me, Mrs Fish. Her father will kill her if he finds out.'

'I'm sorry but I can't help you,' said Jean. 'Abortions are illegal.'

'But please, I'm begging you,' said the young woman.

'No, I'm sorry, I can't help.'

'I'll pay you anything you ask, anything at all. Please, please help me. She's only fifteen. She has her whole life ahead of her. Please help me.'

Jean thought for a few minutes and foolishly agreed. She did not know this woman and it turned out to be a sting. The police had obviously heard about Jean's work somehow and the woman who approached her was an undercover police officer. Sadly, Jean was arrested. She pleaded guilty in court but also pointed out that she had been properly trained and that because of this she was not putting lives in danger. She was sentenced to eighteen months in Strangeways Prison for Women.

To be honest, I never thought of Jean as a criminal. An unwanted pregnancy must be so hard to face. While it was never an issue for me, I saw the desperation of others. Jean was a good woman and was really only trying to help. I visited her in Strangeways every couple of months. I really felt she did not deserve to be locked away: rather, it was more criminal of the legal world to impose such a sentence. On the day of her release, I collected her and took her home. She was a good friend to me and especially to my girls at the café.

39

Wilf Carson

I met Wilf Carson through Jean Fish. He was a short, good-looking man with a baby face. I guess he would have been no more than five feet tall. His father had been an accountant but had passed away some years before I met Wilf, leaving his mother well provided for. They lived in a bungalow in Lytham St Anne's, fifteen minutes south of Blackpool, and home to various bankers, lawyers and doctors. Mrs Carson was a very elegant lady who dressed stylishly and always sported several diamond rings on her fingers.

Wilf had an ego as big as Blackpool Tower – typical Napoleon complex – and he talked constantly about his achievements. He was not an accountant like his dad, nor a banker, lawyer or doctor, but he was a professional – a professional smuggler. One of his tricks was to smuggle diamonds into England from Holland and his tactic was rather clever.

But first I must tell you that channel crossings and border protection were very relaxed then, particularly with large school groups. His *modus operandi* was to find out which of the schools were going on an excursion to Holland – an activity that was growing quite popular in the 1950s – and he would buy the school blazer and cap.

Wilf's research was impeccable. He would establish on which train the schoolchildren were leaving Blackpool and which ferry would take them over the channel. He also made a point of finding out details of the return journey. He would take the train down to Southampton, and before they went through Customs, he would pop on the school blazer and cap, then move through with the schoolkids. Because of his baby face, he could pass himself off as one of the students and therefore no one noticed him.

Once in Holland, he would leave the group, visit his regular sources and buy diamonds. Some were set in rings, others in earrings and some just loose. He would often be armed with a list of special orders. On the return journey, he would arrive at the ferry terminal, slip on the uniform and return with the school. Customs officers never searched schoolchildren nor were they particularly diligent about counting the number of students. Essentially, Wilf bought jewellery on the black market for a fraction of its real worth and sold it off when he returned. I was always worried that he would be caught because he was not the most discreet person, and he paid for his lack of discretion.

One night, he was at home in bed and two fellows broke into his house. Being of slight build, he was afraid he would be beaten up, or worse, so he handed over his latest stash of diamonds. It was a salutary lesson – it did not stop him from continuing to smuggle the gems, but he did learn to be far more discreet.

Over the years, I bought many of his diamond rings at a fraction of their real worth and my girls at the café bought some too. I remember Mary Ebdell really loved a solitaire that Wilf brought back so I put up the money and she paid me back over six months. I used to offer jewellery to a select group of chaps on the dock whom I could trust. They were mainly the trawler owners or the fish buyers, but even the police were up for a bargain. I successfully fenced jewellery for Wilf for probably five years and, with the police in on it, we never had a problem. To my knowledge, Wilf was never caught and I certainly had no issues. Just to be on the safe side, though, I had the loose diamonds I bought set into rings, or, if already in a setting, I would have them remodelled – all by a friendly jeweller in Blackpool. I even bought our Louie a lovely little diamond cluster ring for her fiftieth birthday.

40

Louie and Charlie Steele

As they grew older, Charlie Steele and Louie tended to grow apart and live fairly separate lives. Then in 1957 they officially split up. Charlie initially moved out of Vincent Street into a little house in Park Lane. Louie got a job at the dry-cleaners in Sunderland Street. This job came with a large flat at the back of the shop plus a bedroom and bathroom upstairs. Louie took what furniture she wanted from Vincent Street to furnish the flat and Charlie moved back into their house. She and Charlie remained good friends and would often go out together. Once they had a drink or two, however, the niggly old arguments would raise their heads, then they would not see each other again for a while.

Over the summer of 1957, Jennifer spent the holidays with her Auntie Louie in Sunderland Street. Louie continued to live her life as she had always done, so Jenni discovered a whole new world of takeaway dinners from the chippie. One night it would be fish and chips; another, steak and kidney pudding and chips; mushy peas and chips; or pie and chips. Louie rarely cooked. After tea, she would take Jennifer to the pub, where she would be shuffled into the publican's private rooms to watch television while Louie socialised until closing time when they would wander home.

Our Louie could con anything out of anyone. She had the gift of the gab and a very persuasive way of talking. She was well-known in the Macclesfield community, especially to the landlords in the local pubs, and everyone loved her as she had a great sense of humour and a down-to-earth approach to life.

During Jenni's stay, Louie decided to visit old Mrs Malthouse at a nursing home in Stockport. The old lady was very frail, and her body was so misshapen that it formed the letter 'S' as she lay in bed. Louie persuaded her old friend Jimmy McMahon, the taxi driver, to drive both herself and Jennifer there, wait and bring them home again. Jimmy was a funny fellow, a bit odd to look at, and he mumbled as he had no teeth, but he would do anything for our Louie. So off they all went.

Louie was kindness itself to the old lady, sitting beside her bed and holding her hand.

Mrs Malthouse passed away about a year later, but the frailty of the old lady and Louie's compassion made an impression on young Jennifer as she wrote home about it at great length. I think it was the first time Jenni had been to an aged persons' home and seen the vulnerability of old folk and their dependence on the kindness of others. It definitely moved her, and I recall her telling me at great length, with absolute certainty, that she would never let me live in such a place when I got old.

Jennifer's letters made me realise how much I missed my sister when I was living in Fleetwood. We shared so much history, and with Alice gone, there was only the two of us.

41

Time To Call It Quits

The 1950s represented an era of asset-building for me. I bought property and jewellery, and invested in endowment insurance policies, all of which stood me in good stead when I retired.

However, on the personal front, this was not a happy time. Harry's drinking became worse than ever. I recall one time when he came home from the dog races. I could tell he had lost heavily as he was in a sour mood.

'Get me a sandwich, woman,' he slurred.

I knew better than to argue so I made him a ham, cheese and mustard sandwich as I knew it was one of his favourites and I thought it might help. I could see that Harry was behaving just as his own father, Frank, had behaved, but I am not sure that Harry recognised it.

As Harry was eating the sandwich, he started to pick on our Rodney who was doing his homework. 'So, what's the professor working on now?' he asked in a heavily sarcastic voice.

'Leave him alone, Harry,' I said. 'He's doing no harm.'

'He thinks he's a smart Alec and he thinks I'm stupid,' Harry replied.

'Just leave the lad alone. Why not head off to bed,' I coaxed.

Suddenly he spat his half-chewed sandwich right into my face and said, 'Don't answer me back, you bitch.' With that, he stood up and lurched towards me.

Rodney jumped to his feet; he was furious. He knew his father was violent but had never witnessed it first-hand. Picking up a kitchen knife, Rod yelled, 'Leave her alone or I'll kill you, you bastard.'

I screamed, 'No, Rodney, no, leave him be. He isn't worth swinging for. Put the knife down, Rodney, and Harry, you calm down. Let's talk this through,' I said, trying to diffuse the situation.

'But he can't treat you like this, Mum, it's no way to live.'

As Harry swung around to face Rodney, he lifted his fist and slapped the boy right across his face, toppling him to the ground.

'Leave him alone, Harry, leave him alone!' I pleaded.

Harry had proved his point – such as it was. He was master in his own head. So finally, he shrugged and trotted off to bed.

'Mum, you've got to leave him,' Rod implored me after his father had gone. 'Dad's violence is getting worse and he might end up killing one of us.'

'I know, I know, but let's see how things are tomorrow.'

I went to bed soon after. Harry was snoring away like an innocent child, but his actions were far from innocent. I lay there for a long time, wondering what to do.

Just as the first light of dawn was creeping through, Harry woke and moved over to my side of the bed. He started to make love to me, but it was the last thing I felt like. I pushed his hand away, but he was insistent.

'No, Harry, don't,' I said.

'Why not? It's my right,' he replied.

I used to think of myself as a strong, capable woman but years of abuse left me physically and emotionally cowered by him. I didn't want to have another black eye or a broken rib, so I lay still and unresponsive. He climbed on top, pushed my legs apart and entered me. It was rape, but I had no energy to fight it.

*

Although life with Harry was not all bad, with each act of violence, he betrayed the trust and faith that should exist within a marriage, and he killed off something inside me. But I had chosen to marry him and people in my world did not consider divorce.

Then in February 1955, Harry became really sick. It was a bitter winter that year, and although in Fleetwood the snow rarely stayed around long, this time it lingered, and the daily dumping of sleet crusted in the overnight temperatures, leaving a white carpet. Harry started off with a nasty cold, which turned into bronchitis. He tried to tough it out but then began running a really high temperature and could hardly stand up. Dr Yule diagnosed pneumonia. I immediately thought of our Alice and how she had died from the same illness. Harry at least was a reasonable weight and had some oomph in him.

Again, antibiotics were not widely used, but Dr Yule told me about kaolin poultices. This was a mix of heavy kaolin, boric acid, glycerol and peppermint oil. I would heat the paste to as high a temperature as Harry could stand, spread it on a poultice and bandage it around his chest. Dr Yule said it was the best we could do, as poultices were known to draw out infection while heat killed off some bacteria. During the first week, there was very little improvement. I made clear broth for Harry to sip and changed the poultices three times a day; all this while I was running the café and raising a family.

Initially, Dr Yule called twice a day and it certainly looked as though Harry might not make it. If I am absolutely honest, there were moments during his sickness when it crossed my mind that should he die, I would be free. The very thought of freedom danced around in my mind, and in the occasional idle moment, I imagined what my liberated life would be like. No more anxiety, no more fear, and the ability to speak out and be the person I wanted to be.

But those voices in my head called conscience kicked in and I knew I had to help him fight the sickness. I persevered with the treatment and by the second week Harry seemed slightly better. By the end of week two, he was eating soft foods and the persistent coughing was beginning to ease. I continued with the poultices but gradually reduced them and by the end of week three he was sitting up in the lounge for half a day at a time. It took a full six weeks before he was back to normal.

It was then that I recall him turning to me and saying, 'Annie, I'd never have pulled through this without you. You're my everything in life and I'm so grateful for the care you've given me.'

I know that in his way, he loved me, but it was a controlling love. It was love on his terms, not what I considered real love. For me, real love is unconditional. It involves give and take; it means making promises and keeping them; and it is about allowing the other party in the relationship the freedom to be themselves.

*

Harry was at his best for perhaps six months following his illness but, true to form, it did not last. Eventually, the final straw came. It was a Wednesday night late in 1955. Harry returned home from the racetrack. The children and I saw the car coming up the back road and we all went to bed in case he had had a bad night and lost. I recall that he opened our bedroom door and again demanded his dinner.

'There's food in the fridge if you want it, Harry. There's even a pork pie. I've been up since the crack of dawn and I'm done in.'

'You'll be done in all right, woman, if you don't move,' with which he slapped me across the face and punched my right eye.

That was my tipping point. I decided right there and then, there would be no more. I got out of bed, put on my dressing gown and slippers and told Harry that I was going to the kitchen. However, instead of turning right, I turned left and, as quietly as possible, I unlocked the rear entrance to the café through the Club Room. I lifted my dressing gown and nightie and started running towards the police at the dock gates, a distance of about one and a half miles. Harry must have heard the Club Room door open because, suddenly, he was chasing after me. I started to run faster. I truly thought he was too drunk to follow but he moved surprisingly swiftly.

'Stop, you bitch,' he yelled.

My heart was pounding, and I kept saying to myself, 'Please, God, let me get to the police station. Let me get there before he catches me.' With the adrenalin pumping, I ran down four flights of steps and I could hear him behind me. I ran and ran. I could hear my heart beating in my ears as Harry got closer.

'Stop, you rotten cow. I'm going to kill you,' he yelled.

I glanced round and saw he was only ten feet away. Down Dock Lane I ran, faster than an Olympic athlete, faster than the speed of sound, faster than anyone has ever run in their life. But Harry was getting closer. He was reaching his arm out to grab my dressing gown as it fluttered behind me.

'Please, God, please, God, help me,' I prayed. 'Please don't let him catch me.' If he had caught me, I knew I was dead.

Suddenly, my prayer was answered because Harry slipped and fell. I turned and saw him on the ground. 'Thank you, God,' I remember thinking as I raced on. By the time Harry picked himself up, he had lost distance. I turned the corner and the police station came into sight, just twenty yards away. I willed myself to keep going, hoping that Jerry Cartwright, my favourite constable, was on duty as he knew about Harry's shenanigans. I ran through the station door and fell straight into Jerry's arms.

'Jerry, thank heavens it's you! Harry's as drunk as a skunk and he's threatening to kill me. He'll be here any second. He's chased me from the café. He's going to kill me, I know it. Help me, help me,' I begged in near hysterical state.

'Quick, Annie, into my office and hide.'

I raced down the corridor and scrambled under Jerry's desk. My heart was thumping, and I began to sob. I could hear Harry shouting as he rounded the corner, heading for the police station.

'Annie, stop crying, Harry's coming towards us,' whispered Jerry. 'Be as quiet as a mouse and I'll get rid of him.'

I rolled up the end of my dressing gown and stuffed it into my mouth. I held my breath and listened.

'Hello, Harry,' said Jerry, feigning friendship. 'Where are you off to?'

'I'm looking for my fucking wife,' he said.

'Well, she's not here.'

'She came here, I know she did,' slurred Harry.

'Sorry, mate, she's not here. You can come in and have a look if you like,' said Jerry.

'Are you sure?' asked Harry suspiciously.

'Absolutely sure,' responded Jerry.

At this point, Harry decided not to press the issue any further. I think he assumed that I had gone to Maureen's place, so he turned back towards the café.

Once Harry was out of sight, Jerry helped me out from under the desk, gave me a cigarette and brewed me a cup of tea. 'This can't go on, Annie. I've seen you sporting several black eyes and I know they're not from walking into cupboards. Promise me you'll do something about it.'

I nodded, numb from sheer terror. 'Yes, I must act. I must do something about it. I know I must,' I uttered in my state of shock.

I had no doubt Harry would have killed me that night.

It was around two a.m. by the time I had settled sufficiently for Jerry to suggest that he walk me round to Maureen Bamford's house, where I spent the rest of the night.

Next morning, sporting a severely bruised right eye, I made an appointment with Dr Yule.

He took one look at me and said, 'Annie, you need to file for divorce.'

Despite everything I had been through and my resolve the night before to take some action, I still said, 'Oh, I can't, Dr Yule. What about my children? No one gets divorced. Think of the shame,' I gasped.

'You'll be taken out in a box if you wait another six months and then what will become of your children, Annie? File for divorce and 'I'll stand as a witness for you.'

I think Dr Yule's support was the clincher.

You need to realise that in the 1950s divorce was exceptionally rare.

Getting divorced was something that film stars and socialites did, not something that a mill girl from Macclesfield would do. I was embarrassed for myself, but also for my children. In some ways, I thought that giving up was failure.

When I returned to the café, a very subdued Harry was waiting for me.

'I'm going to file for divorce, Harry, and I want you to move out,' I told him in a resolute voice.

'But I love you,' said Harry.

'Well, you have a mighty funny way of showing it. I'm sorry. It's over. No more chances, no more promises. I've had enough of your temper and your violence. I want a divorce.'

Knowing I had the support of Dr Yule and knowing that it was no way to live, either for me or the children, I set about finding a solicitor and started divorce proceedings. I also found Harry a room in a boarding house on Fleetwood promenade, and I packed his clothing and told him to leave.

He begged me to reconsider. 'I know I've done wrong, Annie; I know I've hurt you. It's because you're so popular with everyone and everyone loves you that I get so jealous. Please let's try again.'

But I had had enough. I could not go on living in fear that one night, he would take my life. So I stood firm.

Even after Harry moved out, he persisted in trying to win me back. A few weeks after he left, he phoned me at the café and suggested we meet. I agreed but decided I would not go alone – in fact, I decided to take Rodney with me. Frankly, I was still afraid of Harry and did not want to meet him by myself. As soon as Harry saw Rod, he admitted that he knew it really was all over. When I think about it now, it was an awful pressure to put on a sixteen-year-old boy. It is not surprising that Rodney always kept his own counsel and, in many ways, withdrew into himself. I guess it was his way of surviving.

The divorce was heard in the County Court in Preston. Dr Yule was as good as his word and appeared as a witness, cataloguing years of abuse. Harry did not contest the case and I was granted a divorce on the grounds of cruelty. We were well-known in Fleetwood as it was really just a small fishing village, so it came as no surprise to read about the decree nisi in the *Fleetwood Chronicle*. Such was the shame of divorce in 1956 that at school one of Jennifer's friends told her that she was no longer allowed to play with her because her parents were d-d-d-i-vorced. The child could hardly say the word, let alone understand what it meant. Sadly, the child's parents had warned her away from my daughter as though Jenni had some sort of contagious disease.

After the divorce, Harry moved from the boarding house to a flat in Dock Street. He continued running his SP bookie business and he phoned me almost every week. If he was short of cash for the business, I was always the first person he turned to and, despite everything, I always helped him out. I guess you cannot wipe away twenty-one years of marriage in the blink of an eye. In many ways, we had grown up together; we had produced three children; and we had nursed each other through serious sickness. I like to think that there was a lot of my father in me: he tried to see the good side of Nellie and I tried only to think about the good side of Harry.

42

George Collier

Once divorced, I had several offers of dinner and invitations to shows at the various piers in Blackpool, but I kept to myself for quite a while. The business and the children kept me busy, and frankly, I did not have the energy to become involved with anyone. Then, sometime in mid-1958 a special person came into my life – George Collier. I had known George for years as one of the successful fish-buyers who frequented the First Class Bar. I recall his kindness whenever I appeared with a black eye. He would guess what had happened and more than once he encouraged me to leave Harry but, as I told him, the café was my livelihood and I could not be the one to leave. If ever I was off colour or came down with a cold, George would always send over some special fish for lunch.

Everybody liked George. He was well educated, tall, slim and softly spoken. He had a head of snow-white hair, often well hidden under his trilby. We spoke many times when he came in for lunch and I was aware he was married. I also gathered it was not a happy relationship, but they stayed together for the sake of the children.

We shared many confidences, all at a platonic level. Then about eighteen months after my divorce was decree absolute, George asked me out. I was forty-three and George was fifty-two, with the last of his brood about to leave home.

He took me for dinner at the County Hotel, one of my favourite places in Blackpool. He sent me flowers; we went to the pictures; and I remember going to see a show at the Central Pier in Blackpool featuring Ken Dodd, a well-known comedian. It was such a relief to laugh again and be paid compliments by a really charming man. We took to going into the country on a Sunday afternoon. I remember one time he parked the car on the seafront and gave me a present. It was a beautiful little leaf-shaped brooch with an emerald in the centre and two tiny pearls on either side. He said it was his commitment gift.

One afternoon, we went over the River Wyre to Knot End and yet another time he took me to Lytham St Anne's for the day. For my forty-fourth birthday, he bought me a beautiful pearl necklace. I truly fell in love with George. He made me feel like a princess. He laughed at my jokes and he cherished me, like a precious gift.

It is funny the things you remember. George and I were on the train to Manchester one day and I was knitting a pair of socks for Jennifer, using four needles.

George was fascinated as I clicked away. 'Annie,' he said, 'you're truly a remarkable woman: you run a business and care about your employees, you have two children, you took in your sister's girl and…you can knit like a professional. I do wish you were my wife.'

I laughed – it was as though the knitting was the clincher. I knew George would never leave his wife. She had been a loyal wife and a good mother to the children, and qualities like responsibility, duty and caring had been instilled in George.

But knowing how he felt about me and how I felt about him, it just seemed right to take the relationship further, so I said to him after dinner one night, 'George, if you could arrange it, perhaps we could go away for a weekend.'

Soon after that, he told me that Myra, his wife, was going to her sister's place for a week and he suggested that we see this as an opportunity. I was so nervous. Despite my wartime dates and escapades, I had never been to bed with anyone other than Harry, but somehow it felt right with George. I left all the arrangements to him and he booked us into a charming bed and breakfast in Windermere, up in the Lake District, well away from prying eyes. We had a candlelit dinner in a little French restaurant nearby and a beautiful smooth cognac before retiring for the night.

'Are you sure about this, Annie?' George asked me.

'I've never been more sure of anything in my life,' I replied.

Although I had had many suitors, my experience in the art of lovemaking was very limited. But George was amazing. He was tender, gentle and powerful.

'You're a very beautiful woman, Annie, and I've admired you for years,' he said as he toyed playfully with my nipples. Then his hand slid smoothly over my stomach and in between my legs. He massaged my clitoris, bringing me to a supreme climax. I was moist, and I wanted him so badly. Gently he slid inside me and his passionate thrusts made me gasp in delicious excitement. It was the most amazing love I had ever experienced.

That weekend led to many other stolen nights. There is a place in north Blackpool called the Norbreck Hydro Hotel. It has turrets just like a castle and is often called the Castle Hotel. One Friday night George booked us in as Mr and Mrs Collier. No one batted an eyelid as we made a handsome couple. We had our usual evening meal and headed up to the room early. Again, we made passionate love, the type that comes only from great affection and caring. Well after midnight we fell into a deep and contented sleep.

At five a.m. there was a loud ringing of bells.

'Good Lord,' said George 'there must be a fire!'

We both pulled on some clothing and stepped into the hallway. To our absolute astonishment, we found people in night attire running up and down the corridors but rather than racing outside, they were entering bedrooms. It was bizarre. We looked at each other and wondered what on earth was going on. Suddenly the corridors were empty, the bells stopped ringing, so with a shrug we went back to bed.

'How extraordinary,' we remarked to each other.

Over breakfast, I struck up a conversation with the people at the next table. 'Did you hear the alarm bell at five o'clock?' I asked. 'We thought it was a fire.'

'Oh no,' said the lady, 'they ring the bells at five every morning so that everyone can go back to their own spouse.'

George and I looked at each other and I began laughing until tears rolled down my face.

'Well, there's a story about adultery if ever I heard one, but I'm not sure whether I could ever tell anyone else as they would want to know how I knew,' I said through my chuckles.

Oh, how I remember that night and smile. It was a wonderful memory. But my relationship with George was bitter-sweet. I was free, we loved each other, but George was married.

I knew it could not last forever and when he came in for lunch a couple of weeks after our visit to the Norbreck Hydro, I could tell that something was amiss. 'What's up?' I asked him.

'It's Myra. She knows about us,' George said. 'I was about to ask her for a divorce when she told me that she had been to the doctor and has been diagnosed with cancer. She has begged me not to go. She's very frightened, and I can't desert her.'

I was shocked. I loved George and I just wanted life to go on as it was.

'I love you, Annie, I always will, but Myra's my wife, the mother of my children and I must do the right thing.'

I was devastated, but in my heart of hearts I expected no less of George. Much as it hurt us both, we agreed not to see each other again. So we parted and, sad though I was, he left me with the warmest of memories. He was really the only man I ever truly loved.

43

Hogmanay

I missed George for a very long time. I would often lie in bed by myself at night and relive our times together. When I was down in the dumps, I used to feel sorry for myself and, in my head, I would query why it had to end. He was everything I ever wanted. But then, knowing I could not change things, I would shake myself and tell myself not to indulge in self-pity.

Thank goodness for special friendships. There was still my dear friend, mentor and benefactor Freddie Thornicroft. He was as attentive as ever and, seeing me so upset, asked me to again join the group travelling to Scotland for Hogmanay. I had been before, and I knew it would be fun.

Hogmanay is the Scots word for the last day of the year and is synonymous with the celebration of New Year. There are many customs associated with Hogmanay, the most common being the practice of 'first-footing', which starts immediately after midnight. It involves being the first person to cross the threshold of a friend or neighbour, bearing symbolic gifts such as salt, coal, shortbread, whisky and black bun, the gift being intended to bring different types of luck to the householder.

Freddie usually organised a group to travel north. There would be anywhere up to twelve of us: Jane Sommerville, a local schoolteacher was one, and another, Jimmy Radcliffe, who owned a tobacco shop. Jimmy took a shine to me and one year gave me a box of cigarettes, each wrapped in different-coloured cigarette paper.

We used to do some silly things; we were really like big kids. There was one chap who was very tall and another who was very short. One day after the races, they changed clothes. The tall man had trouser legs that finished just below his knees while the little chap had to roll up his trousers. They looked ridiculous in their swapped jackets, but it led to lots of laughter.

We all loved the races, as Freddie generally knew the outcome before the race was run, enabling us to place our bets on certainties. It was quite a profitable time for me.

In the new year of 1960, Freddie asked me to go to Scotland with the group, but some sixth sense told me not to go. He phoned me several times trying to persuade me, but I had a premonition that something would go wrong so I decided to stay at home. I am not sure what it was, but whenever I thought about going to Scotland that New Year, a feeling of dread overwhelmed me.

So Freddie went off with the usual bunch of larrikins. They saw the New Year in at a fairground and then, on 1 January while at the New Year race meeting, Freddie had a massive heart attack and dropped dead. He had lived and loved the good life and he died a quick – and good – death. I know it was the way he would have wanted it.

Alice Wall, Freddie's long-term housekeeper and part-time mistress, phoned me to tell me Freddie had died. 'Will you come to Scotland with me, Annie, to collect Freddie's body? I know he was fond of you and I just don't want to go by myself.'

How could I refuse such an entreaty? After all Freddie had done for me, it was the least I could do for him. So we took the train and made arrangements to bring him back.

The funeral was held in Macclesfield on 15 January 1960. Freddie was a prominent businessman, well-known in Macclesfield and Manchester, so there were lots of notable folk, including the mayor, in attendance. Alice and I stood together at Freddie's graveside. Freddie had left her, and her husband Frank, his house, which was typical of his generosity. For me, I simply felt privileged to pay my respects to the one person who had truly believed in me and who had given me my first start in life.

44

The Children

I should step back a little now and fill you in on the children. When Rod came home from the Kings School and started at Baines Grammar, he was twelve and Jennifer was six. He used to walk her from the café on the docks to her primary school, Chaucer, and then catch the bus to Poulton-le-Fylde. He was an independent boy with a great sense of responsibility and always looked out for his sister.

His great passion in life was music. I think I started off his love of music when he was only four years old, and I bought him a wind-up gramophone with a large horn speaker. He loved it and would spend hours playing the same records over and over. I remember when we bought a three-in-one TV, radio and record player; Rod would play music all weekend. At night, he would listen to his portable radio, tuning in to Radio Luxembourg. A couple of times he went to Europe with the school and always came back with the record that was top of the hit parade in that country. He had absolutely no skill in playing an instrument, but he loved listening to music and having others share his passion.

Rod was also highly creative. He could draw and paint, and during the school holidays, when Jenni and my staff's children came to play, Rod would gather them in the Club Room and organise the kids into putting on a concert or a play. Sometimes it would be a fairy story like *Cinderella* or *Snow White and the Seven Dwarfs*; sometimes each child would sing a song. Rodney would get cardboard and paint a backdrop; then he would help the children rehearse. At the end of the day, the staff and I would go into the Club Room to be the audience and all the children would receive two shillings for their efforts.

At other times during the holidays, Rod would take Loraine and Jenni to Blackpool Pleasure Beach. He loved the big dipper, and even though the girls were frightened of it, he would cajole them into going on the rides and revel in the excitement. Inside the Pleasure Hall there were huge slippery slides and he would dare the girls to go to the top and slide down.

The Pleasure Beach was a great source of fun for everyone and it would occupy them the whole day. I can remember Michael, our Louie's son, came to visit at the café for a few days and he took Loraine and Jenni to the Pleasure Beach – something they remembered for a very long time. Loraine loved being seen with her very handsome cousin, while Jenni just adored the excitement of the fairground.

Rodney skipped one of the high-school years, completing his General Certificate of Education (GCE) in four years instead of five, then undertook Advanced GCE to enable university entrance. He was always very nonchalant about his school results.

I would frequently ask him how he had gone in his exams and he would reply that he had 'Done OK,' so I regularly had to phone his housemaster to find out what OK meant. Quite often, he topped the class in English or History, but he seemed to shrug off his achievements. I must say, though, he was never much of a sportsman, but I guess we all have our strengths and weaknesses.

While he was strong in almost all subjects, his one area of struggle was Latin, a prerequisite for university entrance in those days. I remember him swatting Latin for hours on end and then keeping his fingers crossed awaiting the results. He only scored the minimum pass mark; however, with his marks in his other subjects it was enough for him to be admitted to Liverpool University, where he did a Bachelor of Arts, majoring in Geography and Cartography. I was so proud of him, as he was the first person in our family, on either my side or his father's, to go to university. Even Harry was grudgingly proud of his son's achievement, largely, I think, because it gave him bragging rights in the pub.

Jenni was also a capable student, spending her primary school years at Chaucer and her secondary school years at Bailey. She was a helpful child, attended Brownies and Guides and even became a Brownie leader when she was too old for Brownies. She also taught Sunday school classes, was confirmed and was a well-behaved girl. Later in life, she used to describe herself as having been born wearing a Brownie uniform, such was her level of conformity. I can truly say that neither of the children gave me any cause for concern.

By the time Jenni was thirteen, Mary Ebdell, who lived in my house in Manor Road, had moved into a place of her own, so I renovated Manor Road and used it as a weekender. It was a lovely house and a happy one. As Bailey was just around the corner from the Manor Road house, Jenni pleaded with me to be allowed to stay there in the week by herself. Although she was young, she was a very sensible girl and I used to pay our next-door neighbour, Mary Robinson, to cook dinner and keep an eye on her. This lasted for quite a few months, but then the situation changed.

By 1959 I had owned the café for eleven years and, while it was a lucrative business, it was a hard slog. I felt it was time for a change and I looked around for an opportunity. Britain had long been the country of the corner shop. There were no supermarkets in 1959, so I decided to open a discount store where I could sell non-perishable goods. I would go to the warehouses in Manchester every Wednesday afternoon (when all retail shops closed in those days) and buy enormous quantities of toilet paper, different brands of washing powder, soap, toothpaste, washing-up liquid, shoe polish – the product range was extensive – and then sell at a price considerably lower than the corner store. I operated on the basis of large turnover, small profit. The shop was highly successful and for a time I ran both businesses.

Then Maureen Bamford approached me about taking over the café. What a godsend! I sold the business to Maureen and moved into Manor Road along with Jenni.

One of the advantages of my new business, the Bargain Stores, was that there was a flat above the shop. So I painted and decorated that and set it up for Loraine, who was now an independent young woman, and for Rodney when he came home during the university holidays. They both loved the independence.

With the café sold, Loraine also decided to change jobs and she secured a position at the slipper factory in Fleetwood. She loved her social life, going out with the girls to dances at the Winter Gardens in Blackpool, or to the pictures. She had quite a few boyfriends and when she was nineteen, she became engaged to a chap called Harold Haslam. He was a pleasant enough fellow, but I thought he was tied too much to his mother's apron strings as he was unable to make any decision without consulting Mum. I am not sure that augurs well for a new wife, when Mum is always in the background. Anyway, Harold was called up for National Service and posted to Germany, so it became a relationship at a distance.

Meanwhile, Rod was doing well at university and he loved the life in Liverpool. The Beatles were an up-and-coming band playing at the Cavern. Rod would frequently go there on a Friday and Saturday night to hear them. Of course, it was not too long before they became a monstrous success. Later in life, Rod would joke about how his patronage in those early days helped get the Beatles started.

During 1960, Rodney made several audition tapes and sent them off to various radio stations. Radio Luxemburg also ran a competition inviting people to send in tapes of their work and the prize was a six-week stint on air. Rod jumped at the chance and spent hours putting together a demo tape which showcased his style, humour and taste in music. I can hardly describe his absolute delight when he was selected as the winner from over forty entries. I always thought he had talent, but to have that recognised by a third party was wonderful.

He arranged to visit Luxemburg in the university vacation but then the station kept coming up with one reason or another to delay the visit, so ultimately everything lapsed, and he did not get his big break. The experience, however, did whet his appetite and when he heard about a new radio station being established at Gladstone in Queensland, Australia, he sent a tape of his work to Macquarie broadcasting. This ultimately led to a job offer and Rodney migrating to Australia, but I will tell you about that later.

In June 1961, he graduated from university. Oh, what a joy that was for me. I was as proud as a lioness with the most accomplished cub in the pack. There were two places offered for family members at the graduation ceremony and, being a bit of a softie, I thought Harry, as Rodney's father, should be offered the opportunity to attend, even though he had always put the boy down. I phoned him and invited him to the ceremony. Needless to say, he jumped at the chance.

We travelled to Liverpool together and spent a very proud day with our son. On the way home, Harry asked me if he could take me out to dinner the following Saturday and I agreed. We had a lovely meal and repeated it a couple of weeks later.

One night, Harry said to me, 'You've punished me enough now – five years is a long time. I think you should marry me again.'

I looked at him; my mouth gaped open; my forehead scowled; I remember tilting my head as I formed the words. Then, being totally gobsmacked at the idea, stammered, 'Do you think I'm stark raving mad?'

Besides, I was seeing someone else.

45

Charlie Bullen, Australia and the Complexities of Life

Charlie Bullen came into my life about twelve months after my affair with George Collier had ended. It must have been around June 1960. He was one of many fellows from the café who regularly invited me out. I gave short shrift to most of them, but I had a soft spot for Charlie. He was a bachelor living with his elderly father in Mount Street, Fleetwood, and he took really good care of his dad. He was a gentle soul; a bit of a loner; and he regularly manoeuvred himself in the food queue to be sure I served him, and he would always pay me a nice compliment. I just saw something good in him.

He invited me to the pictures and took me for the occasional meal and we drifted into a relationship. I could not say I loved him, but he was a wonderful companion. After about twelve months, he moved into Manor Road with Jenni and me and notionally occupied the spare bedroom. After all, I did want to keep up appearances for the sake of my daughter. Charlie left his job on the docks soon after we met and took up a position at ICI, a chemical processing plant in Thornton, just outside Fleetwood.

Charlie was on shift work, which involved one weekend on and one off. Once I had re-established a friendship with Harry, I used to alternate going out with the two of them; that is, with Harry on Charlie's weekend working and with Charlie when he was home. I can tell you this took some managing! If it was Charlie's weekend, then I would phone Harry at the betting shop and provide some excuse as to why I was unable to see him. Sometimes I would put a peg on my nose and with a very congested voice, tell Harry I had a dreadful cold and could not go out. I got away with this sort of evasion for months. Charlie never suspected as I used to make sure I was home before his shift finished. However, Harry twigged to this pattern of one weekend on and one off, and he became suspicious.

*

I need to digress now to tell you about my decision to emigrate. Rod was offered a job at the radio station in Gladstone and decided to move to Australia. He lodged an emigration application with Australia House and as a young university graduate was accepted quite quickly. He left in 1962. Louie's son, Michael, had migrated in 1958 with his wife Clare and their two children Mark, seven, and Sue, aged eighteen months, so there was a family connection.

When Rodney arrived, he travelled to Gladstone but found that the radio station had not even been built, so he returned to Sydney. He settled in quite quickly and began to write home telling me that Australia was a land of opportunity.

So I said to our Louie, 'I'm going to emigrate to Australia.'

I remember the startled look on Louie's face and she said, 'Well, our Annie, if you're going, then so am I! Michael's there, you'll be there, so I might just as well go too.' Louie sold up everything she had in Macclesfield while the application for emigration was being processed and moved into the Fleetwood flat that Rodney had vacated.

Jenni saw it as an adventure, and when Loraine learnt that Louie and I were going, she said she would come too.

'What about Harold?' I said. 'You're engaged to be married.'

'Oh, I don't think I love him enough, Mum. He doesn't make a move without consulting his mother and I don't think I could live with that.'

So, Louie, Loraine, Jenni and I were all interviewed at the Australian consulate in Manchester and we seemed to tick all the boxes.

*

While waiting for clearance to emigrate, I continued my weekend outings with both Harry and Charlie. One particular Saturday night on Charlie's weekend, Louie, Charlie and I all went out together. As I was dropping Louie off at the flat above the Bargain Stores, there was Harry waiting in the doorway. Louie got out of the car and Harry saw Charlie beside me. Charlie hopped out of the car and was making sure Louie got into the flat OK when Harry started to pick a fight with him. Fists went up, strong words were said, and a full-on brawl ensued. We all do silly things in life and I think my folly was in trying to juggle Charlie and Harry at the same time. I looked at these two grown men fighting and did the most sensible thing I could think of. I drove off and left them to it.

Next morning, I was up early, before Charlie rose, and spent the day with friends in Blackpool. When I arrived home late that afternoon, there was Charlie sitting at the dining table sporting a black eye. I looked at him and thought, nice though he was, there was no long-term future for us. I did not love him. It was then that I broke the news that I missed my son and I was going to move to Australia. Understandably, Charlie was distressed and when I think about it now, I should have ended the relationship sooner, or at least told him of my intention to emigrate. I did hurt him, and I am not proud of that.

*

Shortly after the fisticuffs between the boys, the papers arrived saying our application to emigrate had been accepted. I told Charlie and he skulked back home to his dad. I then had to face Harry and also gain his permission to take Jennifer out of the country.

In so many ways, I had always been Harry's backstop and, in moving to the other side of the world, I somehow felt I was deserting him. Others might think that strange, but that was how I felt. With Charlie gone, I decided to invite Harry over for dinner, and told him what I wanted to do, but I also had an offer to put on the table.

Harry was living in a pretty dingy flat in Dock Street, so I offered to sell him my house in Manor Road for a good price and to finance him into it. We agreed on a purchase price of two thousand, three hundred and fifty pounds, with Harry paying a deposit of one hundred pounds, the balance to be paid off at ten pounds per week. The contract was drawn up, the title deed transferred, and Harry paid the deposit and forty pounds representing the first month of payment. However, he never paid the balance. Once I was in Australia, it was too difficult to chase up, but I always felt that Harry would leave whatever he had to our children, so I did not pursue the issue legally. However, when Harry died, it did not work out that way.

Once we had left and Harry had established himself in Manor Road, Maureen Bamford, who had worked for me at the café, also moved into the house with her then partner of some years, Bill Newby. Bill was ill with cancer and, not long after they moved, he passed away leaving Maureen and Harry together in the house. Over time, they teamed up, so when Harry made his last will and testament, he left everything to Maureen. The only thing she could not claim when he died in 1971 was a war bond to the value of one hunderd and fifty pounds, as she was not Harry's legal wife. This was the only money that went to Rodney as the eldest surviving child. I felt that he had cheated his own children from their rightful inheritance and I was very angry about it for a long time.

*

Let me jump ahead a bit now and tell you how Harry died. He had been running his betting shop and living in Manor Road with Maureen and, as far as I was aware, everything was OK. We fell out over the house payments, so we were not really communicating but Jennifer wrote regularly to her father, so I was across his news. For some reason unknown to me, Harry closed his betting shop around 1970 and given his navy background, went back to sea. He picked up a job as a cook on the *Ella Hewitt*. The crew was fishing in Icelandic waters when around four a.m. on 9 July 1971, Harry got up to start his working day. According to the skipper's report, Harry went to the head about four-fifty and it was there that he had a coronary occlusion. When he was found about ten past five, there was no sign of life. He was fifty-eight years old.

The nearest port was Reykjavik, capital of Iceland, so the *Ella Hewitt* pulled in there and a Dr Ulfur Gunnarsson performed an autopsy. Harry's death was recorded at the British embassy. He was such a died-in-the-wool Englishman that there is irony in his death being registered on foreign soil.

As a sixty-cigarette-a-day man, I should not have been surprised that he died so young, but it did come as a shock. I found out via a letter from Maureen, received ten days after Harry had gone. I remember phoning Jennifer to tell her and she was heartbroken. Even though we were divorced, and we were living on opposite sides of the world, I was immensely saddened by his death. You cannot be married to someone for twenty-one years and not feel a profound sense of loss when they have gone. We shared so much history and I suppose in some ways I thought I would go back to England at a future date and that he would be there. It was not until I returned to England with Jennifer in 1994 and visited the betting shop and the Dock Street flat that I really accepted that he was gone. But all this is way into the future.

*

Coming back to 1963, about three months before we received our sailing date, Loraine went up to Blackpool Pleasure Beach with her girlfriends for a night out. She was riding on the merry-go-round horse when a handsome young fellow hopped on the back. His name was Malcolm Muir and he was on holiday in Blackpool from his home in

London. Loraine was a very attractive girl with a wonderful sense of fun and Malcolm was immediately smitten. They saw each other every day of his holidays and she brought him home to meet us all.

'Mum,' she said, 'I've met this amazing guy. He's cute, he's funny and I think I'm in love.'

He came for dinner about three times during his stay and talked about his family. He was intelligent and was clearly taken with Loraine.

When he returned to London, he invited her to visit. That was just a long weekend and when she came back, there were telephone calls every day. I could tell this relationship had fire, and she clearly was in love. She had pretty much broken up with Harold Haslam in making the decision to come to Australia, but with Malcolm things were different. All of a sudden, she did not want to leave England.

I remember her coming to me at the Bargain Stores and saying, 'Mum, do I have to go to Australia? I'm in love with Malcolm and he's asked me to marry him.'

Loraine was almost twenty-one and I recall saying, 'Well, darling, it's your life. If you feel you're doing the right thing, then you can stay with my blessing.'

So as I was packing up my forty-eight tea chests with all our worldly possessions to send to Australia, Loraine packed her glory box and her clothes and moved to London. It was not possible to organise a wedding before we left, and I was sad that I did not see Loraine and Malcolm married, but in my heart, I knew she would be happy with Malcolm. He was a good man, he had a good career as a draughtsman and, clearly, he was very caring of her.

We set sail from Southampton aboard the *Fairsky* on 10 July 1963. Two months later, at a small wedding in London, Loraine, very proudly, became Mrs Malcolm Muir. It was a love match that was to last a lifetime.

46

A New Beginning in Canberra, Australia

The voyage out was wonderful once we found our sea legs. News aboard ship was pretty limited but the Profumo affair was at its height in the summer of 1963, and as a scandal always makes for juicy reading, we were rewarded with salacious titbits on the newsboard every day.

John Profumo was the Secretary of State for War in Harold Macmillan's Conservative government. Profumo was friendly with an osteopath called Stephen Ward, who moved in quite salubrious circles. Ward introduced Profumo to the Russian naval attaché and military intelligence officer, Yevgeni Ivanov, and also to a call girl called Christine Keeler. Keeler entered into a sexual relationship with both the Russian and Profumo which, when made public, caused great embarrassment. Profumo resigned from Parliament, thereby contributing, in no small measure, to the downfall of the Conservatives at the 1964 general election. There was a risqué joke doing the rounds at the time. Why does Christine Keeler have poppies tattooed on her backside? Answer: In remembrance of those who fell at the front. It always brought a laugh when I regaled it to friends.

But England, and all its political intrigue, was the world we had left behind. On 13 August 1963, Louie, Jenni and I docked in Sydney and began our new life. Our Rodney and Louie's son Michael and daughter-in-law Clare met us in Sydney and we immediately left for Canberra. As Michael and Clare had been our sponsors, we initially lived with them in their two-bedroomed flat in Narrabundah. I can tell you it was very crowded with four adults, one teenager, two small children, two boxer dogs and a parrot. Grateful though we were to have a roof over our head, we were rather like sardines in a can. Very quickly, I bought a car in order to look around for a home of our own.

Canberra had a population of around 63,000 in 1963. The main shopping centre, the Monaro Mall, was celebrating its first birthday and Lake Burley Griffin was still filling. It was a city full of opportunity. I had no problem gaining employment, winning a position at Eva's Fashions, a dress shop at the top of the Monaro Mall.

I did not stay too long there because the proprietor was a bit of a womaniser. He would often say to me that he had a delivery to make and needed help. The first time, I naively agreed, but when we got in the car, he started to touch my knees, run his hand up my skirt and attempted to kiss me. He had more hands than an octopus. I worked hard to avoid him after that, but it became more and more difficult. Eventually, I left. Jobs were easy to come by, so before long before I was working at Paul Coopers Homeware in Green Square, Kingston.

This suited me perfectly because by November 1963 I had bought a brand-new four-bedroom house in what was then the outer suburb of Hackett and I needed curtains, new bedding and a multiplicity of soft furnishing items that were available, with staff discount, at Paul Coopers.

The house cost me eight thousand pounds. Compared to the house we had left behind in England; the Hackett house was enormous. Louie and Jenni used to joke that we would need an intercom system to speak with each other if we were at opposite ends of the house.

Louie picked up a job in the general merchandise part of Woolworths, but very quickly I could see that Canberra was not going to suit our Louie. Despite her only son Michael and her two grandchildren living in the same city, it simply was not enough for Louie. Once the shops closed at five-thirty, the place was deserted until eight-thirty the next morning.

Entertainment took place in people's homes, but the problem was that it took time to get to know people. Louie had loved her life in England; she was at home in the corner pubs, and she missed her friends. We had all committed to come for two years and a return any earlier than that would have meant repaying the Australian government for our fare. So Louie stuck it out.

As the months drifted by, she became more restless and it caused significant tension between us.

She would sometimes disappear for days at a time, which made me worry, and then she would turn up and say, 'Should I throw my hat in first?' She reckoned that if the hat was not flung back at her, she was going to be OK.

'Where the bloody hell have you been?' I shouted, when she turned up after one long-weekend away.

She said that she had befriended a woman from work who had taken her to Cooma for the weekend, where there was 'action'. Cooma was the main town for migrants working on the Snowy Mountains Hydroelectric Scheme and they were great party people. Louie liked that.

She even moved out for a time and took a job as housekeeper to a widower. I thought she might settle and even pal up with him, as he was quite a nice chap, but that was not to be. Unfortunately, she was given the sack because he found her drinking his wine supply.

Then, just as her two years compulsory stay was at an end, a sad opportunity presented itself and Louie returned to England.

Peter Richardson, Clare's brother, who had migrated to Australia in 1957, had a massive heart attack and died at the age of thirty-two, leaving behind his wife June and three little boys. Peter was a larrikin and a charmer. He was good-looking and good-hearted, but his behaviour always used to get the better of him. He was the biggest thief out. He could not go to the shops without pinching something and he always came home with a present for someone.

The youngest of Peter and June's sons was a thalidomide baby who was missing his lower left arm. There was a stump where the left elbow should have been and from the stump grew two fingernails. Thalidomide, a drug developed in 1957, was initially prescribed to reduce anxiety and tension. Later, it was found to be effective in alleviating morning sickness in pregnant women. It was assumed that the drug would not pass the placenta, but children were being born with abnormalities. Research traced these abnormalities to the use of thalidomide, but it was not until the early 1960s that the drug was taken off the market.

Although Peter loved the rawness of Canberra, June never settled. When Peter died, she decided to return to Macclesfield as she felt there would be better medical help for her son as well as greater family support. So June asked our Louie if she would go with her to help with the children on the journey back to England. Louie jumped at the chance.

I saw Canberra as a city of opportunity; she saw it as a primitive backwater with no social life. So, with her two years completed, we said our goodbyes in 1965, but, sadly, we did not part on very good terms. I think she resented me for making the decision to come to Australia. It was somehow my fault that she failed to settle.

47

The 1960s

I now need to tell you about the children and how they settled into life in Australia. As I have mentioned, Rodney migrated in 1962 with the express purpose of working on radio in Gladstone, but that fell through. He returned to Sydney and took a room in a boarding house in Sydenham, which was then quite an unsavoury part of that city, but it was cheap. As his finances were dwindling, he set about finding employment. He applied to the Education Department and was immediately offered a job as a casual teacher despite only having a base degree and no teacher training. Just as he was about to start work, he saw an advertisement for a position with ATN Channel 7. He applied immediately and was offered a position within a few days. The job entailed moving scenery around for various shows being recorded in the studio. The station was located at Artarmon, so Rod hunted around and found a modestly priced flat in nearby Epping.

Wanting to make a good impression, Rod turned up for work on his first day wearing his best suit, as all well-educated British boys do. That particular day there was a baby elephant in the studio. 'Oh, this will be fun,' thought Rod as he patted the animal on its trunk. It was then that it defecated all over the studio floor. The deposit was huge, and the smell was revolting; then right at that moment, the floor manager turned around to Rod and said, 'Hey, boy, clean that up!' What an introduction to the glamorous life of television.

But it did not put him off. He loved it. The station management quickly discovered that Rod had a degree, so he was promoted from moving scenery around to being in charge of those who moved it around. Some promotion! However, he showed real interest and had great talent, so he was quickly promoted again, this time to floor manager of *The Johnny O'Keefe Show*. Within twelve months, he became the show's director and producer.

In 1964, he was invited to work on *The Mavis Bramston Show*, a weekly production that provided a comic and risqué edge to contemporary news stories. In one episode alone, it tackled a visit to Australia by the US vice president, the introduction of female roller-skating, homosexuality, censorship, price-fixing, child endowment, the White Australia Policy and how the introduction of computers would impact on office secretaries. Phew!

The clergy thought the show was outrageous and Cardinal Gilroy in Sydney even told his parishioners to sell their Ampol shares, as Ampol was the show's sponsor. Words never before heard on TV, such as 'bum', invited outrage from conservative folk. However, the show was a great success; it ran for four years and provided much-needed ratings for Channel 7, even knocking off Graham Kennedy's *In Melbourne Tonight* show on Channel 9. A wonderful cross-section of actors featured on Mavis Bramston over the years, but the core team comprised Gordon Chater, Carol Raye, Noeline Brown, Gwen Plumb and Barry Creighton.

During the years 1966 to 1968, Rod directed, produced and wrote scripts for the TV show *My Name's McGooley, What's Yours?* starring Gordon Chater. He went on to direct *Peter, Paul and Mary* at the Opera House in 1973. Rod also directed and produced many children's television shows, including *Now You See It*, which ran for many years during the 1980s.

Rod married Lyn Boyce in June 1966. It is often said that parents believe no one is ever good enough for their child, and I was no different. I could not warm to her. She had been married before and had a son whom she left when he was only eighteen months old to pursue her career in TV. I suppose it was that action which prejudiced me against her, because I can understand a woman leaving a man, but, for the life of me, I cannot understand a woman leaving her child, especially such a little one.

Rod's marriage lasted less than two years before Lyn ran off with a cameraman from the channel. My son was devastated, and I could see how much he was hurting. He was twenty-seven at the time, but he was still my boy, and I did so feel for him. The saving grace was his work: he was passionate about it, he was well-liked, and a great future lay ahead, so he moved on.

*

My children were the antithesis of each other. Rod was bohemian, artistic, impulsive and self-focused while Jennifer was traditional, steady, reliable and sharing.

My daughter completed a secretarial course in 1965 and then joined the public service. Her career was wide and varied, moving from the secretarial to the clerical ranks, finishing up with a senior leadership position at the Australian Electoral Commission (AEC). In fact, when she retired in 2013, she was then the most senior woman in the AEC.

But I am racing ahead. During the 1960s she built up a good circle of friends in Canberra. There were many boyfriends in her life, the first serious one being an ANU law student, Greg Levine, who was boarding with us in Hackett. Greg came from a wealthy Jewish family in Toorak, Melbourne. His home even had its own ballroom. The family owned a chain of fashion stores called L'Officiel, which catered for the socialites of Melbourne and the Gold Coast. Greg and Jenni teamed up for a couple of years, but his family was keen for him to marry into the Melbourne Jewish establishment, so he returned to Melbourne to complete his degree and practise law. Jenni was devastated, but as I told her, 'You kiss many a frog before you find a prince.'

*

In 1965 I met a chap called Dougie Walters. Much like Charlie Bullen, it was no love match, but we did share a friendship. I was lonely, and he was kind. We decided to travel around Australia together, so I gave Jenni the mortgage payment book, the chits for the last three payments on the combined TV/record player and left her with the four-bedroom house in Hackett. She was nineteen at the time, but quite capable of looking after herself. Dougie and I first went to the south coast and I bought a small cottage in Batemans Bay where we lived for a few months. We then decided to travel up the east coast. We made it as far as Cairns then turned back, travelled south, and found an apartment at Broadbeach in Surfers Paradise.

Surfers Paradise was a wonderful place in the 1960s. Development had well and truly started but it was not overdeveloped. It had spectacular beaches and the climate was wonderful – such a contrast to all those miserably cold winters I had spent in England. Dougie found casual work and I picked up a job in the kitchen at the Chevron Hotel, right in the heart of Surfers.

I remember one funny incident. Frank Ifield, the Australian-born singer famous for his recording of 'I Remember You', was visiting at the time and he phoned room service asking for a light refreshment. As it was mid-afternoon, and the chefs were taking a break, I took the call and it was up to me to prepare something for him. Despite running the café for years and cooking thousands of meals, I felt uneasy because I was now being asked to prepare food for someone who was 'famous'.

You must remember that I had grown up in a Britain that favoured Spam and fried-up leftovers. Ridiculous as it sounds, I was actually nervous, feeling that if the light refreshment was not perfect I would lose my job. I decided to keep it simple and lay out a cheese platter – but frankly I had never heard of such exotic delicacies as camembert or goat's cheese, so, filled the platter with what I knew: good old Blue Stilton, Red Leicester and Cheddar. I arranged the cracker biscuits and fruit on the dish like a work of art and, holding my breath, sent light refreshments upstairs. It must have been OK because no one fired me.

*

While we were living at Surfers, Rod decided to pay a visit, driving up from Sydney. I was expecting him around five p.m. but by nine that evening he had not arrived, and I was getting worried. Eventually, there was a knock at the door and I opened it with a wide smile, expecting him to be standing there. My relief was short-lived. It was the police.

Rod had skidded on the road about forty kilometres south of Surfers and had been taken to the Murwillumbah hospital. My heart was in my mouth and the adrenalin surged through me. The police said that the accident had been quite serious. I took a deep breath and whispered to that outer force that I call on in times of need, 'Please, God, let him be all right.'

When I arrived at the hospital, Rod was still in Accident and Emergency. He had cuts and contusions all over his face and he was lying flat on a gurney with his neck in a brace. He had broken his back. Why is it that my mind always jumps to the worst conclusions? I immediately had visions of him in a wheelchair and of him ending his life as a cripple. Fortunately, though, things were not that bad.

Rod spent his whole holiday in hospital. The main positive was that he could feel his toes, which augured well for the long-term prognosis. After three weeks of lying absolutely flat, he was allowed to sit, then gradually he was permitted to stand and walk a limited distance. He spent about five weeks in hospital, then with a collar on his neck, he was able to return to Sydney. In the meantime, I had had his car fixed, so drove him back myself. You would think that once your children were adults, your role as a parent would stop, but it does not always work that way. I could see that Rod would need some help for a few months, so I flew back to Surfers and decided to make a change.

When I arrived back, Dougie was patiently waiting. Oh, dear! It was another sliding door moment. I could have suggested we both go to Sydney and care for Rod, but, harsh as it may sound, I wanted to care for my son by myself. I had never loved Dougie and, at that moment, I did not have space for him in my emotional repertoire. I told Dougie that Rod needed me and that I was going to Sydney…alone. I felt our relationship had run its course. I told him I was sorry, that it had been good while it lasted, but that I was moving on. I gave notice at work, passed in the keys to the apartment, packed up the car and drove down to Sydney. I never saw Dougie again.

48

The Church of England Boys' Home, Carlingford

Rod lived in Carlingford Road, Epping, and right at the end of the street, the Church of England had established a home for boys who had either been left there by their parents or placed there by the court. I was at the shops one day when I saw an advertisement in the window for a housemother, so I applied. The home was run by an elderly English couple, Mr and Mrs Wilson, and they both took quite a shine to me. I am not sure whether it was my English accent, my experience in running a business or the fact that I had raised my own children plus my niece that landed me the job, but I started there sometime in late 1966.

I had fifteen boys of primary school age in my cottage, and what a mixed bag they were! Some had gained a lifetime of experience in a few short years. Many of the boys had been placed there by their mother, generally a single woman. My heart used to ache for the children when the mother would promise to visit on a Sunday but then either not show up, or show up with some fellow in tow, generally introduced as Uncle So-and-so.

I regularly appeared at court hearings and was often asked about the likelihood of boys offending again. So many of the little fellows were simply hungry for attention and affection, hence why they were in trouble in the first place. Whenever we would sit down after tea to watch television, there was always a scramble to decide which two boys would sit next to me, such was their need to feel close to someone. I found it sad but touching. I taught them table manners, a sense of responsibility, and what was morally right.

There was no way I could clean house, make beds and do laundry for fifteen people each day, so I gave each boy a task, but I would make a game of it. Polishing the floors was their favourite. I made soft pads for the boys to tie to their shoes and they would slide up and down the hallway to make the lino shine. First to make their bed perfectly would get a chocolate and those who scored the worst job – cleaning the showers and toilets – were given the best pick of dessert.

I really loved those boys. If it had not been for my dad, who cared so much about me, I could have become a street kid, finishing up in care, just as these boys had. I could empathise with them. I knew what it was like to feel neglected. They took to calling me Mic Kirk, and when Rod visited, the little ones assumed he was my husband, not my son, only because he was taller than me. These little fellows did not see in my face that I was so much older.

I had one little boy in my cottage who was barely five and there because his older brother was with me and he was frightened to be away from him. Fortunately, Mr Wilson bent the rules to keep them together. They had been neglected and had been placed in care under a court order. When they arrived, they were the filthiest little chaps, both with lice, and I thought then – not for the first time – that some people did not deserve to be parents. I took such a shine to these brothers and it used to break my heart to see them waiting for their mother to collect them at the weekend and then witness their utter disappointment when she would phone with some excuse as why she would not be coming. A promise to be there the following week raised their hopes, poor boys. But she rarely kept her promises. I knew that I could not show obvious bias to any child, but these brothers tore at my heartstrings and whenever I could, I would give them a little extra treat.

Obviously, we had behavioural problems from time to time but there was nothing that I could not manage. I generally found that patience, kindness and humour went a great deal further than punishment.

I was very fortunate to be offered a place on a course at the University of Sydney during the summer of 1969. It was an eight-week course, designed for carers of children in institutional environments. I attended with staff from a wide range of places such as St Vincent de Paul and the Salvation Army and learnt a great deal from these people, who knew how to cope with drug users, alcohol-induced violence and abused children. It was challenging, and confronting, at times, but I was quite proud of myself for completing the course and receiving a Certificate of Commendation at the end.

At the boys' home, there was one fourteen-year-old lad, the brother of one of my charges, who told me that he had had sex with his older sister because his mother had told him it was OK. I had to sit him down and explain that not only was it not OK but that it was also illegal. He was astonished. I tried to teach him about respect for women and that the sexual act should be about love and caring. I could only imagine what sort of a home he must have grown up in, to have his own mother condoning such behaviour. At fourteen, he was already hardened in the world. I tried to turn his thinking around, but I doubt that I was very effective.

I stayed at the boys' home for about five years, spending my days off with Rod. Over that time, we renovated his house in Carlingford Road. It was a bitter-sweet time in so many ways. I became very attached to my charges and in fact I managed to arrange a proper adoption.

We always appealed to the community to take the boys at Christmas and Easter; one couple who were unable to have children took Stuart, one of my little ones, and grew very attached to him. Even though his mother did not really want him, she was not willing to surrender him for adoption, so I pushed the couple to take it to the court. I provided evidence of the number of times the mother had promised to visit the boy and had let him down. Eventually, the court granted long-term guardianship to this couple. I heard that when he was about twelve, they applied to adopt him, and were successful.

Once the boys reached their thirteenth birthday, they moved to the next cottage and stayed there either until they finished school, obtained an apprenticeship or until they secured some type of employment. Several of the lads stayed in touch with me after they left, even visiting me in Batemans Bay. I would like to think I made a difference to the lives of those boys, that I was someone they could turn to, someone who would not let them down, someone who would not turn away. Being abandoned was their greatest fear.

49

Jennifer, Loraine and Louie

When the boys were placed with families over the holidays, I took off to the south coast and stayed at my cottage in Batemans Bay. Over the Easter holidays in 1967, Jenni phoned asking whether she could come down and bring someone 'special' with her. His name was Brian McMullan. He was tall, good-looking, had a mop of dark curly hair, the most wonderful smile and a voice like melted chocolate. However, the minute I clapped eyes on him, I had a sixth sense that there was something amiss.

At a convenient moment, I made up some excuse to get Jenni by herself and the first thing I said was, 'He's married, isn't he?'

'Well, he was,' she replied, 'but he divorced in 1966 and he moved to Canberra in March this year.'

'And what does he do for a living?' I asked.

'He works in radio,' she replied.

'Does he have children?' I queried.

'Yes, two girls, Leigh who's seven and Karen who's four.'

'Goodness me!' I said. 'Why did you have to choose someone with baggage?'

She just looked at me, smiled, and said, 'But he's gorgeous, Mum, and I really like him.'

She had been out with so many good prospects. There was Greg, now a lawyer; Damian, the medical student from Brisbane; Bill, the maths teacher at Narrabundah College; Gary, the aide-de-camp to the Governor-General – all of whom were single – and she had to choose someone with a maintenance order out against him and two little girls he would have to support for the next ten years. I was not happy.

But one thing I do know is that you cannot make decisions for your children. Brian and Jenni were in love, so it was a question of accepting the relationship or losing my daughter. There was no way I would jeopardise losing her, so I set about supporting them. As a divorcee, Brian had no assets whatsoever, so when they became engaged in August 1968, I helped finance them into their house at Watson.

In December 1969, they were married. I remember watching my baby walk down the aisle and promise her life to someone else. We had been on so many journeys together, from the moment she entered my world, and while I was happy for her, I felt a profound sense of loss. Of course, marrying and having a family is the natural order of life and while I was genuinely pleased she had found her soulmate, for me, there was a sense of melancholy. My little girl was not mine any more.

Much as I had reservations about Brian, he grew on me over time. He worshipped my darling and he treated her like a princess. This is what every mother wants for her daughter.

*

Around 1971, I decided to leave the boys' home and return to Canberra. I still had a house there, although it was rented, but I wanted to be nearer to Jenni.

I had only been back in the city for a couple of weeks when I bumped into Pat Redmond, whom I had worked with at Paul Cooper's shop in Kingston. She was working at the Church of England Girls' Grammar School in Deakin and she told me they were looking for a housemother. Of course, my experience in the boys' home stood me in great stead and my reference from Mr Wilson was very flattering, so I won the job.

You could not have found children from such polar backgrounds. My boys had mostly come from disadvantaged homes, brought up with domestic violence, money shortages and often in an environment where drug use and criminal activity was prevalent. The boys also came from families who did not value education. My grammar school girls, on the other hand, came either from defence force families or were the children of senior public servants posted overseas. There were a couple of girls whose parents lived in Canberra but whose social life was such that the children were something of a nuisance, so they were placed in boarding school.

While their backgrounds may have been different, the girls needed just as much love and affection as the boys had needed. I spent many an evening listening to them discussing their problems and worries. Many of them would turn to me to seek approval for the decisions they took. I became so fond of several of the girls that in the holidays, those children unable to join their parents often came down to Batemans Bay with me. I only had a two-bedroom cottage, but they brought their sleeping bags and it was nothing for me to have eight or ten of them spread out on the lounge room floor.

Some of them were cheeky buggers. I discovered that once I was in bed, they would sneak down to the golf club at the bottom of the hill and pass themselves off as eighteen, so they could get a drink. I caught two of them out when they arrived home smelling of alcohol and did I read the riot act! Not only was it illegal for them to be drinking under age, but had they been caught when they were holidaying in my care, I stood to lose my job.

*

In March 1973, I decided to take a long period of leave and return to England for a holiday. There were several reasons for my decision.

Firstly, I wanted to see Loraine and her children. She and Malcolm had welcomed Dawn on 2 August 1964. Funnily enough, Dawn was born on my father's birthday – a good omen, I felt. Then two and a half years later, on 7 January 1967, she gave birth to identical twin boys, Simon and Aaron.

Secondly, I felt I needed closure in a couple of areas. My mother had died in 1969, having inhaled carbon monoxide poison from the gas fire poker. I am absolutely convinced that she committed suicide She had moved to the almshouses in Buxton Road and I know that twice before she had put her head in the gas oven and turned it on. However, both times she did so when she was expecting visitors and, of course, they saved her. This time, no one arrived, and she died. She had been a lousy mother to me and my sisters, but she was the only mother I had, and I felt the need to walk the old streets she had walked, call into the old pubs she frequented, and somehow put her to rest in my head. While we were not close, I still wanted to visit her grave to say my goodbyes.

And my third reason was our Louie. We had parted on such poor terms that I did not want to go to my grave with harsh words being my lasting final memory. We shared so much history and I felt overwhelmingly sad that not even a letter had passed between us in the eight years since her return to England. I planned to take six months off, spend a couple with Loraine and then go north.

It was a real pleasure for me to see Loraine so happy with her little family. Malcolm was a good provider, a great husband and a wonderful father to the children. They had a charming little house in Twickenham, with the prettiest garden. As the children grew up, Loraine found herself part-time work helping supervise school lunches. She converted to Catholicism, Malcolm's faith, and she became an active member of the church community. I could see that life was good for her; that she had made the right decision in remaining in England, and I was happy for her.

Two months into the trip, I journeyed up to Macclesfield. I knew from Louie's son Michael that she was living in Roe Street, so I checked into a hotel nearby and took a taxi to visit her. She was living in the poorest part of town and her front door looked shabby. With butterflies in my tummy, I took a deep breath, walked up to her door and knocked. I was anxious as I had no idea what sort of a reception I would receive. I waited and then knocked again.

I heard a little shuffle and slowly the door opened, and a small face peered round. 'Yes, what do you want?' she asked feebly.

'It's Annie,' I said, 'and I've come all the way from Australia to see you.'

'Bloody hell,' she said. 'Our Annie, I never thought I'd see you again.'

'Well, are you going to keep me on the doorstep or are you going to invite me in?' I asked.

With that, she flung open the door, wrapped her arms around me and we hugged each other tightly, both of us shedding tears of joy. I was not sure what to expect, but I could not have asked for a better welcome. I was shocked at her appearance. She looked very frail and very thin. Although she had always been petite, now she was like a tiny wizened goblin. Her little flat was meagre and I had the sense that life was a struggle. She asked me where I was staying and when I told her the hotel's name, she insisted that I check out and come to stay with her.

I moved in the next day and it did not take me long to work out why she looked so fragile. She was drinking very heavily and eating practically nothing. It was quite common for her to go to the pub by eleven a.m. and come back about two p.m., have a snooze and then go back in the evening.

The first day she was gone, I just had to clean the flat as it was filthy. In all our years growing up, and through her married life, Louie had always maintained a good standard of cleanliness, but not any more. I stripped her bed and mine, cleaned the bath and toilet, swept out the living area and then set about buying some groceries. Her pantry was bare. It saddened me to see her living like this. I cooked for her many times while I was there, and coaxed her into eating something, but she took food like a sparrow. Alcohol now governed her life.

I caught up with my cousin, Jimmy Gidman, but most of my other relatives in Macclesfield had either moved or died. You must remember that I had left in 1948 to move to Fleetwood so it really was no surprise that I knew so few people. However, I did have a funny incident one evening at the Waters Green Tavern.

I was sitting up at the bar with Louie when Elsie Brown, one of my old weaver friends from the mill, walked up and exclaimed, 'Well, I never. It's Annie Gidman! I haven't seen you in a while. How've you been?'

It was as though I had been away a couple of months and she wanted to catch up, but it had been twenty-five years.

Macclesfield in 1973 looked depressed and dirty; tragically, Louie was a lost cause; and I began to wonder what I was doing there. Then a month later, I received a letter from home with some wonderful news.

*

'Dear Mum, I'm writing to tell you that you're going to become a nanna.'

Those words were music to my ears. Jenni and Brian had been married for four years and I knew that they were keen to have a child, but nothing was happening. Jenni had surgery but still nothing seemed to work. So to learn that a new little person would soon join our family was fantastic. I was over-the-moon with excitement and wanted to race back to Australia there and then, despite the baby not being due for another six months. The letter was all the impetus I needed.

With immense sadness, I said my goodbye to Louie, knowing that I would probably never see her again, although we did promise to write. I stayed with Loraine for another couple of weeks then headed back to Australia. I had planned to be away much longer, but my children were in Australia, so my heart was there too – after ten years in my new country, I felt that it was home.

Elizabeth Ann arrived on 28 December 1973, which ironically was Louie's birthday. The baby was beautiful, with big saucer-shaped eyes, incredible eyelashes, and a mop of dark hair, which eventually fell out and regrew as blonde. I fell in love with the little girl the moment I saw her. She had made me a nanna, something I had longed for, and I was overjoyed to have a new baby in the family again.

Elizabeth's arrival was not without its drama, as the umbilical cord was tight round her neck. At birth, she was blue, the result of near-strangulation; however, Dr Cutter acted quickly, cleaned out her airways and gave her a whiff of oxygen.

I was delighted Jenni had given Elizabeth my name, Ann, as a second name. For me, it was the golden thread linking me to my first grandchild. Elizabeth brought such happiness to my life, but this joy was followed two years later by great sadness.

*

It was 28 December 1975 and Louie had gone out to celebrate her sixty-sixth birthday. I later learnt that she drank rather more than usual before reeling home. Being the middle of winter, the ground was thickly frozen; as she climbed the stairs to her front door, she slipped on the black ice. She somehow managed to drag herself into the flat and into bed. When she woke, she could not get out of bed because she had broken her leg and hip. She cried out for help but her desperate, feeble entreaties fell on deaf ears.

Being bedridden, she was unable to use the toilet and her embarrassment at having anyone see her in a soiled state would have been acute. She was incredibly thin and being without food or water would not have helped.

It was about 4 January 1976 before her neighbour, Ada, realised that she had not seen Louie for several days, so she knocked hard at her door. 'Louie, are you there? Are you all right?' she called out. Some sixth sense told Ada that things were not all right. She called out again and thought she heard the faintest of responses. Ada immediately realised something was very much amiss.

'I'll go back to my place and get your spare key,' she called out. She rushed back, grabbed Louie's key, unlocked the front door and raced inside.

What a sight she found! Louie was barely conscious; her bedding was heavily soiled, and she was in incredible pain. Ada told me in a letter that when she walked into the room, she sensed Louie was not alone: Death was dancing beside her. An ambulance was called, and Louie was taken to the Macclesfield Infirmary. Ada trawled through Louie's address book, found Loraine's number, called her and, in turn, Loraine called me at Batemans Bay.

I could do nothing from the other side of the world, but I sent up a prayer for her to fight back, to not give in, to show some of the fighting spirit that I had known her capable of. But Louie had no fight left in her. All her strength had been sapped away.

The hospital made her comfortable, gave her a saline drip and painkillers and she slipped away on 10 January 1976. I have thought many times of how awful it must have been for her lying in agony, unable to move, with no family close enough to check she was OK. If only she had remained in Australia, I could have looked after her. If only she did not drink so heavily. If only things had been different – but I could not change what had happened. It was a sad way for her life to end. She was my angel in adversity, my partner in crime, but most of all, despite our cross words when she left Australia, she was my big sister and I loved her.

I will forever be grateful to Loraine and Malcolm, who drove north on the M1 to Macclesfield, battling snowdrifts and some of the worst winter weather England had seen for years, to make appropriate arrangements. I sent money to cover the funeral expenses. It was a modest affair, with a few of her old cronies attending. Loraine and Malcolm then emptied out her flat and disposed of her few meagre possessions. All that I have are her photographs, which Malcolm sent me, and my memories.

50

Phil Ward

In 1975 I decided to leave the Girls' Grammar School and retire to my little cottage at Batemans Bay. It was a happy little house. I was only a two-hour drive from Canberra and the village-like nature of the place appealed to me. I knew a few of my neighbours and liked them; I joined the bowling club and made some lovely new friends.

Around mid-1977, one of my neighbours mentioned that the secretary manager at the Soldiers' Club was desperate to find himself a housekeeper: someone who would look after him, keep his place tidy, do the laundry plus the odd bit of shopping. I was not that keen to work again as I was financially quite comfortable. He had hired two different ladies but neither had worked out. Reluctantly, I said I would help short-term until he found someone else.

The secretary manager's name was Phil Ward. He was fifty-four years old, about my height, with fair hair and a real twinkle in his eye. A reformed alcoholic, he had not touched a drop of alcohol after suffering a cardiac arrest some years before, which resulted in the installation of a pacemaker. He was a divorcee with three adult daughters, all living interstate. I must say he was a gentleman, a quiet achiever, and I found him very easy to look after. He was rarely home as he spent long days at the club, only taking Fridays off.

I must have been looking after things for about a month when I thought it might be nice if I left him some home cooking. I used to tend his place every Monday and Thursday, so one Thursday evening I left him a chunky casserole, some crusty bread and a note on how to heat it up. On the following Monday, he left me a lovely note of thanks. I took to making something for him on a regular basis. Really it was easy and much nicer to cook for two than one.

After leaving him several dinners, I received a phone call from him. He said, 'As a thank you for all your cooking, Mrs Kirk, I would like to take you out for dinner.'

Well, I thought that was considerate of him, and, since I found him quite attractive, I was tickled-pink with the invitation. The following Friday evening, he collected me from my cottage. He was quite formal, but I liked his quaint, old-fashioned way.

He took me to the Lincoln Downs and we had a lovely evening. I learnt all about his girls and his son Peter,, who had died in his twenties in a motorbike accident. There seemed to be much to talk about and when he took me home, he told me that he had enjoyed a lovely night, had not talked in ages to anyone about his family and he asked if we could do it again. At sixty-two years of age, it does come as a delightful surprise when someone takes a shine to you, so I was rather flattered and said yes. Of course, I did not tell him how old I was. I have always felt that my age is my business.

One dinner led to another and then I took to inviting him home for meals. He was highly appreciative of everything I did for him but when you like someone, nothing is too much trouble. After about three months, he asked me whether I would like to meet his mother. She lived at Springwood in the Blue Mountains. Her name was Sarah Grace Ward and she was about eighty years old. Of course, this meant a weekend away with Phil. I was actually quite nervous about the prospect because, up to this point, we had only been walking out together.

As I had such a close relationship with Jenni, I phoned and asked her what I should do.

'Well, Mum,' she said, 'what do you want to do? If you want to go away with him, you're a big girl and you should go.'

'But what if he wants sex?' I asked.

'Just let things take their course,' Jenni replied with a smile in her voice.

So we went off to Springwood. I met Sarah Grace. What a delightful lady she was! She confided in me that she was happy Philip had found a new friend as he had been on his own for some years. I also met Phil's sister, Maisie, and she too was a treasure. What a lovely, supportive family, I thought; no wonder Phil is such a gentleman. In some ways, he reminded me of my father: he was old-world, gentle, and caring, especially with his mother.

But I was unsure whether I wanted another physical relationship. To be on the safe side, I packed my 'nanny-like' nightie, made of soft cotton, fastened high at the neckline, with sleeves to the wrist and a hemline to the ground. It had been nine years since my friendship with Dougie had broken up and I had carved out a life for myself. Also, at sixty-two, I certainly did not have the figure that I had had twenty years earlier. Gravity had arrived. I no longer had firm, perky boobs and a pancake-flat stomach. It was more a case of two wobbly jellies and a floppy soufflé; much more of a 'comfort' figure.

However, my shape did not seem to worry Phil. Jennifer was right. Somehow, things just did take their course and by the end of the weekend, we were a couple. Although we each still retained our own houses, we had lots of sleepovers and spent most of our evenings together.

About a year into our relationship, I fell ill. Pain invaded every limb of my body. Food made me nauseous. I had overwhelming exhaustion, and everything was a supreme effort. I also lost quite a bit of weight. Frankly, I felt so awful that I thought it was the end.

My GP at Batemans Bay referred me to a specialist physician in Canberra, Dr Marcus Faunce, who immediately hospitalised me and ordered a whole barrage of tests. Three tentative diagnoses were proffered: first, arteritis, an inflammation of the arteries leading to the brain; second, bowel cancer; and third, multiple myeloma, which is cancer of the bone marrow. I had two spinal taps which were very painful but produced no definite diagnosis. Lying in bed, feeling so ill, I reflected on my life and thought that if this was the final curtain, then I was content: I had seen my children grow to adulthood; I had seen continuity of the family with the arrival of my granddaughter; and I had loved and been loved in return.

My illness became a case that was discussed at the weekly meeting of professionals from across the various disciplines in the Canberra Hospital and, by a process of elimination, eventually it was established that I had polymyalgia rheumatica or PMR as it is colloquially known. PMR is an inflammatory disease which causes stiffness and pain, and while the cause is still unknown, there is some evidence that environmental triggers or a virus are responsible. I was put on a course of cortisone tablets and the improvement was dramatic.

During the month in hospital while undergoing all these tests, every Friday – rain, hail or shine – Phil drove up from Batemans Bay to see me. He would arrive at my hospital bed with a bunch of flowers and some treat he thought might tempt me to eat. He was kindness itself and I recognised that this man was a keeper.

I returned to my little cottage at the Bay and slowly, over many months, I recovered. Initially, the cortisone stimulated my appetite and I transformed from a scarecrow to a dumpling in no time at all. The medication was gradually reduced, and eventually I returned to a normal weight, but it was a full three years before I finally came off the cortisone. Phil was very supportive and thoughtful throughout the whole ordeal, never once complaining if I took to the bed for the day. He cared for me with such compassion and I counted my lucky stars to have him in my life.

One Friday, when I was recovering, he took me for a drive north of the Bay and we found ourselves at Maloney's Beach. Right on the beachfront there was a block of land for sale and Phil suggested we buy it and build a home together. What a bold thought! We visited the block three or four times. The outlook was wonderful. We had a 180-degree view of the ocean; the sand was clean and golden, and as it was not a surf beach, it tended to attract young families, who were a pleasure to watch. The block itself was level and just the right size. I felt that our relationship had been tested and had come up trumps, so I agreed.

However, up to this stage, there were two things that I had never told Phil; one was being eight years older than he was. The second was the fact that I was a divorcee. Jenni said to me that I should tell him the truth before we got too financially committed. I knew she was right, but I had kept quiet about my age and marital status for so long, I worried that in bringing it up after such a long time, Phil might think I was deceitful. I had in fact told Phil that I was a widow, which was true, but I had failed to mention that I divorced Harry before he died.

'OK, girl,' I said to myself one Saturday afternoon, 'here goes.'

'Phil, before we make financial commitments on the land and house, there are a couple of things I feel I should tell you.'

'Oh, are you already married?' he asked.

'No, no, it's not that, it's that…well, um…well, I'm actually a little bit older than you are.'

'Are you eighty?' he asked jokingly, 'because, if that's the case, then I'd be going out with someone as old as my mother.'

'No, I'm not bloody well eighty, it's just that I am older.'

'Well, if you're not eighty, then it doesn't matter, does it? I love you just as you are.'

He never did ask my true age, so I never told him.

That was enough 'non-confession' for one afternoon, so I left the bit about being a divorcee until we were planning a holiday to China and we both had to apply for a passport. He had his birth certificate and his decree absolute papers on the desk.

Ever so casually, I picked up his decree absolute and said, 'I've got one of these too.'

Again, he never questioned it, so all my anxiety had been for nothing. It is amazing how often we sweat anxieties in life only to find that the problem, once aired, is not nearly as big as it initially seemed.

It was time to turn my energies into our new home. We had bought the land outright. Phil sold his house and moved into my cottage while we built the new place. I felt like a young bride again, working with Phil on the design, selecting bricks, tiles, kitchen and bathroom fittings – the myriad of things that go into building a home. It was an exciting time; a whole new adventure. Working together on something as big as this was a wonderful bonding experience. It took about twelve months from the start and we project-managed the build ourselves, eventually moving in in 1979.

I bought *Home Beautiful* magazines for furnishing ideas; selected beautiful fabric for the curtains, chose Berber carpet, which was highly fashionable then, and the house became everything I had ever dreamed of. It had three very large bedrooms, the main with an en suite, a huge country-style kitchen, a dining room, a living room that overlooked the ocean, and we also had a small TV room. We installed two five-thousand-gallon water tanks under the courtyard, plus solar heating panels, and together with the vegie garden, which Phil established, we were substantially self-sufficient. Phil was very handy with tools and made quite a lot of our furniture. He was a true craftsman. This was a really contented period of my life. I had a beautiful home, a gorgeous partner, and two children who were doing well in their careers. I also had my darling Elizabeth Ann.

Then another blessing was bestowed upon me. Jenni produced Kathryn Ellen Cecilia on 16 September 1979. She arrived just as Phil and I were about to move into the new place, but I was so excited that the move had to go on hold while I rushed up to Canberra to see my new little granddaughter. What a beauty she was. Like her older sister, Kathryn was born with large saucer-like blue eyes, rosebud lips and a mass of dark hair, but unlike her sister, Kathryn's mass of hair stayed put and just grew thick and curly. She was a treasure.

I now had one blondie and one brunette, and they both brought a wonderful dimension to my life. When they were little tots, I knitted whole outfits for them, then as they grew, I produced sweaters with animals on them and knitted whatever they fancied. Once they attended school, they frequently came down to the coast for the school holidays. I would take them to the beach, then to the Ulladulla Amusement Park, and finish the day off with fish and chips. My home became my grandchildren's holiday house.

As they grew up, they brought their friends and my orderly life would temporarily be turned upside down. There were teenage girls and boys wandering in and out; beach towels flung over the washing line; the fridge crammed with extra food; card games and dominoes littering the living room floor. While their visits were chaotic, the house reverberated with chatter and laughter and I have only the best memories of my beautiful girls.

Phil and I lived at Maloney's Beach for twenty-three years. When he turned sixty-five, he decided to retire from the Soldiers' Club. It was only about six months into his retirement when he declared himself bored. I suggested he continue with his woodwork and I with my knitting, and that we should share a stall at the local Sunday market. We went to Candelo, Moruya and even the Jamison Market in Canberra, and in no time at all we had established quite a business. Phil made bookcases, occasional tables, sideboards, dressers, children's furniture, toy chests, with the bonus of numerous toilet roll holders produced from the timber offcuts. I knitted baby clothing and sweaters and took orders. After a couple of years, we found ourselves busier than when we had both held down full-time jobs.

A beautiful incident occurred once as we drove to the Jamison Market about four one Sunday morning. We had stopped in Braidwood, about halfway between Canberra and Batemans Bay, and while sipping a cup of coffee from our thermos, Phil said, 'Annie, I have something to ask you.'

'OK, shoot,' I said, wondering what on earth he was leading up to.

Then out it popped. 'How about we get married?' he said.

You could have knocked me over with a feather, as it was the last thing I expected. It took me completely by surprise. 'Married!' I mumbled to myself. 'Do I really want to get married?'

'No pressure with your answer,' said Phil, 'but if you could let me know by the time we reach Bungendore' – about forty minutes away – 'that would be good.'

His proposal was serious, but I tended to treat it lightly, and when we arrived in Bungendore, I fobbed him off with a reply along the lines of, 'Well, Phil, what a wonderful offer but I couldn't get married because I'm too old to wear white.'

Over the years, I guess he would have asked me to marry him at least six times. The trouble was, in my head and in my heart, I still felt as though marriage was a once-in-a-lifetime thing. I had done that. I had married Harry and even though I divorced him, and he was dead, it was the one and only commitment I felt I could make. I am not sure I ever really explained that to Phil. Also, I did not want to spoil what we had.

Life at the coast was magic. There was nothing more I wanted or needed. I had a wonderful circle of friends, a great social life, and regular visits from my children and grandchildren. I would often look at the grandchildren running up the beach, chasing each other, then stopping to draw love hearts in the sand and write their name next to mine. I would watch the sun glisten on the beautiful blue waters and feel mellow as I saw them building sandcastles. It made me think back to 1932 and my visit to the Potteries with Marjory Finlow. The fortune teller had told me that one day I would live beside golden sand and clear blue water. It had taken more than fifty years, but her prophesy came true.

At Christmas time, and often at Easter too, Jenni, Brian, the children and Rod would join Phil and me – my whole family together. I truly counted my blessings. I took great pride in knowing I had given both my children a better life, supported them in their dreams and paved the way for my grandchildren. It also made me reflect on the childhood I had known – so much deprivation, so much hardship. I was born into poverty, but my children were raised in comfort; I left school at fourteen, but my son was a university graduate; and I had traded on my looks to survive, but my daughter had no need for coquettish behaviour.

You cannot live your children's lives, but you can prepare them for the challenges that life brings. I just hope that my children, grandchildren and great-grandchildren, when reading my story, will come to realise that they were born in a fortunate time. I hope they never experience the hardships I have known but, if they do, I hope they have the strength of character and self-belief to overcome the odds and contribute to society in a thoughtful, constructive way. I hope they treasure the start they have had in life and I trust they will always feel my love, even when I am gone. I hope they recognise that to get something worthwhile out of life, you need to invest. You need to give back, you need to think beyond yourself. You need to demonstrate that you care, because caring is its own reward.

Afterword

The later years of my mother's life were good ones. She and Phil opened their home and their hearts to us. During my marriage, there were many financially lean times, so with no spare money, Maloney's Beach became our holiday haven. Elizabeth and Kathryn spent many school holidays with their Nanna and Uncle Phil. Phil was generous with his time and treated all of Mum's family with kindness and respect.

Mum befriended many people at Batemans Bay, as was her nature. She attended the senior citizens gathering each week, played bingo at the Soldiers' Club, and went away with the seniors to various places around Australia: Bright, Port Macquarie, Sydney and Bowral/Mittagong to name a few. Phil was less interested in going but she would trot off on her own, generally sharing a room with one of the other ladies. Mum was partial to a drop of sherry each night, and she and her roommate would regularly have a tipple before going down to dinner.

She had a great sense of fun and usually there was a dress-up night on these seniors' trips. I recall photos of one trip with everyone wearing hats. Mum had not taken a hat with her, so she rolled up to dinner wearing the motel's bedside lampshade, to which she had attached a few corks and went as a 'real Aussie'.

As my children grew up and went through the usual round of childhood illnesses, Mum could always be relied on to zip up from the coast and look after the girls while I went to work. Elizabeth, in particular, was sickly as a small child. She had pneumonia when she was two and again when she was three, then had her tonsils out and when she was around seven, had a tumour removed from her foot. Mum was there on every occasion, doing the bedside vigil in hospital while I was at work, then going back to our place to cook dinner when we relieved her at the end of the working day. Mum was my lifeline, my severest critic when I did something foolish, but my rock in times of adversity.

She came on holidays to Surfers Paradise one year and when Elizabeth was splashed with droppings from one of Birdland's inmates, Mum smeared a bit of the bird's droppings on her arm to show that she was 'lucky' as well. She had a wonderful way with children: firm but kind; tolerant; and full of fun.

Apart from the usual aches and pains that occur with age, Mum maintained quite good health until around 1998, when she was diagnosed with an aortic aneurysm. Unfortunately, this was not a straightforward aneurysm. Rather than just one swelling in the wall of the aorta, it turned out that the whole of the aorta was an aneurysm and therefore inoperable. It was then that she and Phil gave up doing the markets. Essentially, she was living with a time bomb in her chest.

She still continued with her pleasant life but in early 2002 she woke up one morning to find her arms covered in bruises. As I was at the coast when this occurred, I took her down to the chemist, who suggested I get her into a doctor as quickly as possible. The doctor referred her to a haematologist at the Canberra Hospital and she was hospitalised within twenty-four hours. She was placed on a huge regime of medication which knocked her around quite a bit.

When she came out of hospital, in a relatively stable condition, I took her for afternoon tea one Sunday to Federation Square in Canberra. As we left the café, she fell and was very shaken up. She thought she had simply bruised herself, but I took her for an X-ray to be on the safe side. She was given the all-clear, but six weeks later we received a call from the hospital saying her rib was broken. It was no wonder she felt poorly almost the whole six weeks. She became progressively frail and as a result stayed on living with us in Canberra.

By this stage, Brian had retired and became a house husband while I still worked. So much of Mum's care fell to him and he was kindness itself. In August 2002, she complained of being unable to see from her left eye. A visit to the eye specialist revealed that she had developed a melanoma in her eye. We took her to the Sydney Eye Hospital for further advice. The specialist talked about resecting the eye but there was the added complication of the aneurysm and the strong possibility that she could die on the operating table.

In typical Annie style, she slept on the diagnosis overnight and then said, 'I'm an old dame, I've had a good innings and I'm not going through the drama of surgery. I'll just let nature take its course.'

As she grew more poorly, she repeatedly asked Brian when I was at work what medication she could take which would end it all. Of course, he told me, and I found it very distressing as frankly the thought of her not being there was something I did not want to face.

In May 2002, Loraine came out from England with Simon, one of her twins, and stayed for a month, as we knew things were not going to improve.

It was a very happy time and I recall over a glass of wine one night, Loraine said to me, 'Mum took me in when no one else wanted me. If it had been left to Nellie and Louie, I would have finished up in an orphanage – only Mum cared. I've come out to see her because I just want to hold her one more time and tell her I love her, and I want to thank her for everything she did for me.'

Mum spent eleven of her last thirteen months in Canberra. This was hard, as she missed the coast and her house and Phil missed her. We took her down to the Bay every month for a long weekend, but it was not really enough.

Then I managed to get some help from the Illawarra Retirement Trust. Over Christmas 2002, when we were all at Batemans Bay, someone from the trust came out to assess both Mum and Phil and determined that between them they qualified for fourteen hours assistance per week. This was a boon. It meant Mum could return home, and she did.

In January 2003, I packed up all her Canberra belongings and we settled her back at the coast, with the lovely Annabelle coming in each day to care for both Mum and Phil. Brian and I went down every second weekend with prepared food parcels and checked on things. I remember taking Mum to get her hair cut and coloured in early February.

When the hairdresser finished, Mum patted her hair, looked at herself coyly in the mirror and said, 'You know, our Jenni, I could pick up with a hairstyle as good as this.' She maintained her devilish streak right to the end.

Rod decided to take some time out and stay with Mum at the coast in February 2003. On the 25th, he phoned me and said that Mum had again come out with bruising all over her and was in considerable pain, so he was taking her to the doctor. The doctor immediately admitted Mum to Batemans Bay Hospital and ordered further tests in Moruya the next day. I said I would take time off work and come down. About five on the morning of 26 February 2003, Rod called to say the hospital had phoned and Mum was failing fast. He and Phil rushed straight there. Brian, Kathryn (who was still a student and living at home) and I hopped in the car and drove like the wind to the coast. We did not phone Elizabeth because she was newly pregnant with my first grandchild – Mum's first great-grandchild – and we wanted to assess the situation first.

Kathryn drove the whole trip to the coast. It is normally a two-hour journey, but we made it in one hour and forty minutes. All the way down, I was saying a prayer to some outer force, pleading that she would still be alive, that I could hold her, kiss her and tell her I loved her. The minutes ticked away; the trip seemed endless.

I kept saying to Brian and Kathryn, 'She'll be alive, won't she? I must see her again.'

Brian, in his usual calm and accepting way, patted me on the arm and said, 'What will be, will be.'

Rod saw us arrive at the hospital and came out to meet us. 'She's gone,' were the first words he uttered.

I knew it was coming but I could not believe it; I did not want to believe it. She had been there my whole life. I thought she should still be there. We entered the hospital room and she was lying peacefully on the bed. I lifted her into my arms and hugged her so tightly, letting the tears stream down my face. As I write these words, I can still recall the pain in my chest, the true feeling that my heart was breaking in two. My mother's death was my first experience in losing someone I truly loved: my grief was raw and profound.

We all sat in the hospital room with her: Phil, Rod, Brian, Kathryn and I, taking in the reality of what it all meant. Kathryn phoned Elizabeth and she immediately drove down to the coast, as she too wanted to say her goodbyes to her much-beloved Nanna.

Sometimes even when you see the reality of death before you, it is hard to take it in. We must have spent about three hours in the room, none of us wanting to move. Annie's spirit seemed everywhere. I remember looking at every one of us around the hospital bed and thinking of what she meant to each of us: she was parent, grandparent, lover, friend, but most of all she was an indomitable spirit that had touched all our lives. I gently removed her wedding ring and pushed her hair back from her head. Then I smiled as I remembered her comment at the hairdressers. 'I could pick up with a hairstyle as good as this.' Oh, Mum, how very you!

The funeral was held in Canberra. My cousin Michael, Louie's son, played the keyboard; we sang the wonderful old Vera Lynn wartime song, 'We'll meet again', and I delivered the main eulogy.

I spoke of Albert Facey's book *A Fortunate Life* and of how he was an ordinary man who lived through extraordinary times and how in the living he became extraordinary himself. I hope that in my telling Annie's story you gained a feel of how the events of the twentieth century shaped my mother, how she came from humble beginnings, worked, saved, married, had children, lived through the war, became a successful businesswoman, helped others, divorced, laughed, cried, loved and was loved. This fabric, this tapestry, gave to Annie Gidman a Fortunate Life indeed.

Jenni McMullan

Postscript

You might be wondering what happened to some of the key people in Mum's story, so I have provided a little about each of them.

Phil Ward

Phil missed Mum terribly. He had not been well himself for a couple of years, with poor kidney function, his pacer and limited mobility. He was also lonely, rattling around in the house he and Mum had built at Maloney's Beach. He took a fall in September 2003 and passed away eight months after Mum died.

Michael Steele

Michael lived to be eighty-five years old. He passed away on 29 May 2019, leaving behind his second wife Margaret. He was an excellent pianist and until four weeks before his death played the organ for his church as well as touring retirement villages in Canberra and on the New South Wales south coast playing some of the old wartime favourites for the retirees in the villages. Michael was awarded a medal in the Order of Australia in 2016 for his musical charity work.

Brian McMullan

Brian retired in 1991 and became a wonderful resource for the women in his family. He took over much of the running of the family home while I worked, and he supported Elizabeth and Kathryn. He played around with shares, lunched with his friends and generally led a relaxed life. He was also a wonderful grandpa to Elizabeth's son, Tom. Lucy was born on 16 September 2005, two years and two months after Tom, and the family was elated. But the joy was short-lived, as four days after Lucy's birth, Brian was diagnosed with multiple melanoma brain tumours. He underwent three brain operations over four days in October 2005, then further surgery in February 2006 to remove a tumour from his bowel. He was stoic through it all, but in his ever-calm way, he took it all in his stride. For seven months, he fought the cancer, but it spread into his lungs, spine and aorta. He told me that he was not afraid of dying, but he was afraid of leaving all his beautiful girls behind. He died in my arms on 30 April 2006, with Elizabeth, Kathryn and Karen, a daughter from his first marriage, at his bedside.

Loraine Dutton

Loraine and Malcolm raised their family in London. She visited Australia for her fortieth, fiftieth and sixtieth birthdays and there was regular communication with the family. She became a grandmother to five granddaughters: Kelly, Kirsty, Jodie, Amy and Abby and great-grandmother to six children. She was active in the church and in musical drama, often taking a leading role in the Christmas pantomime. Loraine had a wonderful sense of humour and was the very heart of her family. She developed cancer around 2011 and put up a brave battle but passed away, surrounded by her family, on 1 July 2016.

Rod Kirk

Rod left Sydney and moved to Brisbane, working for Fremantle International, a large film distribution and TV company, where he made children's television programs. It was initially intended that he go to Brisbane for thirteen weeks, but his shows became so successful that thirteen weeks extended to thirteen years. He rented his house in Carlingford Road to the owners of the greengrocery store next door; they used the living room for an office and the kitchen/laundry for food storage. Rod returned to Carlingford Road a couple of times to collect clothing and documentation for a passport, but he never again stayed there.

When retirement loomed, Rod did not want to return to Sydney and began looking for a place on the New South Wales central coast. The greengrocers made Rod a good offer for his house which he accepted. He eventually settled on a lovely little property at Mylestom, a village about twenty minutes south of Coffs Harbour. He had the Bellinger River on one side of him and the Pacific Ocean on the other. It was a perfect spot.

Rod returned to Sydney to pack up his house. He intended to donate his furniture to charity, particularly his queen-sized bed, which had been gathering dust for thirteen years but to his enormous surprise when he began to dismantle the bed, he found it was warm and beautifully aired. He had left the electric blanket on number one and it had been on for thirteen years! It is amazing that the place had not caught fire.

Rod worked for three different community radio stations in and around Coffs Harbour, playing the music he loved, and he brought immense pleasure to his listeners, many of whom baked him cakes and dropped them into the studio. He and a mate renovated the Mylestom house and, like our mother, Rod found immense pleasure living by the sea in retirement.

In August 2014, while I was overseas, he visited Canberra, before being admitted to hospital in Sydney for surgery on his mouth. He was staying with Elizabeth and complained of severe backache. He blamed his broken back on the car accident he had had in the 1960s and asked her to heat a water bottle for him. On the way to the bedroom, he collapsed. Elizabeth called an ambulance and Rod was taken to Calvary Hospital. She phoned her sister Kathryn and together they met at the hospital and waited for the doctor to join them. He asked them many questions about Rod's upcoming surgery with the girls answering as best they could. They were fully expecting to be shown into his ward. Then the doctor delivered the bombshell, saying that Rod had been placed on life support, and there was nothing they could do. It was an enormous shock. That morning he had been walking and laughing, and now they were told there was no hope.

Elizabeth and Kathryn entered the room and each of them held his hand as the machinery was turned off. He simply slipped away. The girls assumed it was a heart attack, or perhaps a stroke, but the autopsy revealed that he had died from a ruptured aortic aneurysm, just as our mother had.

In line with the showbiz life he lived, Rod finished up with a showbiz exit from this world. He had three funerals, one in Canberra while I was overseas; then, when I returned, we held a memorial service in Canberra for the many people who knew him, and finally a further memorial service in Mylestom. At the end of the last service, we gave him a royal send-off. In keeping with his freewheeling way of life, we placed his ashes in a large palm leaf that had been fashioned into a boat. We covered the ashes with rose petals and took him to the estuary, where the river meets the ocean, to send him out to sea. I waded into the river and launched Rod on his final journey, but back he came, so I waded out further and launched him a second time, but again he returned. As I am not a strong swimmer, John McNee stripped down and swam Rod out to the sea lane, and eventually down he went. How typical it was of Rod to come back for three encores!

John McNee

Finally, although he was not a character in Mum's story, I want to pay tribute to John McNee, who strongly encouraged me to write this book. I met John in late 2007, almost two years after Brian died. John had lost his beautiful wife Bettie to cancer in 2002. We were introduced by mutual friends at a dinner party and we found we had so much in common. When I was posted to Melbourne for work in 2009, John came with me. What began as a lovely friendship blossomed into love. When in Florence in 2014, John asked me to marry him and we tied the knot in October 2015 in the garden of the home we had bought together.

www.ingramcontent.com/pod-product-compliance
Lightning Source LLC
Chambersburg PA
CBHW071810080526
44589CB00012B/741